23. 00

12/12/89

EDMUND WILSON'S AMERICA

EDMUND WILSON'S AMERICA

❧

GEORGE H. DOUGLAS

THE UNIVERSITY PRESS OF KENTUCKY

Library of Congress Cataloging in Publication Data

Douglas, George H., 1934–
    Edmund Wilson's America.

    Bibliography: p.
    Includes index.
    1. Wilson, Edmund, 1895-1972—Knowledge—United
States.   2. Criticism—United States—History—20th
century.   3. United States—Civilization.   I. Title.
PS3545.I6245Z595   1983   818'.5209   83-19696
ISBN 0-8131-1494-2

Contents

Introduction

This book is a study of Edmund Wilson's views about American life. It is primarily a work of exposition, but I have sought, through analysis and interpretation, to make intelligible a long and varied professional career, to synthesize Wilson's moods and ideas over several generations.

But why such a work at all? Wilson has spoken eloquently for himself, and there have already been several biographical and general studies of his work. My assumption is that the breadth and diversity of Wilson's work has made it difficult to obtain a sharp focus on some of the most powerful and enlightening strains of his thought. As the great man of letters of our time (some might say our *only* man of letters), Wilson was a generalist, an eccentric, and an individualist. He read the books he wanted to read and wrote essays on those that struck his fancy. He wrote substantially on topics as diverse as the Dead Sea Scrolls, sleight-of-hand magic, Canadian politics, Hungarian verbs, Russian poetry, the history of upstate New York, and the literature of the Civil War. Throughout his career he wrote not only literary criticism but also intellectual history, political analysis, travel books, novels, poems, and plays. The result of this splendid diversity has been that Wilson is somewhat elusive. Most frequently he has been the object of study by literary scholars, and a look at the many articles written about him will show that they are devoted almost exclusively to Wilson's literary ideas and opinions, although a fair number have also been concerned with Wilson as a social and political thinker and reformer. Of course these areas do present rich materials for study and investigation, and I have not neglected them. I have tried, however, to narrow the scope of my study so as to locate one major area of Wilson's work within a coherent intellectual framework. I do this because I believe that Wilson's views about American civilization are worth preserving—indeed, they are among the most challenging and rewarding of the twentieth century.

As a result, some readers may find scant consideration being given to what may be their favorites among Wilson's books. I have done very little with *Axel's Castle,* long considered Wilson's masterpiece of literary criticism. I have done nothing with *The Scrolls from the Dead Sea,* a superlative scholarly treatment of the subject. I have discussed *To the Finland Station,* not, however, for its detailed history of the intellectual background of European socialism but because it reveals a dimension of Wilson's heroic response to the economic upheavals of the 1930s and the seeming vulnerability of American values and traditions at that time. On the other hand, as a part of my historical and cultural approach, I have given considerable space to works like *Apologies to the Iroquois,* which would merit only marginal treatment in a study of Wilson's literary ideas. In addition, I have relied more heavily than earlier writers on Wilson's diaries, letters, and personal essays in an effort to render the texture and intimate feeling of his response to the American scene. Wilson is a writer who uniquely combines intellectual analysis and imaginative synthesis, and to comprehend his work in all its dimensions one must enter freely into his various moods and attitudes.

This book is arranged roughly in a chronological sequence. But only roughly. There is advantage in treating Wilson, as I have done, decade by decade, so as to uncover the shifting values and viewpoints that controlled his work during different periods. But it is also important to do as much as possible to show the unity of Wilson's thought over time. I have a chapter, placed near the end, that reflects Wilson's views about the condition of scholarship in America. But here I have referred to several essays on the subject that Wilson wrote over a period of forty years. Wilson's well-known attack on certain forms of academic scholarship, which brought him some unpleasant notoriety in the late 1960s, is clearly foreshadowed in numerous essays that he wrote in the 1940s and before. His ideals of scholarship were also clearly revealed in his beautiful essay on John Jay Chapman, first published in the *Atlantic Monthly* in 1937. Still, it seemed sensible to place a discussion of Wilson's ideals of scholarship in the decade of the 1960s, at which he was stirring up controversy on the subject of institutionalized scholarship.

There is a great deal in this book about Wilson's views on politics and on the strengths and weaknesses of American democracy. So much, in fact, that it would not be possible to gather it all in one chapter. Furthermore, it is not desirable to do so, since Wilson's political philosophy underwent marked changes over time, despite a substratum of early American republicanism. I have found it advantageous to treat Wilson's political views in several different places.

Altogether, though, the aim of a book like this is to urge its readers back to a fresh reading of the original. This book offers a convenient framework for Wilson's ideas that he himself did not provide. It is true that no serious reader could treat himself to very many of Wilson's works without coming away with a strong impression of the moral force of the man and without the notion that his central concern was the quality of life and civilization in his homeland. The cumulative effect of Wilson's work over the years has been a striking one, and my intention in this book has been to capture that effect, to bring it between the covers of a single book. I hope to share with my readers the full thrust of Wilson's historical imagination and moral intensity and to reveal his stature as one of the great spiritual voices of our time.

To my mother
Harriet Elizabeth Douglas

1

The Man and
His World

For a period of almost ten years Edmund Wilson failed to file an income tax return. When the Internal Revenue Service finally caught up with him in 1955, a friend offered the advice that this neglectful and eccentric behavior had put Wilson in such a tangled legal mess that it would probably be best for him to move abroad and become a resident of some other country. But Wilson took the risk and stayed in the United States. As he later explained in his book, *The Cold War and the Income Tax,* the idea of going into exile "seemed fantastic. . . . I had no wish to live abroad; I was more interested in and involved with the United States than I could imagine being with any other country" (13-14).

The incident, and Wilson's response, seems pregnant with meaning. Edmund Wilson was always a highly idiosyncratic personality, always somewhat estranged from his native land, somewhat out of joint with it. But at the same time he was powerfully committed to America, deeply involved in understanding its spiritual life and historical particularities. Despite his tremendous range of interests, despite the fact that he had traveled abroad extensively and written on subjects as diverse as European literature, religion, and sleight-of-hand magic, despite his great appetite for foreign languages, Wilson was first and foremost an Americanist; he was primarily interested in the American scene, and his writing became more saturated with this interest as his life progressed. He is, when the entire body of his life's work is taken into account, one of the great critics of the American experience, able to stand comparison with Tocqueville and Henry Adams.

When he died in 1972, the obituary writers typically characterized Wilson as a "man of letters," perhaps even our "great national man of letters." Unfortunately, since the time in 1840 when Carlyle spoke of "the hero as Man of Letters," glorifying that figure as "our most important modern person," the term *man of letters* has come to mean a writer of the second rank, perhaps a kind of higher journalist. Whatever the popular reputation, the general man of letters is always hard to define, especially in America, which seems to have had so few of them. Being a nation of determined pigeonholers and conceptualizers, we provide no niches where there are no heroic statues to go into them. Wilson was neither a watered-down philosopher nor a higher journalist. During his later years he always seemed to stand alone in a category of one.

Wilson's luck—or bad luck as the case may be—to find himself adorned with the label "man of letters," is largely a result of the tremendous diversity of his work over the years. He was the author of two novels, numerous volumes of poems, plays, personal essays, many hundreds of book reviews and journalistic pieces of various sorts, and other books and articles that defy easy classification. If Wilson had written more than two novels he might have become known as a novelist. If his plays had thrilled Broadway producers, he might have gained a reputation as a playwright; but as the years went by Wilson came increasingly to think of himself as a journalist or essayist, and the sheer breadth and diversity of his work defied any of the usual classifications accorded to writers. As time went on the popular press tended to refer to him as Edmund Wilson the literary critic, but since Wilson himself saw his mission to be a wider and more rigorous one than that, we probably do best in the end to describe him as a man of letters.

Wilson's career as a writer spanned over fifty years, beginning in 1920 when he joined the staff of *Vanity Fair* as managing editor. Wilson's earlier education at the academically stringent Hill School and at Princeton University would seem to have prepared him for a scholarly or academic career; indeed, an academic career is what Wilson's old Princeton mentor Christian Gauss hoped for the bookish young Wilson. But on graduating from Princeton in 1916, Wilson turned his back decisively on graduate school, taking instead a fifteen-dollar-a-week job as a reporter on the *New York Evening Sun.* This job, in the whirlwind atmosphere of New York, with its daily diet of murders, suicides, horse races, society gatherings, and ferry boat accidents, whetted Wilson's appetite for an active and involved literary career, a career that in time might most nearly resemble that of the scholarly writer.

As an undergraduate student at Princeton, Wilson had come to accept literature as a genteel occupation, somehow separate from the larger social world. But this notion crumbled under the weight of his experiences as a general reporter and perhaps also as the result of the turmoil and trauma of the grim war years. So it is not at all strange that the still youthful Wilson who returned from the war, where he had served first in a hospital unit and later in the intelligence service (gaining the rank of sergeant), sought to identify himself with active literary circles in New York. He and his friend John Peale Bishop began writing and publishing satirical poems and stories that eventually appeared in *The Undertaker's Garland*, Wilson's first book.

Still, a purely independent literary life seemed economically unfeasible in 1920, just as it would today, and the young Wilson took a job on *Vanity Fair*, then one of the numerous smart magazines appealing to upper-crust New Yorkers and suburbanites. Wilson could hardly have shared the overall philosophy and aims of *Vanity Fair*—its editor-in-chief, Frank Crowninshield, once described the main concerns of the magazine to be "things which society, money and position bring in their train: paintings, tapestries, rare books, smart dresses, dances, gardens, country houses, correct cuisine and pretty women"—but the magazine was jaunty and sophisticated, quite flexible enough to foster young and imaginative writers on the rise.

Salaried journalism continued to be Wilson's lot for many years. His novels and plays never brought the financial rewards enjoyed by his friend and fellow Princetonian Scott Fitzgerald, so after a year at *Vanity Fair* Wilson moved on to a nineteen-year association with the *New Republic*. During the 1940s, Wilson also served for five years as literary editor of the *New Yorker* and thereafter maintained strong ties with that magazine, which kept him on a retainer and continued to print his essays on a multitude of subjects for the rest of his life. Between some of these assignments Wilson attempted to eke out a living as an independent writer, taking whatever assignments he could get to provide for himself and his family. Sometimes this was painfully difficult, but starting in the 1950s, with a number of solid books to his credit, and with the rise of the new "quality paperback" publishers to reissue some of those out-of-print titles, Wilson began to survive comfortably as a miscellaneous man of letters—a rare

American phenomenon. Journalists and muckrakers apart, the serious essayist devoted to journalism has never been a common commodity on the American shore.

Whether we call him a critic, a man of letters, or a journalist, it is clear that Wilson himself preferred to believe that he was first and foremost a critic of ideas, a historical thinker and writer. Like the gentlemanly historians of the nineteenth century, he was a writer of personal vision, a sojourner in the world of his own time and country. He believed a writer to be essentially a creator of a moral universe, a Prometheus struggling to make some sense out of the phantasmagoria of events rocketing past. The writer must first find his own footing, his own patch of permanent ground, before he can say anything useful to the reading public.

In a lecture delivered in 1940 at Princeton entitled "The Historical Interpretation of Literature," Wilson explained that the outlook of the historical critic is in some sense the defining characteristic of humanity. Above all, permanence of vision is what we really want from our thinkers and creative minds. What is an intellectual but a person who attempts to give meaning to our lived experience—"to make life more practicable; for by understanding things we make it easier to survive and get around among them." For example, a mathematician like Euclid, working in a field of abstractions, shows us the relationships between distances in our cluttered environment on which we may rely and depend. Similarly, a drama of Sophocles indicates relations between various human impulses, makes coherent patterns out of things that otherwise would appear confused and dangerous. Thus there is a kinship between science and art in that both are intellectual activities; they have a historical goal, that is, a goal embedded in the strivings and aspirations of human experience.

The experience of mankind on earth is always changing as man develops and has to deal with new combinations of elements; and the writer who is to be anything more than an echo of his predecessors must always find expression for something which has never yet been expressed, must master a new set of phenomena which has never yet been mastered. With each such victory of the human intellect, whether in history, in philosophy or in poetry, we experience a deep satisfaction; we have been cured of some ache of disorder, relieved of some oppressive burden of uncomprehended events.*

Whether or not this is a perfect definition of the human animal as thinker, it is certainly an accurate definition of Wilson's aspirations

*This address was later reprinted in *The Triple Thinkers* (1948 ed.), 257-70.

as a writer. Wilson's talents were spent confronting the world of his own time. This did not mean that he tried to take on the universe or hurl himself against the complex and massive world of twentieth-century America in its entirety and immensity. Instead he sought to articulate his own personal reading of the world before him, always attempting to bring his singular erudition and style of learning to the task of explaining the spirit of the day.

Wilson's life work, and this became progressively more evident as the years passed and his voluminous diaries and personal memoirs came into print, was never devoted to historical objectivity and detachment but to personal authenticity and involvement. Wilson's lifelong struggle was to dredge up from his own past a personal style and perspective from the vantage point of which he could look out at the world around him. Accordingly, not only his subject matter but his angle of vision was peculiarly American. Even when he was writing about Russian literature or the Dead Sea Scrolls, Wilson was writing for Americans and addressing American concerns. Above all he believed that he was thinking with a uniquely American mind—a mind grown to maturity in a very definite social and intellectual environment, then alternately mellowed and reinvigorated over the years by a constant dredging up of the memories of the wounds and glories of his personal environment.

Wilson was a man driven by an obsessive concern for the locales and the cherished happenings of his younger life. Back he went, time and time again, in an almost Proustian fashion, to the scenes of his childhood, to his family, to the homes that his family had lived in for generations, to the effects that a new industrial and commercial America had had on the early Jeffersonian Republic. Because of a compulsive need to comprehend the spiritual changes and upheaval in his own family, he developed the sensitivity to fathom and interpret changes going on in American life as a whole; to make some sense out of them; to dull the cutting edge of the destructiveness; to render them meaningful and orderly.

Wilson's brand of historical criticism was thus highly personal, the genius of it carved out of psychologically colored response to the world. Anyone who would understand Wilson's critique of American life, indeed, the style and substance of his work, must first have a firm view of who he was, where he came from, and why he continued persistently and painfully to draw on his early family life, why he returned over and over to the sparsely inhabited regions of upstate New York and an old stone house he loved there, why he sought some transfusion point between the lifeblood of an America that was going and another that was coming. Edmund Wilson is a writer who created a vision out of the particularities of individual autobiography. In many writers these individual readings of the world, these highly personal responses bear little fruit—the weak perfume of the local historian or topographer comes immediately to mind. But Wilson's love and understanding of America was a deep and undying intellectual passion; his vision was a mighty one. It would be difficult to find anyone in the twentieth century who worked harder at interpreting America to itself. He was, perhaps as Dante said of Aristotle, *il maestro di color che sanno*—the master of those who know. Wilson knew us well, we Americans, and in explaining us to ourselves he has been among our most spectacular intellectuals.

Edmund Wilson was born at Red Bank, New Jersey, on May 8, 1895. His family, like many New Jersey families of the day, had deep roots in New York state and New England. Wilson's New Jersey birthplace, like that of James Fenimore Cooper or Grover Cleveland, seems somehow accidental and inappropriate. He more properly belongs to that spacious and isolated world of upstate New York to which, after the Revolution, his individualistic forebears had gone to escape the cramped spaces of New England.

Red Bank, a scant five miles from the Atlantic Ocean, is now a bedroom suburb, within easy commuting distance by rail from New York City. In 1895 it was already an older settlement with a sedate country air about it. The part of the New Jersey coast lying between Red Bank and Long Branch was then fairly fashionable and was dotted with small estates of those whom Wilson called "the second-rate rich." It was certainly not a bad place to grow to maturity: there was space, there were trees, and, above all, there were remnants of the early American individualism that had nourished Wilson's family for many generations—there was the North American Phalanx nearby, a Fourierist community that Wilson visited as a child and that his physician grandfather had visited regularly as a general practitioner. All the amenities of life were available, but by the time Wilson was born in 1895, Red Bank was somewhat in a state of decline; daily commuting to Wall Street was already a reality, as was the flashy presence of the *nouveau riche.*

On his father's side, the first American Wilson came over from Londonderry in the eighteenth century, "equipped, according to the family legend, with nothing but a fishing rod and a silver onion watch." Some later members of the Wilson family came from New-burgh-on-the-Hudson and elsewhere in New York state. The Kimball family, on Wilson's mother side, also had ties to New York state, but later it too had become part of the landed gentry in New Jersey. The male members of the Wilson and Kimball families were most often successful preachers, lawyers, and doctors, but, because of the inti-macy of this society, because of their strong sense of tradition and the historical past, they had become a kind of local landed aristocracy that, by 1895, was somewhat out of phase with industrial America, weakened and attenuated: "people who had large farms and had been there since the eighteenth century, the doctors, the lawyers, the preachers" (*Prelude,* 31).

On his mother's side, Wilson's roots went back to an earlier and more primitive kind of aristocracy, represented tangibly in Wilson's mind by an old stone house in Talcottville in Lewis County, New York, not far from Lake Ontario. Wilson's maternal ancestors, the Talcotts, who built the old stone house, were Tories who sought freedom in the open spaces of western New York after a treaty with the Oneida Indians had made settlement there possible after the Revolution. The Talcotts' hope was to build a community somewhat along New England lines, and at one time they had a complete manor settlement with numerous buildings, some of which served public functions for the community. But such a civilization was not to persist—Fenimore Cooper had been quite well aware of its de-cline at the beginning of the nineteenth century—and by the time Wilson's mother came into possession of the property, the commu-nity was long gone, and the main house was all that was left of the buildings.

The house, made from stone that had been quarried and brought out of the river, had walls a foot thick. It had the simplicity and solidity of a fortress. The house, said Wilson—one of the few of its kind among later wooden houses and towns—"was an attempt to found a civilization. It blends in a peculiar fashion the amenities of the Eastern seaboard with the rudeness and toughness of the new frontier" (*American Earthquake,* 497). Doubtless the dual appeal of civilization and roughness, solidity and wildness, was the source of the lingering attraction it had for Wilson thoroughout his life. The old stone house at Talcottville makes its appearance again and again in his writing: it is the subject of a lyrical essay in 1933, is much in evidence in later autobiographical works such as *A Prelude* and *A Piece of My Mind,* and is a commanding presence in one of his last works, *Upstate.*

The wildness of the country near Talcottville and the solidity of the house must have been sources of inspiration and refreshment to Wilson and his forebears. It was a place where a man could breathe freely, a place to cultivate the expansiveness of rugged individualism. It also served as a symbol of the loss of the earlier frontier, as a point of focus for memories of a sovereign race of men "who had owned their pastures and fields and governed their own community," a race whose descendents today are performing mainly minor functions in a machine that they do not control. It was at one and the same time a symbol of a distinguished civilization and a place where the imagination might soar to its wildest heights. For years Wilson had a recurrent dream about this land:

I take a road that runs toward the west. It is summer; I pass by a strange summer forest, in which there are mysterious beings, though I know that, on the whole, they are shy and benign. If I am fortunate and find the way, I arrive at a wonderful river, which runs among boulders, with rapids between alders and highspread trees, through a countryside fresh, green and wide. We go in swimming; it is miles from anywhere. We plunge in the smooth flowing pools. We make our way to the middle of the stream and climb on the pale round gray stones and sit naked in the sun and air, while the river glides away below us. And I know that it is the place for which I have always longed, the place of wildness and freedom, to find which is the height of what one may hope for—the place of unalloyed delight. (Ibid., 505)

Something of the same dream was apparently also the balm and comfort of Wilson's father throughout his life. Edmund Wilson, Sr., acquired the large house at Talcottville through his wife's family, but it was he, rather than his wife, who felt at home in the wilderness of upper New York state. Apparently he saw in the house some kind of lifeline, a retreat from the complexities of his urban law practice— a refuge from the moral impurities and imperfections of twentieth-century life, where the mind could go to be refreshed.

Wilson, Sr., was a lonely and isolated individual, somehow out of tune with the post-Civil War world that violated everything that Talcottville and the old stone house stood for. He was, nonetheless, an extremely successful attorney, who dabbled in Republican politics in New Jersey, even becoming attorney general of the state under Democratic governor Woodrow Wilson. (President Wilson apparently thought well enough of Republican Wilson to consider him for a seat on the United States Supreme Court.) He had at one time served as an attorney for the Pennsylvania Railroad (which he came to loathe) and the New Jersey Board of Railroad Commissioners. He was an extraordinarily skillful and resourceful trial lawyer. He only lost one case in his entire career, and that one very early in his practice. "In court he attacked the jury with a mixture of learning, logic, dramatic imagination, and eloquence," a description that might apply equally well to his son's powers as a literary critic.

But apparently the elder Wilson's success had little to do with the characteristically American urgings toward success. He kept his law office above a liquor store; the fashionable life of Red Bank meant nothing to him. Although nominally a Republican who insisted to his skeptical son that "business had done a great deal to develop our natural resources," he found businessmen generally boring; he strenuously opposed the establishment of a business school at his alma mater, Princeton. Politically, as his son was also to be, Edmund Wilson, Sr., was a kind of instinctual Jeffersonian Democrat with a Tory coloring—a libertarian who had little faith either in big government or in big business. His greatest desire was to be left alone.

Wilson's mother, Helen Mather Kimball Wilson, possessed a different sort of temperament from her husband. She was an extrovert who preferred social activities, gardening, women's clubs, and teas. In his writings Wilson always took pains to emphasize the temperamental differences of his mother and father, although socially the differences were not great. Both mother and father belonged to a small and somewhat clannish local gentry, the young members of which had very little choice when it came to selecting marriage partners. Although it may be true, as Wilson insisted, that his mother might never have picked his moody and introverted father if anyone else had been available, both were bound by a similarity of family style and social outlook. Both came from families with deep roots in the American past, roots that were still solid and unbroken; both came from families that loathed the commercial ethic of post-Civil War industrial America and preferred to live on the outer fringes of high society, regarding the mainstream of American life with a kind of scornful detachment.

Wilson's maternal grandparents are described in a nostalgic essay, "At Laurelwood," centered around another house, this one at Lakewood, New Jersey—a house that also seems to have made a deep impression on Wilson. Wilson's maternal grandfather was a physician, a general practitioner who was much loved by his patients, and in his home at Laurelwood he tried to provide his family with genteel and aesthetic surroundings. Wilson's essay is a loving description of the ambiance of this house with its books, its games of chess, its conservatory, its flowers, its gardens. Grandmother Kimball "engendered about her a singular amenity and brightness. The essence of it seemed to reside in the exquisite odor of her house: the fresh fragrance of flowers combined with the seasoned smell of oriental rugs." Edmund also remembered a large cookie jar that his grandmother provided for the children. The "cookies were rather rich, and each was stabbed in the middle with a raisin. The jar in which they were kept was like a symbol of our grandmother's life: dignified and decorative without, full of comfort for human appetites within" (157-59).*

Grandfather Kimball was a man of science and a man of learning; but his library was as full of satisfactions for human appetites as grandmother's table and cookie jar. The library, the bookcases of which reached nearly to the ceiling and were ornamented by two small stuffed owls, contained the inevitable works expected in the collection of a medical man. Mainly, though, the books of Grandfather Kimball were suggestive of a wide-ranging, perhaps eccentric individual—a liberally educated man in the best old sense. Histories and old Bohn translations of the classics made up the foundation of the library. There were works on philosophy and religion, Spencer and Mill. He had J.A. Symonds's *Greek Poets,* Bulfinch's *Age of Fable,* and other works on classical mythology. "But he had also many out-of-the-way books that appealed to his taste for the marvelous: the Finnish epic, the *Kalevala,* from which Longfellow had taken the meter for *Hiawatha;* a fascinating book on Russian folklore by that pioneer scholar William Ralston; several works of which all I can remember is that they contained rather terrifying pictures of prehistoric animals and oriental gods." He would not have owned a five-foot shelf, or a great books series. "He preferred these long, old-fashioned, formless books full of amusing or curious things, such as Burton's *Anatomy of Melancholy* and the *Noctes Ambrosianae,* which one does not so much follow through as drop in from time to time, like the house of a learned friend" (159-60).

No doubt Wilson's own fierce scholarly independence and his wide-ranging reading habits were formed in that library at Laurelwood. There he may have established his preference for an individual style as opposed to specialization in learning. From his grandfather he may have absorbed the notion that it is better to cultivate oneself by means of an individual set of interests and proclivities than it is to follow some narrow pathway to innocuous and

*"At Laurelwood," which first appeared in the *New Yorker,* November 18, 1939, is reprinted in *Night Thoughts,* 157-77.

unimaginative professional certainty. Grandfather Kimball's library was the library of a freeman who was also something of an aristocrat.

Wilson's forebears on both his mother's and father's sides were aristocratic republicans of the early American type, like the majority of the signers of the Declaration of Independence. But the essay on Laurelwood also makes it clear that Grandfather Kimball stood in opposition to the commercial aristocracy of the new age. The essay discusses a visit that young Edmund had with a family that lived near Laurelwood, a family that was not only richer than the Kimballs, but much richer. This family, called Finch in the essay, although this was not their real name, had a boy of Edmund's age, and the two occasionally played together. The boy's father was the son of a great robber baron and railroad magnate, and he had built for himself a pretentious estate, surrounded by a black iron grille. The estate contained, among other things, a gymnasium, bowling alleys, a shooting gallery, a large swimming pool, and Turkish and Russian baths.

Wilson never really liked the Finches and felt uneasy in their home; the garish display of wealth pained him. In later years he remembered a sunken Italian garden with statues of classical gods and goddesses. The walks were carefully graveled and meticulously maintained. But he was "amazed and somewhat embarrassed to observe that there was a man standing by with a rake whose role was to smooth the gravel when anyone had walked or driven over it." Especially offensive to Wilson's democratic sensibilities was another incident that lingered in his memory all his life. One day, when Wilson, young James Finch, and the latter's governess were riding around the estate in a pony cart, James spied some apples that he wanted. He called for the footman to bring him some. At first the man hesitated, but young James became insistent. And "when the footman had gone after the apples, he turned to the governess and said: 'These men must do their duty, Anna!' " Even to the boyish Wilson these words were revolting. "I was shocked by them and did not like them. I should never have been allowed to behave like that, and it would never have occurred to me to speak like that to or about a servant. The incident dropped a partition between the Finches and me" (170, 172).

In his diaries and autobiographical fragments written over the years, Wilson took pains to emphasize the fact that his family belonged to a tradition of Jeffersonian individualists, of simple democrats; people like the Finches with their ostentatious spending, their hauteur, their misuse of people, left Wilson uncomfortable. Undoubtedly Wilson's liberalism in the 1930s, his sympathy for Lenin and the

Marxist movement, grew organically from the antiquarian democratic outlook that he had sniffed in the air at Laurelwood and Talcottville. A hostility to the grotesque excesses of capitalism that had
also troubled Henry Adams became a persistent theme in Wilson's
writing over the years.

The noncommercial aristocracy from which Wilson sprang,
whatever its strengths, seemed to be lost, floundering, in an America
that had turned another way. This is a major point in one of Wilson's
best autobiographical fragments, "The Author at Sixty," written in
1955. The difficulties found by the civilized elite of an earlier but
more fragile American society were never better described than in
this passage from that essay:

The period after the Civil War—both banal in a bourgeois way and fantastic
with giant fortunes—was a difficult one for families brought up in the old
tradition: the generation of my father and uncles. They had been educated
at Exeter and Andover and at eighteenth-century Princeton, and had afterwards been trained, like their fathers, for what had once been called the
learned professions; but they had then to deal with a world in which this kind
of education and the kind of ideals it served no longer really counted for
much. Such people, from the moment they left their schools, were subjected
to dizzying temptations, overpowering pressures, insidious diversions of purpose, and the casualties among them were terrible. Of my father's close
friends at college, but a single one was left by the time he was in his thirties:
all the rest were dead—some had committed suicide. (*Piece of My Mind*,
213-14)

These casualties, these psychic disasters, are rife in Wilson's family on both sides. On his mother's side there was Uncle Reuel, a
physician, a man of great charm, pillar of the family, much loved of
all who knew him. Although highly successful professionally, he
suffered from aimlessness, a poorly defined sense of purpose, which
gave way in middle life to serious periodic bouts with drinking. This
drinking, a kind of dipsomania, Wilson saw as a neurotic escape from
the world, a symbol that his Uncle Reuel's well-ordered professional
life had no ultimate meaning or significance.

Then on his father's side was his Uncle John, who had studied law
at the University of Virginia and had married the daughter of the
head of the school, "a delightful Virginian woman, full of humor and
charm, with no grasp of the practical life." He later moved with this
wife and young children to Pittsburgh because he had some college
friends there and assumed (for no rational reason) that it was a city
of great opportunity. But the place did nothing for him and he died

at the age of thirty-eight. His wife, who could never bear the cold Pittsburgh winters, returned to Charlottesville. Both seemed too fragile, too tender for the world in which they lived.*

Of course the most compelling example of this isolation and social alienation, the one that had the most impact on Wilson as a child and young man, was that of his own father. Despite the brilliance of the elder Wilson, despite his dramatic flair as a trial lawyer, he was obviously an uprooted man, a displaced and wounded soul. By the time he was thirty-five he was beginning to suffer neurotic eclipses, and in time these became longer and longer in duration and more difficult to combat. His neurosis took the form of hypochondria, and he spent nearly all of his later years in and out of sanatoria.

Wilson was convinced that his father's neurosis (what it would be called today is hard to say, since psychiatrists have largely abandoned the term *hypochondria*) was due to his lack of objectives in life. He had given up his political ambitions; he had had every possible success at law, but law, in the long run, bored him. With every passing year he had to spend more time in sanatoria, or on a plantation in North Carolina, or shut up at home in a room with a felt-covered door. But reflecting years later on his father's tragedy, Wilson marveled that a person of his class or his temperament could have survived at all. "To have got through with honor that period from 1880 to 1920! . . . I have never been obliged to do anything so difficult" (*Piece of My Mind,* 235).

But Edmund Wilson, Sr., had an even more reliable safety valve than that provided by sanatoria or the felt-covered door—the wide open spaces of Talcottville and the simple society provided by the people of the village nearby. Talcottville became, in fact, the elder Wilson's only true home. Although it came to him through his wife's family, and his wife never really liked it, he found it to be the only place where he could forget the pressures and demands of professional life. He had a devoted friend there with whom he made countless fishing trips and who was "a man of such imperturbable placidity that one felt it would be difficult for anyone to try to impress himself with neurotic complaints." He liked to talk to the people in the blacksmith shop and the general store. He gave splendid picnics for the local folk and took an interest in their affairs. (He was elected an honorary member of the Grange and enjoyed attending its meetings —which he would not have done in New Jersey.) Indoors he would

*Uncle Reuel and his bouts with alcoholism are described in *A Prelude,* 19-22; Uncle John is described in *A Piece of My Mind,* 216-17.

calm himself by inspecting tackle or by whittling sticks into slender cones. Above all, like his son after him, the microscopic community of Talcottville and the solid old stone house offered a balm for the hurt mind: "He would relax here as I can relax—at home with his own singularity as well as with the village life, at home with the strangeness of this isolated house as well as with the old America that it still represents so solidly" (237-38).

In his lengthy reminiscence of his father in "The Author at Sixty," Wilson concluded that the generation just before the First World War was subjected to pressures and forces every bit as devastating as those inflicted on his father and his uncles. This generation started out rejecting the materialism and priggishness of the late Victorian era and believed that they could refashion American life, having a little more fun than their fathers in the process. But, said Wilson, "We, too, have had our casualties"—suicides, breakdowns, premature deaths. "I myself had an unexpected breakdown when I was in my middle thirties . . . exactly the age at which my father had first passed into the shadow. I must have inherited from him some strain of neurotic distemper, and it may be that I was influenced by unconscious fear lest I be doomed to a similar fate" (235-36).

All of Wilson's autobiographical essays, all of the available letters and biographical fragments of friends and relations, suggest that Wilson's boyhood was marked by isolation and a search for sustaining cultural roots—roots that could not be supplied by his own parents, who came from the rapidly weakening aristrocratic classes. Whatever relief and escape might have been enjoyed by Edmund Wilson, Sr., through the mechanism of his neuroticism, or the withdrawal behind the green, felt-covered door, or the wilds of upstate New York, they must at first have provided little relief to an adolescent boy who was going to have to live in the standardized urban world of twentieth-century America.

Wilson's mother did not prove to be much help either. Unlike her introverted husband, Mrs. Wilson was outgoing, gregarious—a clubwoman type almost. She was interested in bridge playing, gardening, horses, and dogs. More than her husband, she savored the trappings of wealth, and the comforts that are usually accorded the genteel classes. But she had no intellectual interests to speak of and in later years never read any of her son's works. She was an enthusiastic follower of college sports and even in her old age continued to attend football and baseball games at Princeton. When Wilson was a boy, she inappropriately presented him with a baseball suit.

On practical grounds Wilson sided with his mother against the whims of the unapproachable father he adored. He admired the fact that his mother could seemingly stand up to the world, that she was brusque, forceful, and forthright. But he felt little in common with her and found little basis for affectionate closeness. In fact, he feared his mother somewhat, because it was she who did all of the disciplining and organizing. (Wilson, Sr., frequently threatened to whip his son "to within an inch of his life" but in actual fact never touched the boy, and Mrs. Wilson had to do whatever strapping needed to be done.) Mainly, though, the young Wilson did not share the same interests as his mother, and as he grew up he found nothing to talk to her about. As a teenager, anticipating coming home from prep school, Wilson once tried to compose a list of topics that he could discuss with his gregarious and outgoing mother but found himself hard pressed to come up with a single one. Her hearty effusiveness was a frequent source of embarrassment to him. When Mrs. Wilson took Edmund to his prep school—the Hill School at Pottstown, Pennsylvania—she referred to him in front of the other boys as "Bunny," a nickname that unfortunately stuck with him throughout his life.

Nor was the community around Red Bank, or the social class of his father's and mother's family much support for the adolescent Wilson. Around the time he was sent away to prep school Wilson recalled: "I had known hitherto almost no one but the members of my own family, and such marginal persons as surrounded these in their habitats of Red Bank, Seabright, Shrewsbury, Eatontown, and Talcottville. My first intimation of the fact that there existed other self-centered worlds had occurred when my mother took me on one of her annual March holidays to Atlantic City." Here he met some children from Philadelphia, a place every bit as insular as Red Bank, although naturally much larger. When some children he was playing with found that he was not from Philadelphia, they ran at once to their mother. " 'Never mind,' said their mother, 'he may be a very nice boy even if he doesn't come from Philadelphia' " (*Prelude*, 45).

If the young Wilson was generally a lonely and introspective child, which we must accept from his own testimony, he had nonetheless been able to put down some firm roots that would serve him faithfully throughout his life. There was his grandfather's library, and, in time, the much larger world of books; like so many writers to be, Wilson's youth was filled with reading and all the fancies of the imagination. He found his first real intellectual haven at prep school, which he entered in 1909 at the age of fourteen. The choice of a school for Wilson was eccentric and inexplicable, like most such decisions made by Mr. and Mrs. Wilson—it was the Hill School of

Pottstown, Pennsylvania, slightly removed in style and spirit from the typical schools selected by wealthy Easterners intending to send their sons on to Princeton, Yale, or Harvard. The school had been founded by the Reverend Matthew Meigs, a Presbyterian minister from Connecticut, and in Wilson's day was run by Reverend Meigs's son John—a man of imposing and upright presence—who had whipped the school into first-class shape by sheer moral energy. The Hill School's aim was to serve not the genteel Eastern seaboard but the industrial towns of Pennsylvania; not the sons of Wall Street, but the sons of anthracite barons and coke-oven princes. Instead of being snooty it endeavored to be stern and academically sound.

John Meigs himself was a formidable man but not at all what would be called a pedant. He had a certain smartness about him, although this was not the smartness of the Episcopalian headmasters found in the more refined and fashionable New England schools. He was a figure who inspired confidence and in whom one could feel pride. Above all he ran a first-rate school—financially sound, meticulously organized, and without "any of those moral leaks which cause favoritism, ill-feeling and inefficiency." The Hill School was scholastically at the top of the heap. Apparently Meigs had spared no expense on education and had expended a certain amount of imaginative effort to bring the school up to the highest standards and to obtain the best masters.

There were a few reasons for complaint from the students' point of view. The school was somewhat *too* efficient, *too* demanding, allowing the boys almost no time for themselves. But though Wilson, like most of his classmates, chafed under this stern regimen, he also profited from it. The school had a demanding curriculum, and there was a legend at the time that no Hill student ever failed to get into college; so tough was the work, so rigorous the drill, that most students found the college examinations child's play.

The teachers were demanding at Hill School, but they were never mere drill masters. Wilson's most memorable teacher was Alfred Rolfe, the Greek master, who later became the subject of a nostalgic memoir in *The Triple Thinkers*. A New Englander, Rolfe gave Wilson a genuine feel for high civilization of the Concord period. Most important, he taught Wilson the value of combining erudition with softer humanistic flavorings. When he taught Homer he made the students "translate every word into an English not unworthy of the original." He was a man who would make you get everything right, who would force you to respect precision and exactitude. But he did this not merely to be fussy or pedantic; rather he wanted his students to feel the true being and essence of the classics. He could impart a soaring vision of life in ancient Greece, "and the first time you heard him read a passage of Homer aloud in class you knew what Homer was as poetry." In addition, Rolfe was a highly personal teacher. He took a strong interest in Wilson, opened his personal library to him, shared with him his opinions and prejudices.

The Hill School obviously had a strong impact on Wilson—it gave him his lifelong faith in the value of a thorough and well-disciplined education as well as his first opportunities for social intercourse with intellectuals, indeed the first sustained social intercourse with anyone outside his small family circle. At the school he made friends to visit during summer vacations and some friendships that would last all his life. It gave him the first feeling of human identity and social permanence he had known. Above all, the school offered him his first opportunities as a writer—his first tales and poems were published in the *Hill School Record.*

If it had been for the Hill School alone, Wilson might well have gone on to become a scholar or teacher by profession. But in his college years, the lure of a literary career must have beckoned to the youngster, who once more became an editor of the student literary magazine, but now something of an observer of the social scene as well. Wilson moved back to his home state of New Jersey in 1912, joining the freshman class that year at Princeton University. After the academic rigors of the Hill School, Wilson found Princeton almost a breeze. In the atmosphere of Princeton, half respectable college and half country club for the sons of Wall Street bankers, Wilson found quite enough leisure time to broaden his interests while spending his spare time as he saw fit. Like so many other undergraduates, he neglected certain academic subjects. The record shows, for example, that Wilson hardly bothered to master the rudiments of chemistry and mathematics.

The years at Princeton were both fruitful and invigorating, expanding Wilson's horizons in a number of directions. He encountered inspiring teachers, especially Christian Gauss, who kindled his interest in European literatures and initiated his lifelong study of foreign languages. He established himself—at first under the editorship of T.K. Whipple—as a writer on the *Nassau Literary Magazine,* familiarly known as the *Lit.* He made numerous contributions to the *Lit*—a few rather weak poems and stories but some first-rate essays and criticism. He continued to be something of a loner during those years and struck students who knew him as a bit stuffy—a fastidious "poler" or "grind," perhaps. Nonetheless, he was far from antisocial

The
Nassau Literary
Magazine

Volume LXXI

APRIL 1915   MARCH 1916

EDITORIAL BOARD

EDMUND WILSON, JR., *Managing Editor*

HAMILTON FISH ARMSTRONG   JOHN PEALE BISHOP
B. B ATTERBURY   ALEXANDER L. McKAIG
W. S. DELL   J. S. NICHOLAS

BUSINESS DEPARTMENT

DOUGLAS H. KENYON, *Business Manager*
KIRK MOORE, *Circulation Manager*
JAMES M. GARVEY   EDWARD F. McNICHOL

FOUNDED BY THE CLASS OF 1842

Published by the Undergraduates of Princeton University

1916

and used his college years to develop and enlarge his circle of friends. He naturally gravitated toward the literary bunch—to professors like Christian Gauss, and young writers like Scott Fitzgerald and John Peale Bishop, with all of whom he would maintain long-term relations.

In his senior year Wilson served as managing editor of the *Nassau Literary Magazine,* a position that must have directed his thinking toward a future career as a practicing journalist. Doubtless, too, it put him in good stead for the years ahead when he held editorial positions on both *Vanity Fair* and the *New Republic.* The *Lit* carefully reflected the Princeton of the time—a Princeton that still had one foot in the Puritanism of the eighteenth century, another in the twentieth-century world of American capitalism. Princeton did not quite know whether it wanted to be a seminary for starched-collar dons or a resort for young playboys—a moral dilemma that certainly appealed to Wilson's complex sensibilities. The literary magazine itself dabbled both in politics and literature—two persistent forces in Wilson's career.

It was also strongly concerned, naturally, with matters of academic politics and college life. In this area the *Lit* directed itself to establishing complete individual freedom, to the elimination of compulsory courses, and to the abolition of required attendance at chapel. It generally addressed itself to the kinds of concerns that have always occupied the minds of undergraduates—pricking the balloons of adult authority being one of its special delights. On the other hand, insofar as the *Lit* represented the intellectual elite at Princeton, it also scoffed at athleticism, the superficial trappings of club life, and the anti-intellectualism of the typical undergraduate. The editors of the *Lit,* following the guidance of men like Gauss, sought to cultivate intellectual interests that were serious but not pedantic, playful but not frivolous, genteel but not fussy. Couldn't students be induced to attend a play by George Bernard Shaw rather than the "dismal farces" of the Triangle Club? Couldn't they be induced to read novelists like Wells and Bennett rather than slavishly following the musty old classical curriculum, the only release from which was the weekend orgy?

His experiences on the *Lit* and his observations of college life must have convinced Wilson that his destiny lay in the direction of journalism, or at the very least, some kind of writing for the general public. At the time he was convinced that he was headed in the same direction as friends like Fitzgerald and Bishop, and this belief steered him away from any kind of permanent academic attachment. Wilson had discovered that the academic profession, as it had developed in the twentieth century, held too few charms. Student life in general (except for a few enclaves carved out by isolated individuals) was frivolous; on the other hand, with the exception of a few playful and far-ranging scholars like Gauss, the typical professor was rigid and unimaginative, uncurious about the larger world outside his specialty. Partially stifled himself by the limited associations of his childhood, Wilson was now boundlessly curious about the world outside. He wanted to bustle around in it and find out what made it tick. Above all, he wanted to write.

Edmund Wilson's first published book did not appear until 1922. This was *The Undertaker's Garland,* a literary miscellany written with his Princeton classmate John Peale Bishop. A lot of water had gone over the dam since Wilson's graduation from college in 1916. Like most young men of his generation, Wilson had been sidetracked by the war, his goals and objectives held in abeyance until this great conflict that meant so much to his elders finally came to an end. The wartime interregnum was not as traumatic for Wilson as it had been for some of his contemporaries, especially after a little assistance and influence from his father got him assigned to military intelligence. His wartime reminiscences were bitter, as we can see from some of the poems and stories from *The Undertaker's Garland,* but his final months of army life were primarily filled with a kind of intellectual lethargy and ennui. Wilson's voracious appetite as a reader was apparently not affected however; at the end of his book *The Prelude,* he appended a list of about two hundred books that he read between the summer of 1917 and the armistice of 1918.

But Wilson's return to civilian life, like that of many of his fellow doughboys, was marked by a mood of disillusionment. It was not just the war itself; it was this nagging question of what was there for young Americans on their return home. Wilson, already witness to the deterioration of his father's mental health, began his youthful writing in this bleak mood of questioning despair. *The Undertaker's Garland* contains a preface, two stories, and four poems by Wilson; five poems, one short play, and a story by Bishop, the theme of all being "death"—not, of course, the literal death that the two authors had so happily eluded in the war but the death of the spirit; the death, as it seemed to them, of cultural life in America. The war itself could be endured, hinted Wilson in the preface; but a grimmer side of death awaited the chastened veterans on their return to their homeland. One could survive the war, but what was there to come home to? Only, it seemed, to an America in which the old traditions of liberty had been lost, in which the culture was low and tawdry, the spirit stale and weary.

The Undertaker's Garland is a grim book, laced with a mood of complete cynicism about the war and corruption of life on the home front. It is a youthful jihad against Puritanism, sexual repression, the standardization of manners and morals, the dead hand of convention and propriety. Nevertheless, in his preface Wilson blithely insists that the book was written "in a spirit which we hope is one of loyal Americanism." This manifesto on death was an attempt to clear away the cobwebs, to wipe the slate clean, to start over. The younger generation, Wilson believed, had come back to discover a new faith, to find out what in the American cultural landscape they could believe in.

Wilson's journalistic career, in full swing right after the war, probably dissipated those moods of despair. So, too, did life in Greenwich Village, where all the hopes and expectations of the young sought fulfillment. But those grim satirical poems and stories of the postwar period, however callow and superficially idealistic, foreshadowed Wilson's later literary career. He had not yet found the optimum blend of his literary efforts, but he had clearly found the major ground of his intellectual concern. He would be a writer, a critic of ideas, most specifically, a critic of American ideas. He was never gripped by the desire to become an expatriate, to live abroad; no, as he said in the preface to *The Undertaker's Garland,* the antidote to death is to look around and see what is alive, what fruits will still grow. What is out there for Americans? Where can we turn, what should we do? His literary career thereafter was a kind of intellectual search for some release from that "ache of disorder," or "burden of uncomprehended events," that he later spoke about so vividly in his essay "The Historical Interpretation of Literature." Wilson had his own personal reasons for asking. He had seen his family lose its moorings, he had seen the virtues of the older, republican America disintegrate. In any case, the pre-1914 world, which had once had a meaning of its own, had died. Wilson's all-consuming project was now to make some sense out of the welter of events that seemed to be passing by so recklessly as the decade of the 1920s dawned.

2

The New Wilderness

The distinguished American historian Richard Hofstadter once remarked that "the United States was born in the country and has moved to the city." He might have gone one step further to observe that America has always been shaken by change and tumult—we are a people born to one set of conditions and then rudely jostled into another. Like all people, Americans crave certainty, stability, a degree of permanence in social life, but perhaps more than any other people in history we have repeatedly faced economic upheaval as a result of the cycles of boom and bust that have characterized most of our history from the first days of the Republic. Sometimes the American finds the social world he knew in his youth falling apart with no new and clearly distinct world to take its place. He may find himself prepared for a vocation that is no longer in demand; he may find that the training and upbringing that formed his individual style count for nothing and have to be discarded.

For many generations the volatile character of American social life and the cruelty of boom and bust economic cycles went unrecognized by the nation's intellectuals because there was always general growth, prosperity, and a mood of national self-confidence and optimism. Between the Civil War and World War I there was a period of tremendous euphoria and self-assuredness, and the average American had not the slightest doubt that everything would work out for the best, even in the 1870s and 1880s when many of the nation's farmers were starving, or in the terrible depression of 1893 when thousands of the urban poor wandered city streets in threadbare desperation. There was enough general prosperity and spiritual gusto in this period to cover up the darkness. But, as Edmund Wilson once remarked of his father's generation of Americans, "To have got through with honor that period from 1880 to 1920" was little short of startling; even their sons who went through the war as they emerged from college did not have it so bad. Very often those of Edmund Wilson, Sr.'s, generation fought blindly against forces they only imperfectly understood. Sometimes they went to the top; sometimes they were crushed or caught in the gears of some mysterious social mechanism that life had not prepared them to avoid.

But the young writers and intellectuals who came to maturity just before the war, who weathered the war years either at home or abroad, and who began their creative life in the 1920s, were clearly a different breed. They had no intention of suffering in silence; they were questioners, doubters, skeptics, often cynics. They struggled to understand American life and their place in it even when it meant that they were ruined in the process. Although they were ruined as often as their parents who failed to cry out, they did speak out, loudly and eloquently; hence the twenties provide us with a clue to the typically American style, to our own unique pattern of enlightened world-weariness. It may be that times since have muffled the essential truths about ourselves, but the young writers of the twenties saw what had to be seen with precision and clarity.

Edmund Wilson gave us one of our richest and most enlightening literary panoramas of the twenties, not because he was of the famous "lost generation," as Gertrude Stein called it, but because he continued to be an American and wrote voluminously of his most intimate, native experiences in the twenties. He was not an expatriate but one of those who stayed home to grapple with the diversity and complexity in the life around him, and, for that matter, to do some living himself. He traveled during the twenties, primarily in the United States; for the greater part of the time he lived in Greenwich Village in close proximity to his job on the *New Republic* and to the largest cluster of young writers and intellectuals that has ever gathered in America in any one place. In Greenwich Village Edmund Wilson learned to live, he learned what in himself was stale and should be cast aside and what was capable of growth and development. At the same time he was cultivating a sensitive understanding of his contemporaries: he was given to agonizing over their fates, their dreams, their disasters—the interaction of their careers and the social milieu.

Wilson has provided us with a rich legacy of material dealing with the America of the 1920s. Not only did he write a number of stories and plays with a distinct flavor of the decade and the interesting first novel, *I Thought of Daisy,* he also wrote the many fine literary sketches later published under the title *The Shores of Light,* perhaps the most remarkable collection of its kind about the culture and literature of the 1920s. Throughout his life Wilson continued to think deeply of writers that he had known in the twenties, constantly and regularly revising his ideas about them. He did not issue one official white paper on Scott Fitzgerald, H. L. Mencken, or Edna Millay and then leave them buried for posterity, but he wrote repeatedly about these writers who for one reason or other had moved him or impinged upon his existence in earlier years. At the end of his life Wilson was editing his notebooks from the twenties (published posthumously as *The Twenties* in 1975), writing fresh interpretations and explanations for a book that now seems to be his most intimate and highly personalized vision of the decade.

The appearance of Wilson's notebooks in recent years is an especially valuable addition to the long-available novels, plays, poems, and critical essays. They contain so much excellent journalistic writing that it is a pity that this work had to be withheld from the public for so long. It was undoubtedly withheld because the notebooks were too personal for publication in the dignified literary publications and magazines Wilson contributed to throughout the period. But, as Edmund Wilson himself must have recognized later on, his reputation as the American Defoe is due in no small part to his highly personalized accounts of contemporary events. Indeed one can learn a great deal more about the ambiance of Americans in the 1920s from reading the notebooks than from reading *I Thought of Daisy*.

Whatever the case, a careful reading of everything Wilson wrote about the twenties either at the time or from the vantage point of a fifty-year remove gives us a splendid and rich account of the period. At the same time, it allows us a sweeping vision of American life. The period of the twenties is a microcosm of the American experience; it was then that the velocity of social change began to hurt; it was then that young American writers began to react.

When Wilson began his work on *Vanity Fair* after his return from the army, he quite naturally took up residence in New York. His diaries from the 1920s reveal that he made many trips around the country during this period—trips to Red Bank to see his parents or to California or the Southwest—but Greenwich Village was his home, the place he sought to understand. His first novel, *I Thought of Daisy*, is set in the Village like many of his early sketches and stories. Wilson's youthful preoccupation with the Village environment is tightly wrapped up with his vision of American life. The Village was not only a haven for writers who had tasted success, but also for bohemians, ne'er-do-wells—perhaps the estranged son of some New England mill owner; the dilettante daughter of some prosperous suburban doctor; a drunk; a failure; a lost soul. Not a microcosm of American life, exactly, for here were no Carol Kennicotts, or Babbitts, or Clyde Griffiths, but a place where the sensitive writer might discover himself in a congenial and thought-provoking environment. Above all, Greenwich Village mirrored the growth and decay, the inspiration and desperation in America at the time.

The Village as a haunt of artists and intellectuals did not begin with the twenties but in the decade before the war. In fact, by the mid-twenties the Village became so popular with middle-class people looking for "atmosphere" that the artists and intellectuals were pressed out and had to find cheaper quarters in Chelsea, Brooklyn Heights, or even Hoboken, New Jersey. Some had begun the long trek to southern California or Taos, New Mexico. But before high rents and land values squeezed out the artists, Greenwich Village came as close as any place we have had in our history to a spot where people of intellectual or artistic interests could congregate and express their feelings of revolt and alienation.

Wilson was not a bohemian or arty type, and later he found that many others who had sought the Village as a nesting place—Edna Millay being a good example—were also *in* it but not *of* it. Still Wilson relished the sexual freedom of the Village, the fluidity of the social situation where one could mingle freely with a great variety of people that one would never meet in Red Bank or in a college community like Princeton. Wilson was never a joiner, and he did not seek out the Village as a way of reaching notoriety on someone else's coattails—a typical pattern of the place. Rather he came and stayed as an outside observer, a watcher of the passing scene. Yet he came to join in a sense. As a somewhat stuffy and inhibited scholar he still needed to rub elbows with the masses, to make love with women who rode the subway from Brooklyn rather than the well-groomed and sheltered types he knew in the suburbs. But intellectually Wilson never joined the Village core; he held himself aloof, always the skeptic, always the outsider.

The unnamed narrator of *I Thought of Daisy*—loosely based on Wilson himself—attaches himself to an old school chum named Hugo Bamman who is a more typical and standardized Village product. Wilson makes clear, through the words of his narrator, that in his initial contact with the Village he was breathing in the air, catching the flavor of things, but holding his own attitudes in suspension. He would go along with the prevailing mood in a vague way:

My whole point of view at this period was still largely taken over from my old school-friend, Hugo Bamman; he had come, after the War, to live in Greenwich Village, and I had been brought there by his example. It was Hugo who had taken me around and who had told me what to think of what I saw; and I had seen through Hugo's eyes. The people whom Hugo thought important seemed important to me too: he and they, I believed, were leaders, leaders of the fine social idealism which cut under capitalistic politics. To them the social revolution seemed as real as their love affairs; and I had often a guilty consciousness that it was not real enough to me. (6)

But if the various slogans and life-styles of Greenwich Village were not quite real to Wilson, if somehow he stayed apart from them all, he did manage to get from his Village experience something of far greater value. He was able to capture and put down on paper impressions of the kaleidoscopic motion of life in the Village that also expressed the spirit of the twenties. What he found were people drifting into the Village from all parts of the country, from all social spheres—people grasping for some ideology, some pattern of habitual behavior, some permanent home, and then discovering either nothing at all or some temporarily solid ground that in turn got knocked out from under them.

Near the beginning of his collection *The Shores of Light,* Wilson presents two sketches from this period under the general title "Greenwich Village in the Early Twenties." The first of these sketches, "The Road to Greenwich Village," is taken from life; the second, "Fire Alarm," is imaginary. Both are powerful and moving vignettes of American life. Both give us a vivid idea of what Wilson was feeling in the 1920s.

"The Road to Greenwich Village" is a first-person account of a woman who leaves the narrow constricting environment of the West for a job as a seamstress in Greenwich Village. The narrative has something of the quality of a Sherwood Anderson short story: the luckless woman, like Anderson's grotesques, is perpetually out of joint with her surroundings. As a child she receives very little education. Her father, an itinerant "half-doctor" puts her in a narrow-minded girl's school in Greeley Valley, Colorado. After looking at her father's medical books she tells some of the girls that a baby looks like a tadpole before it is born. For this she is bawled out by the teachers and eventually socially ostracized.

She is married when she is fourteen and goes to Washington state. In a passage eerily reminiscent of Anderson's prose she reports: "On the train when I was on my way up there, a man got in from

Idaho, and when he heard I was going to Washington, he said, 'You're going to Washington, are you? Well, when you've been there a little while, you'll be all covered with moss—you'll have moss growing on your eyebrows and hanging out of your ears, and your hair will be full of moss' " (74).

But loneliness, not moss, is to be her worst enemy. Her husband is cruel and mean—he is supposed to have Indian blood and to have played tricks on her. One time he tries to poison her with strychnine. She has two children in fifteen years but always she is trapped, hemmed in by a cruel and uninspiring environment. She tries to get her hands on books, anything that will carry her away. In the wilds of Washington she has to settle for an almanac and a seed catalog, but later, from a circulating library in Seattle she is able to obtain E.P. Roe's *The Opening of a Chestnut Burr* and *He Fell in Love with His Wife.*

Leaving her husband she returns to her father who has set up medical practice in Oklahoma. But Oklahoma is, if anything, even more constricting and culturally barren than Washington. She does manage to see movies that deal with New York or other romantic places, but she finds out that anybody who claims to have read a book is the object of suspicion. ("They didn't even read the Bible.") She reads Darwin and *The Wandering Jew* by Eugene Sue, later D.H. Lawrence and Michael Arlen, but this makes her a marked woman. People begin to talk about her as if she were some sort of wild eccentric; they point her out whenever she walks along the street.

After a number of indignities she decides to try New York, which in her mind is the acme of sophistication and the source of freedom's light. "So finally I came to the Village. I did sewing. Now I run this little store, and I like it, because I always had a sort of original taste in decorations and things. . . . Another thing is that nobody cares what you do down here—nobody expects you to cook or to go to church—and you can always talk to interesting people. I tell you, the West is all right, but it's a great relief to get some place where you can feel a little bit free. I know all about those great open spaces" (81).

The road to Greenwich Village represented a distinct inversion of the early American pattern. Wilson's ancestors, who built the stone house at Talcottville, followed a road that led away from the settlements; they believed that freedom was to be found in the wide open spaces. But the call of Greenwich Village was the reverse.

People in the twenties believed that freedom could be found in urban impersonality, not in the small towns of rural America, where people cared what church you belonged to, how clean your apartment was, and whether you lived with someone other than your spouse. The people who came to Greenwich Village wanted to make interesting new associations, but their main motivation was to cut loose from their old, restrictive environments and, perhaps, from any sense of duty.

But it was far from clear what value was really being gotten from these new associations. Many of those who came to the Village in the twenties or before were achieving freedom from something, but what were they achieving freedom to do? In the case of this working woman from the West there was a little shop and some sewing to do. In the case of numerous young bohemians there was the promise that one could hobnob with a real poet or a real painter. In neither case was there any promise that the Village would make a gift of anything. But that is what young Americans were looking for—a gift of the abdication of responsibility and a promise of security. With the right place to live and the right job, they believed they would have it made.

But in Wilson's experience there was no such thing as certainty and security. In the Village of the twenties you did not really know who you were or what was lying ahead. If you went to a party you did not know whether you were being introduced to a real poet or a phony one, in part because of the fragility and artificiality of Greenwich Village social life, but also because of the tremendous upheaval that was taking place in the arts, and the consequent lack of certainty that this or that art was going to be held in esteem by the public a few years hence.

In the second part of Wilson's portrait of "Greenwich Village in the Early Twenties," the so-called fictional part entitled "Fire Alarm," Wilson pins this motif down further. (Interestingly, though Wilson labeled the first part factual and the second part imaginary, he blurred the distinction between the two; he was reporting critically and imaginatively in both essays.) "Fire Alarm" is about a play of the same name, written, produced, and acted in by a miscellaneous lot of Greenwich Village characters. The action of the play concerns the nervous breakdown of a worker in a paper-box factory. There are eighteen scenes—absurd in itself—but the absurdity of the plot and the language show that Wilson was also amusing himself with a spoof of the then fashionable expressionistic drama about which he was writing reviews in the *New Republic*.

Beneath the surface of the lighthearted satire is a deft and incisive comment on Village characters and Village life. The playwright,
DeGross Wilbur, is "a pale vain young man, who not only had never
seen a paper box factory, but had never even been near the textile
mills where his father made bathing suits." When asked why he
wrote a play about workers in a factory when he neither knew nor
cared anything about workers or factories, Wilbur replied that "he
simply believed that the time had come for that sort of play to be
written." Here, then, is a singularly mindless fellow who has no ties
to the world that created him and who is floundering aimlessly,
comically, in an environment that he knows nothing about.

Then there is the director, Bob Mott, "who had done a little of
everything in the Village." He cultivates a unique style in dress and
manner, perhaps foreshadowing "the real thing." He is impressive:
"He would sit in a corner and smoke with a homely or rugged assur-
ance that seemed to mask treasures of subtlety and wit, and people
would gather about him to hear his judgments on all sorts of subjects." Unfortunately, when you get beneath the surface there is little
more to Bob Mott than to DeGross Wilbur: "When you really got to
know him, you found out that the basis of his character was a smug
invincible limpness" (85).

But far and away the most interesting character to appear in this
sketch is a woman who attends the last performance of the play (its
run, needless to say, is short). This woman pops out of nowhere—
what could be more characteristic of Greenwich Village life, this
turbulent melting pot of melting pots? "After the performance," says
the narrator, "a strange rigid woman—a spinster of about forty-five,
who wore spectacles and was dressed in hideous clothes of some
remote age and place—appeared at the stage door and desired to
meet the author." She talks nervously and sounds not a little mad. Or
so the narrator thinks. But, as was so often the case in the Village,
things are not what they seem.

The mad lady turns out to be Isabelle Griffin. "I did not know that
she was eventually to become the first woman dramatist of importance in the history of the theatre. And I was even further from
guessing that this immature and incoherent play of Wilbur's was
actually to show her the way to her own creative development."
Apparently she is influenced not only by the silly play itself but by
the jokes and accidents of the last performance. She is a schoolteacher from Gibson, Colorado, who heretofore "had read almost
nothing but seventeenth-century poetry," but in passing through
Greenwich Village she hits upon something that is to spark an im-

mense creative vision; later, she comes to be talked about in the same breath as Strindberg. A farfetched and even grotesque character, she forcefully makes Wilson's point about the fluidity of Village life.

Isabelle Griffin, flung like a meteor as if from outer space, and not one of the Greenwich Village "authentics," is mentioned with Strindberg. Here she is, dressed not in the expected garb but "in some hideous clothes of some remote age and place," not having arrived anywhere, just in transition. Hers is the archetypical American pattern: up and down, backward and forward, ebb and flow. There are social backgrounds that seem to promise much and deliver little; there are others, wildly implausible, from which genius may spring. Nowhere could these truths about spiritual and creative life be seen better than in the Greenwich Village of the nineteen twenties.

Another side to the tenuousness and fragility of Greenwich Village life was the economic unreliability and unpredictability of the superstructure that must support the artist or intellectual in any society. This side is dramatically illustrated in the second of Wilson's portraits of the Village later reprinted in *The Shores of Light,* "Greenwich Village at the End of the Twenties." This portrait, like the earlier one, is divided into two parts, the first of which, "15 Beech Street," is said to be fiction, the second, "Hans Stengel," fact. The theme of both these vignettes was the deterioration of the Village and of its residents under economic pressure. The first, "15 Beech Street," written in 1927, deals predominantly with physical changes in the Village caused by rising land and rent values that were driven up by an influx of middle-class respectables looking for excitement. The narrator visits his old friend Jane Gooch, a long-time Village resident who has been struggling to keep her little magazine *Vortex* alive. In the description of the large rooming house on Beech Street, and in the narrator's conversation with Jane Gooch, we learn something about the pattern of change: the names on the letterboxes are different, some apartments are vacant, people have moved away, died, or committed suicide. Above all, economic conditions have created new life-styles. Ralph Davis, the poet whose address the narrator hoped to get from Jane, is now a writer for the magazine of a Detroit automobile firm. Another young writer who had been living with a girl got a job working for one of the tabloids and married a "respectable girl." His old girl friend, in turn, married a saloon keeper "who made enough money to live uptown by selling bad whiskey and gin to people who came from uptown to drink it."

The second of these two pieces, "Hans Stengel," makes the same point in a less diffused, more carefully focused way. Hans Stengel was a German-born artist who had at one time been associated with the group in Munich that produced *Simplicissimus* and who emigrated to the United States hoping to turn a profit from his knack for caricature. Shortly after his arrival in this country he sought out the offices of *Vanity Fair,* with which Wilson was then connected. Stengel's caricatures were vigorous and often repulsive drawings of the German school, "harsh, mordant, sometimes monstrous, sometimes gruesome." They were, said Wilson, the sort of thing that did not fit in commercially in the twenties. "The prevailing taste at that time was for the agreeable triviality and the thin distinction of line of French or English drawing: and Hans Stengel was not merely too harsh, but also in a sense, too serious." No magazine would touch his work, and although for a short time he was the principal caricaturist for the Sunday *Herald Tribune,* he was always an outcast, an outsider; he spent the year before his suicidal death doing a silly daily feature for a cheap evening paper. In these features he had been forced to eliminate all the distinctive qualities of his work and he refused to sign them.

Stengel, who apparently had great wit and charm, was a man of the world. Even with only a small amount of money to entertain he became one of the most popular hosts in Greenwich Village: Mencken, Dreiser, and Robert Chanler were among his friends. He was one of the few people toward the end of the Greenwich Village era capable of attracting a regular company of friends and admirers. "He displayed, on these occasions, a vein of ironic commentary, fantastic but also acute. . . . He was also, for all his Prussian pose, capable of generosity and a certain sensitive feeling." Altogether, a remarkable man. His personality far transcended his professional achievements. He was, to be sure, a gifted caricaturist, though not, according to Wilson, of the highest rank. On the other hand, little things like his German accent, his Prussian air, worked against him in the commercial field. "It is possible," noted Wilson, "that a caricaturist of the very first rank might have been able to force New York to accept him." But Stengel, who had the raw talent to be commercially successful, fell somehow between the interstices for vague, hard-to-define reasons. In the end, although always admirable and socially successful, he knew himself to be a failure in the eyes of the world. At one of his evening parties he shut himself into a coat closet, tied a rope to his neck and the doorknob, and strangled himself by pulling against the door.

Wilson admitted that we could look on this human failure as attributable to the fact the Stengel was foreign, not assimilated. Yet he was unwilling to place all of the blame for Stengel's "failure" on the man himself:

> It is natural to put down a failure to survive in one's own community—where we ourselves have no difficulty in prospering—to the deficiency of the person who fails; but it is sometimes a good idea to inquire into the deficiencies of one's civilization from the point of view of what it destroys. (366)

Wilson raises an issue here that was of deep concern to him throughout his career. Could it be that a great material civilization (and "Hans Stengel" was written during the height of the twenties' prosperity) that holds out everywhere the promise of unbounded success, actually breaks many people, especially many of the wrong sorts of people, many rare and unusual people. In Greenwich Village everyone was supposed to be free; there was said to be total freedom of expression. Ultimately, however, the economic system, and the commercial ethic that it embraced, was more often shoddy and cruel than noble and uplifting.

Of course it was not until the thirties that Wilson was confronted with this problem in its full and awful intensity, but many of his writings—critical essays, diary entries, stories, plays—were devoted from the first to the stifling quality of commercial and industrial America. In the preface to his first published work, *The Undertaker's Garland,* Wilson drew a grim parallel between the killing war from which the young men were returning and the spiritual killing that was going on at home, the deadening of culture, the stifling of manners and morals. Later, in his early stories such as "After the Game," "Emily in 'Hades,'" and "The Men from Rumplemayer's" and in plays like "Cronkhite's Clocks" and "The Crime in the Whistler Room," Wilson deals, however immaturely and ineffectively, with the theme that was so dominant in his thinking during the twenties, namely, the inability of a strong and vigorous culture to survive in an industrial and commercial society that insisted upon rigid conformity of social behavior.

In recent years, with the publication of Wilson's diaries and notebooks from the twenties, we get a clear idea of another strong concern of Wilson's that echoes this grim view of America's too-rigid social structure and dead morals. This is a belief that the landscape is being cluttered up, that the great open spaces, like those that beckoned Wilson's forebears to Talcottville, were being filled by urban sprawl, by worthless industrial development over which there was no governance and against which the individual was powerless.

There is in Wilson's diaries some powerful descriptive writing—far more striking and effective than anything in his stories—descriptions of the American landscape written after his travels around the countryside. Always in these passages we have the stark contrast between a world of industrial might and another of spiritual suffocation. Here is Wilson riding on the Pennsylvania Railroad back home to Red Bank, or perhaps back to Princeton, as the train emerges from the tunnel under the Hudson River to encounter the industrial marshes of northern New Jersey near Newark:

Coming out of the Hudson tunnel, one finds oneself emerging from a hill on whose barren sides are seen the straggling frame houses of suburbs, the last city streets of some New Jersey town which is itself a suburb of New York; one stark church stands up in the sordid landscape, where one is surprised to see even the outer semblance of a religion; if it is actually the house of a religion and not merely a building designed mechanically, in an obsolete form and by architects who had more taste for designing factories, as an inexpensive recognition of a respectable convention; it is a religion hardened and begrimed and divested of beauty, which has assumed protective coloring in order to live at all. It is a country forever tarnished by a dingy haze of dampness and smoke. At the foot of the hill lies a vast marsh of swamp grass, bleached by the fall, with patches still persisting in a feeble verdancy and with stagnant pools corrupted by a vivider green; the whole of this dead meadow is laced with telephone wires and occasionally traversed by muddy roads that seemed to be foundering. The one touch of color and life was the series of large board signs that advertised New York hotels and theaters, underclothes, candy and shaving soaps. Then one saw the factories with tapering smokestacks; one of them had four chimneys and lay like a ship in the marsh. The landscape bristled with chimneys and with cranes along the railroad tracks. And there were human habitations: feeble-looking houses, unpainted and gray, which, but for an occasional line of clothes drying in the tainted air, would have seemed bleached to as complete a death as the sea they were islanded in. At last, after ten minutes' ride in a world of factories, one reaches a body of water, perfectly black and still, where the hulk of an old steamboat, as black as the river, has been rotting and sinking slowly for several years and shows only its warped upper deck and its blackened wheel. This is Newark Bay, and the city is Newark: more factories here, but jammed together; small factories and machine shops, pattern-makers and electroplaters, press close beside the train—manufacturers of castings, blowpipes, paints, chemicals, mattresses, fountain pens, ketchup, refrigerators, phonographs, bacon, chewing gum, safety razors, cigarettes, carpet sweepers, licorice drops, flours, letter openers, typewriters, umbrellas. The city and the bay produce a curious impression of mingled life and death: there is business, one can see that; there is lots of work being done; there is prosperity in the cheap stores and solid buildings; but in the dirtiness of the streets, the dull colors of the city, the lack of any sign of a love for cleanness or brightness, the impression of life grown heavy and sordid in those thousands of brick-walled rooms behind those dirty windows, one felt that death was rotting and blackening the city, as it had that old steamboat hulk which no one had thought to destroy or save. (*Twenties,* 21-23)

This, of course, is a description of the urban blight of which Wilson became an adroit and sorrowful reporter in the twenties.* But everywhere around him he saw signs of the encrustation of dead forms of urban life over what had at one time been a vital civilization. As he reached home on his Pennsylvania train, far from the streets of New York or the smokestacks of Newark, he saw the older, freer America being choked out even in the spacious and genteel surroundings of Red Bank. In the boom and prosperity of the twenties he saw houses being pressed in on other houses, lots being filled up, roadhouses or night spots being slipped in, always with the result that civility and comfort are squeezed out. Following is a typical description of Wilson's of the New Jersey coast only a few miles from his family home in Red Bank:

The Jersey coast. Swiss chalets bleached out like mussel shells, Italian villas with elephantiasis, turreted medieval castles like Maxfield Parrish worse debauched, giant mosques, English half-timbered manor houses swollen to a toneless hugeness, enormous stiff wooden pergolas standing bare and vine-less on the treeless unfenced lawn, great pedestaled silver globes and crouching marble dogs and lions drowned in a flat sea of grass—infinitely dilapidated hotels with signs in Yiddish and English, exact concrete-sided lakes bordered by dusty motor roads, dreary gray boardwalks, the infinitely desiccated bones of trees, flimsy cottages with bizarre ornaments and disconcerting excrescences ready to capsize like sand castles as a result of the lack of human care and the deadly breath of the sea, gigantic barn-like auditoriums dropped inappropriately in vacant lots, for which their bulk is much too great, extinct soda fountains boarded desolately through summer and winter alike. All this must once have been thought attractive, have possessed the charm and the movement of life—there must have been a spirit of holiday-making to have produced such monstrous bizarreries—but a blight has fallen upon it—the houses gape hideously at the road, ogling, winking and peering with the horror of the corpse of gaiety. (121-23)

In diagnosing American social life there is perhaps a convenient analogy between the kind of problems Wilson was addressing in his

---

*See also in *The Twenties* the descriptions of Johnstown (25), Bethlehem (130), and Pittsburgh (134-36).

Greenwich Village skits and the decay of the physical landscape. What tortures Americans, what drains their hopes for an enduring civilization, is a lack of permanence in things, a lack of permanence that would be fine if it resulted in freedom and flexibility but that instead results in deprivation and restraint. The latest roadhouse or gas station or hamburger place adds the promise of some kind of liveliness, fills some felt need; but this progress is attained at a steep price—something permanent and fulfilling is removed and lost forever. Similarly, Americans believe that some new setting, some new industry or vocation, will be their salvation. Most of us believe in upward mobility, in new and different life-styles as a way of salvation. But this is most often illusory; in addition to motion and vivacity, the good life requires a degree of permanence, of changelessness. We must know who we are and where we came from. We must know that if we have to go back where we came from that it will still be there.

One aspect of the twenties that makes it such an interesting period in American history—and such a fascinating period in Edmund Wilson's writings—is that it displays so accurately the recurrent American theme of a surface vivacity and buoyancy with an undercurrent of decay and stagnation. We may have a colorful and lively social life without a healthy and productive one. We may be able to build homes made of the best materials and equipped with the latest conveniences, but it will do us little good if a hamburger stand and parking lot are put in down the block. And the hamburger stand and the parking lot are put in because there is no restraining hand of civilization—only material progress counts.

What the United States lacked as a nation, as an advanced civilization, was becoming clearly evident in the nineteen twenties. What many of its prominent writers (Mencken, for example) were decrying was a lack of tradition, a lack of a spiritual community to fall back on, a lack of any kind of higher folkways. This deficiency was precisely the source of Wilson's skepticism and youthful cynicism during the same years. Many of the characters in his sketches and stories, and in *I Thought of Daisy*, were helpless refugees, fleeing from a world that had reared them but that finally seemed to offer little. However, they were fleeing to an unknown and inscrutable future, to a world of traps and illusions. Sometimes, as in the case of the fictional Isabelle Griffin in "Fire Alarm," a coherent life-style could be carved out of a kind of austere independence and self-direction (perhaps this is always the way of art), but in the main Americans spend their time reaching out for some bauble or tinsel made possible and manufactured by the riches of an unstable industrial economy. In the end, most are doomed to a sense of frustration and a lack of personal fulfillment. For Wilson America had declined rather than advanced in the postindustrial world. The phantasmagoria of popular American culture he saw as a lure and a distraction, a Lorelei.

During the 1920s Edmund Wilson's own activities as a writer were in a fluid state and he had not yet established his reputation as a literary critic or man of letters. During the time that he was dramatic editor of the *New Republic* he was experimenting with the theater—he wrote a number of plays, followed the doings of the theater crowd, even married an actress. He wrote a novel and numerous stories and poems. Still, when one looks back at Wilson's writings of this period, we can see that he had already developed his propensity for historical criticism. His central concern was with the literature of his own nation and how it fit into the social environment from which it sprang. If we look at the shorter pieces of criticism that Wilson chose to reprint in *The Shores of Light*, we will see that his main concern was with young American writers of his time and with the place of contemporary literature in the scheme of things. Is our literature of any value? Does it do anything for us spiritually? Are we saddled with dead forms and styles that do nothing for our civilization? Is poetry or the novel going to be replaced by the motion picture or the radio or other forms of mass media?

In answering these and similar questions Wilson's underlying assumption seems to have been that American writers, like Americans generally, were in a state of flux and agitation during the twenties. They reached out here and there for this or that—they tried salvation through politics like Dos Passos or through religion like Eliot; they tried living abroad like Pound or Hemingway or Gertrude Stein; or they stayed at home and tried to capture some distinctively American style like Mencken or Sherwood Anderson. But the main point is that most American writers were afloat, adrift, with no clearcut civilization from which to draw sustenance, no literary culture that had any manifest usefulness.

It is peculiarly hard for such men to get an intellectual foothold in our world: New York, in particular, just now, is like the great glass mountain of the *Arabian Nights*, against which the barques of young writers are continually coming to grief. And this is true not merely of the United States, but more or less of the whole Western world. Industrially, politically and socially,

Europe itself is becoming more and more like America every day; and the catastrophe of the war has demoralized America, too. It is up to American writers to try to make some sense of their American world—for their world is now everybody's world, and, if they fail to find a way to make possible in it what T.S. Eliot desiderates: "a spiritual and intellectual coördination on a high level," it is improbable that any one else will be able to do it for them. (*Shores of Light*, 440-41)

A "spiritual and intellectual coördination on a high level" was what Eliot was looking for, and although Wilson found no evidence of such a coordination in the twenties, he was by no means pessimistic about the future of American writing. As his various literary essays and his reviews for the *New Republic* clearly show, he had a kind of guarded optimism about a few strains in American literature that seemed to hold some hope for the future.

To a reader of Wilson's "The All-Star Literary Vaudeville" of 1926, the verdict may well seem to be otherwise. In this originally anonymous essay Wilson ticked off the various forms of literature and found most of its best-known practitioners wanting.

The novel, for example, is "commonly assumed to be our principal glory," but Wilson found very few American novelists that he cared to read. He held that "we have no novelist of the first importance, of the importance of James, Joyce or Proust; or of that of Balzac or Dostoyevsky." Dreiser, according to Wilson, commands our respect but writes so badly that it is hard to read him or believe in his literary permanence. (Wilson seems not to have written appreciatively of Dreiser until the forties.) Hergesheimer writes nearly as badly in a fancy way as Dreiser does in a crude way. Sinclair Lewis possesses a vigorous satiric humor but tells us nothing profound about life. And his novels are lacking in beauty both of style and form. "Willa Cather is a good craftsman, but she is usually rather dull." Sherwood Anderson is a different matter—and more of him shortly. Wilson professes to be most interested in John Dos Passos and F. Scott Fitzgerald but found it too early in 1926 to pronounce judgment on where they were going and what they would do.

As for the dramatists there is only O'Neill, who, for all his efforts, remains less than first rank. Although there was much going on in popular theater in the twenties, Wilson looked for little of enduring value to come from it.

The outlook in poetry was somewhat brighter. The new movement in poetry that was in flower on the eve of World War I held great promise at the time. "But who can believe in its heroes now? Edgar Lee Masters did one creditable thing: *The Spoon River An-*

thology." But he has done little since. An "incurable cheapness and looseness" are rampant in the poems of Vachel Lindsay. Carl Sandburg's ideas seem obvious, his emotions meager, despite his forceful language. "Robert Frost has a thin but authentic vein of poetic sensibility; but I find him excessively dull, and he certainly writes very poor verse." Ezra Pound deserves all honor as a pioneer, but somehow he does not affect us as the highest poets do. His cantos seem entirely composed of fragments. They seem like ornaments from some masterpiece on a grand scale. He has created a mosaic that fails to reveal a pattern. In its lack of cohesion, its lack of driving force or a center, it would seem to lead "to a kind of poetic bankruptcy" (240).

Wilson deals at somewhat greater length with several female lyrical poets—Edna St. Vincent Millay, Elinor Wylie, Lizette Woodworth Reese, and Louise Bogan, among others—and concludes that "on the average I find them more rewarding than the men." The most admirable poets of the time Wilson found to be T.S. Eliot and Edwin Arlington Robinson. Although deploring a "fatigued and despondent mood that seems lately to have been drying up both his criticism and his poetry," Wilson nevertheless believed that no passion for poetry as serious and as intense as Eliot's "can be permanently shifted or numbed." Robinson he believed to be (with "the happiest flashes of Emerson aside") the most important of the New England poets. Robinson was one of the few writers living in the middle twenties who seemed able to successfully maintain ties with older American literary traditions.

Still, elsewhere in American literature there were signs of freshness and power. One writer who appeared to be enormously gifted was Sherwood Anderson. In Anderson Wilson saw an authentic American voice and a literary artist of some importance. Not only is Anderson mentioned favorably in "The All-Star Literary Vaudeville," but Wilson reviewed Anderson's books as they came out in the twenties. He followed up these reviews with more searching essays in later years. As early as 1922 Wilson had written to Stanley Dell:

Of recent books, I have found Sherwood Anderson's *The Triumph of the Egg* about the best thing in current American fiction. . . . It's not at all like *Main Street, Moon-Calf* et. al.; Anderson has something quite different from the regular realistic formula. He has a seriousness about life and a gift for making a local story seem of universal significance that make me think he may be the best of this generation of American novelists. (*Letters,* 79)

Wilson admits to being disappointed with Anderson's longer works; he tires before the end of the "vagueness of the characters and the constant repetitiousness of the form." But, when he is at his best, "Sherwood Anderson functions with a natural ease and beauty on a plane in the depths of life—as if under a diving-bell submerged in the human soul—which makes the world of the ordinary novelist seem stagy and superficial."

Admitting that Sinclair Lewis had greater resources and Willa Cather greater technical virtuosity, Wilson believed that Anderson's short stories and symbolist prose-poems have a kind of artistic authenticity not found in Lewis or Cather. Anderson never really learned the tricks of the trade, but in the best of his stories he "has shown an almost perfect instinct that fashions from what seems a more intimate stratum of feeling and imagination than our novelists usually explore, visions at once fresh and naive of a slightly discomfiting strangeness" (*Shores of Light*, 93, 233).

Another bright spot in our literature was that represented by our popular humorists. In 1924, Wilson held out some hope that Ring Lardner would be able to give us another *Huckleberry Finn*, and thus continue one of our strongest native literary traditions and one of the American's strongest character traits—our willingness to laugh at ourselves. Admitting that Lardner had not yet reached the stature of either Lewis or Anderson—for he lacked the former's satiric fury and the latter's poetic sensibility—and admitting too that Lardner had shown an unwillingness to leave popular newspaper journalism and work on a higher level, he nonetheless believed that Lardner had "come closer than anyone else among living American writers to possessing the qualities that made *Huckleberry Finn* a masterpiece. For one thing, he has ready invention—which most American realists did not, and for another—what is even rarer—an unmistakable personal accent which represents a special way of looking at things." Even such important works of American realism as *Main Street* and *Babbitt* have been put together "out of literary materials that the author found ready to hand—the pre-war English novel of Bennett and Wells." But Lardner is a native original who created all his materials afresh.

Ring Lardner seems to have imitated nobody, and nobody else could reproduce his essence. You have to read the whole of a novel of Lewis to find out that there is anything remarkable about it; but there is scarcely a paragraph of Lardner's which, in its irony both fresh and morose, does not convey somehow the sense of a distinguished aloof intelligence. And he has shown an unexcelled, a perhaps unrivalled, mastery of what since the publication of Mencken's book, has come to be known as the American language. Mark Twain, in his foreword to *Huckleberry Finn*, explained that he had taken

great care to differentiate between "the Missouri Negro dialect; the extrem-
est form of the backwoods Southwestern dialect; the ordinary 'Pike County'
dialect; and four modified varieties of this last." So Lardner has marked the
distinction between the baseball player's and the prize-fighter's slang, can
speak the language of the Chicago song-writer of *Some Like Them Cold,* who
has come to New York to make his fortune, and has equally at his command
the whole vocabulary of adolescent clichés of the young girl who writes to
the songwriter, and of the quite different set of clichés of the middleaged
man from New Jersey who goes to Florida for his golden honeymoon. And
he understands the difference between the spoken language of these semi-
literate types and the language they will use when they write. Finally, what
is most important, he writes the vernacular like an artist and not merely like
a clever journalist—as George Ade or O. Henry did. There is nothing artificial or forced about the use of slang in these stories; it is as natural as it is
apt. Lardner's language is the product of a philologist's ear and a born
writer's relish for words. (96-97)

There was in Lardner an ear finely tuned to the subtle discrimi-
nations of the American language, and, by implication, to the various
subtleties in American life. This was something that Wilson believed
could be cultivated further, and in the mid-twenties he looked for
much to come from Lardner. Unfortunately, Lardner's literary career was cut short by alcoholism. He was never able, as Wilson
feared, to cut loose from his journalistic moorings. But he represented a rich vein in our national letters that remains insufficiently
mined to this day.

The highest hope Wilson found in our national letters during the
twenties was in the area of criticism, both literary and social. We
Americans have shown some genuine talent for self-criticism, and
the field was represented brilliantly at the time by Van Wyck Brooks
and H.L. Mencken. Both of these writers were to figure prominently
in Wilson's thinking for the next several decades, and he apparently
never abandoned his belief that they were critics of the first rank,
even when Brooks abandoned his tough-minded criticism for mellow
descriptive histories and when Mencken's career foundered (in the
opinion of many) because of Tory political ideas that were seemingly
so inappropriate in the thirties.

Of the two, Mencken was surely the more important, and in the
1920s he was a sparkling public figure, wildly popular with young
writers and intellectuals. Shortly after joining the *New Republic* in
1921, Wilson made it a point to deliver himself of a full-scale essay
on Mencken's achievements as a writer. Although troubled by the
ruthlessness and rigidity of Mencken's stance, he nevertheless saw

him as an original and indigenously American genius. What is the most important thing about Mencken, the thing which makes him such a towering figure in American literature today?

It is the fact that here we have a genuine artist and man of intelligence who is thoroughly familiar with, even thoroughly saturated with, the common life. The rule has been heretofore for men of superior intelligence, like Henry Adams and Henry James, to shrink so far from the common life that, in a country where there was practically nothing else, they had almost no material to work on, and for men who were part of the general society, like Mark Twain, to be handicapped by Philistinism and illiteracy; but in the case of Mencken we have Puritanism and American manners in a position to criticize itself.

By Puritanism, of course, Wilson is referring to that peculiarly American form of social disorder delineated so well by Mencken himself. Make no mistake about it, Mencken is first and foremost a kind of social critic who held the highest ideas for the advancement of American society.

Most Americans—even of fine standards—have long ago resigned themselves to the cheapness and ugliness of America, but Mencken has never resigned himself. He has never ceased to regard his native country with wounded and outraged eyes. The shabby politics, the childish books, the factories turning out wooden nutmegs have never lost their power to offend him. At this late date, he is, I suppose, almost the only man in the country who still expects American novelists to be artists and American politicians gentlemen.*

Later, in "The All-Star Literary Vaudeville," Wilson remarks that "although it is true that Mencken's style lends itself to excesses and vulgarities, especially in the hands of his imitators who have taken over the Master's jargon without possessing his admirable literary sense, I believe that his prose is more successful in its way than that of these devotees of beauty usually is in theirs." This is due not so much to the intrinsic quality of Mencken's ideas as it is to "some strain of the musician or poet" that "has made it possible for Mencken to turn these ideas into literature; it is precisely through the color and rhythm of a highly personal prose that Mencken's opinions have been so infectious" (*Shores of Light*, 235).

Much the same kind of theme and approach is found in Wilson's review of *Notes on Democracy* ("Mencken's Democratic Man," in the *New Republic*, in 1926). What kind of political thinker is

*"H.L. Mencken," in the *New Republic*, June 1, 1921, 10-13.

Mencken? Not at all a superficial one as the later mythology would have it. He was a thinker of the highest order, albeit not strictly a philosopher.

His new book *(Notes on Democracy)* is certainly not to be taken as a contribution to political science: it is simply another of his "prejudices" treated on a larger scale than the rest. But, though *Notes on Democracy* is not precisely politics, it is quite remarkable as literature. Poe said of his philosophical system, *Eureka,* that it was to be taken as neither philosophy nor science, but as a "prose poem," which was, nevertheless, in its own way, true. Mencken might say the same of his new book. (Ibid., 294)

The extraordinary dual power of artist and thinker is something that has always meant more in Germany, the land of Mencken's forebears, than in America, but Wilson quite aptly recognized its presence in Mencken.

Wilson was to continue to write appreciatively about Mencken over the years. In his review of Edgar Kemler's *The Irreverent Mr. Mencken,* entitled "Mencken through the Wrong End of a Telescope," written in 1950 and reprinted in *The Bit between my Teeth,* Wilson maintained that Mencken represented the best that was going on in American letters in the 1920s. Mencken himself was firmly rooted in the virtues of an older America. Relying on his German-American sense of propriety and solidity he attempted to serve as a critic of American popular culture, not by removing himself from it, not by surrendering to its baseness and wild indirections, but by clashing with it head on, thus pointing the way out of the tangled mess of the twenties. If a writer like Mencken is the example, we Americans can be adjudged fairly accurate self-critics. We might yet learn to hold ourselves to good account, to develop an inner sensitivity to hypocrisy, an immunity to dishonesty in politics and social life. Mencken, of course, being an old-line Tory federalist, thought that our social institutions had become too diseased to cure, and occasionally all he offered the intelligent man was the opportunity to *enjoy* the idiocies of democratic man. Wilson, sharing the progressive's vision of the future, believed that changes could be made. Above all, both Wilson and Mencken discovered that some of the pain and agony of living in American society could be assuaged simply by living in it and loving it, sometimes just laughing at it.

Even with his belief that the area of criticism would provide a strong sense of direction to American letters in the years to come, Wilson could have been only slightly aware in the 1920s that this same decade would be witness to the origin of American studies as a distinct field of scholarly study. Even before World War I, men like George Santayana and Van Wyck Brooks had been drawn to a systematic study of American literature and culture, and a few years hence Wilson would himself become intrigued by Brooks's massive study of American letters known as the *Makers and Finders* series. But these books would not begin to appear until the thirties, although Brooks remained active in the twenties, with individual studies of American writers—Mark Twain, Henry James, and Emerson.

The decade would also see the appearance of Vernon L. Parrington's impressive history of American ideas, *Main Currents in American Thought*. This work, an attempt to study the whole range of American letters from a liberal, Jeffersonian viewpoint, gave a rather sudden birth to the field of American literature as a specialized discipline. The work won the Pulitzer Prize in 1928 (the year after its publication), and its brisk, passionate style spawned an entire generation of scholarly Americanists and gave rise to a roster of new fields in the area of American studies. In the wake of Parrington's magnum opus, new courses in American literature and studies suddenly appeared in American colleges and universities, and learned chairs were established in these fields, which only a short time before had been looked on with not very mild contempt and disdain.

Of course Parrington was not the only academic scholar of the twenties to devote himself to American literature. Irving Babbitt and Paul Elmer More at Harvard and Princeton, and Stuart Pratt Sherman at the University of Illinois, did not hesitate to praise traditional (mostly nineteenth-century) American literature from a moralistic and rationalistic stance. Similarly, young scholars in college during the twenties began to turn to American literature as a field unto itself. Young F.O. Matthiessen as an undergraduate at Yale in the early twenties had found that "literature" at Yale meant exclusively English literature (Matthiessen insisted amusingly, if not perhaps truthfully, that *Moby Dick* was listed in the Yale Library as late as 1930 not under American literature but under cetology); but Matthiessen was deeply moved by reading Whitman. Later he read *Walden* while on vacation in Europe steaming up the Rhine and immediately found himself responding to the clarion call of Van Wyck Brooks that "it is time for the history of American literature to be rewritten." Thus began in the twenties Matthiessen's vocation as an Americanist, leading to the publication of his spectacular study *American Renaissance* in 1941.

In his "All-Star Literary Vaudeville" of 1926, Wilson makes no mention of this impetus toward a rapidly growing devotion to American literature and American studies (Parrington's book had not yet appeared; Matthiessen was still a graduate student), but he does concentrate intently on the seemingly precious gift for scholarly criticism in America. Citing a tradition that went back to James Gibbons Huneker, he mentions the persistence of a hale and hearty American penchant for attention to the various arts, and he lists among other contemporaries Paul Rosenfeld, George Jean Nathan, Gilbert Seldes, and Lewis Mumford. Mencken, of course, must be added to this company, since in his days as an editor of the *Smart Set* he was also a spectacular literary critic as well as a social and cultural critic. Wilson mentions the presence of some good historical writings in the twentieth century, offering as an example of especially effective writing Samuel Eliot Morison's *Maritime History of Massachusetts*. He also mentions a rather lively interest in biography, based primarily on Strachey and psychoanalysis, to be sure, but with a number of effective practitioners: Katherine Anthony, Van Wyck Brooks, Thomas Beer, and M.R. Warner. At the time he only found Brooks's *Mark Twain* to be a first-rate work in this genre.

Perhaps the whole field of critical literature had still not completely ripened in 1926, but it is clear from Wilson's survey of the field that big changes were in store. Of course, in 1926 Wilson himself was a little-known but quite respected theatre and book reviewer for the *New Republic.* As for himself, he had not thought how he might fit into the coming scheme of things, and it would be another generation before he would find, like Van Wyck Brooks and F.O. Matthiessen, that it was the role of "critic of things American" that suited him best. An all-absorbing devotion to the American scene may not have seemed a real possibility in 1926, and even those who were so inclined formed no coherent whole as yet. But in another generation this would change.

3

Women of
the Twenties

Edmund Wilson's reputation as a writer continues to rest largely on his work as a literary critic. On the other hand, toward the end of his life, and with the flurry of literary revelations in the years since his death, another, interesting side of Wilson has come to the fore. With the publication of his diaries and letters from the twenties (the most personal of the letters, unfortunately, are still being withheld from publication), we are able to identify a resurgence of Wilson's poetic and imaginative side to counterbalance the somewhat misleading image of Wilson that held sway before his death. Wilson's diaries from the twenties reveal him not as a peripheral or backseat figure of the period, a kind of anemic junior scholar put in the shade by the young giants of the postwar generation—men like Fitzgerald and Hemingway—but as one of the most perceptive and forceful writers of his day. As a historian of life in the twenties he had perhaps few if any equals.

Wilson wrote about the America of the twenties not only intellectually and historically but also with the full force of passion and rage. He was never entrapped by intellectual fads or dominating ideologies of the day; rather he lived life with a fierce intensity and sometimes wrote with a reckless abandon. He knew its grittiness, its richness and diversity, firsthand and *con amore.* Reading a novel like *Babbitt* today, George F. Babbitt and the members of the Realty Board of Xenith, Ohio, seem singularly drained of life. They are stick figures of an age that has passed from view. The college girls of Fitzgerald seem to come to us in a dream. But the ambiance of the twenties as found in Wilson's diaries is vivid, human, and true.

Interestingly, for example, few writers have written more sympathetically and colorfully about American women than Edmund Wilson. It has not gone without notice that Wilson's first novel, *I Thought of Daisy*, is dominated by several female figures—usually thin disguises of women he encountered and knew intimately in his Greenwich Village days. But in his diaries of the twenties we find a cascade of women of all social classes and dispositions, and they are of exceptional interest not only for the part they play in the development of a literary imagination but because through Wilson's sensibility they become intrinsically interesting in themselves. Of course Wilson has also written formal literary essays on the women writers he knew in the twenties—women like Edna Millay, Elinor Wylie, and Dorothy Parker—and these are valuable both intellectually and historically; but Wilson knew a large number of women in his younger days—actresses, waitresses, factory girls, and others—all of whom are richly portrayed in his diaries. He responded to these women openly and warmly. He liked them for what they had to offer as individuals; he liked them in their fullness as social beings; but, what is most important, he put them down on paper in some of the most poignant, eloquent, and generous language that has ever been devoted to women in American literature.

Wilson's sexual intensity in the twenties was doubtless fueled by earlier sexual starvation. His adolescent celibacy, enforced by a scholarly and diffident manner, gave him the typical stored-up sex drive of the artist. Moreover, as the only child of two parents incapable of demonstrating affection, Wilson began his young manhood in a more or less desperate sexual situation, which was heightened by the isolation of army life. Wilson's young adulthood in Greenwich Village in the twenties opened a new world of sexual delights with which he was not wholly prepared to deal. Apparently he was attractive to women of different social and ethnic backgrounds and established sexual liaisons with a good number of them, but the sexual experimentation was psychologically tiring and disorienting. He was also to have two wives in the 1920s, Mary Blair, whom he married in 1923 and by whom he had a daughter, and Margaret Canby, whom he was to know from the mid-twenties and marry in 1930. But his life was always hectic during these years, and his first marriage to Mary Blair, a young actress who specialized in playing O'Neill heroines, fell apart because of the conflicting careers of the two partners. Mainly, though, Wilson was not of a monogamous bent in his younger years and moved regularly from one sexual exploit to another throughout the 1920s.

It is often said that the sexually promiscuous male is secretly contemptuous of women; that the Don Juan, far from being a lover of the female nature is hostile, antagonistic toward women. But this cannot be said about Wilson. If he was a Don Juan, it was not because he was hostile to women—even secretly or subconsciously. He was one of those males who had been overpowered by his mother, and apparently he was always deeply moved by female power, but this attraction was usually a healthy, heterosexual one that allowed him to appreciate women in the fullness of their charm and magnetism.

Where Wilson's sexual prolixity may have been unhealthy was in the general feeling of insecurity that it imparted to his life at a time when he probably needed more than anything else the quieting influence of a wife and family, or at least some kind of cohering or solidifying influence. His literary genius may well have been nurtured by personal insecurity and rapid change in interpersonal relationships, for genius usually is, but the twenties were trying and difficult times for Wilson. He became a heavy drinker, as he was to be throughout his life. At times his condition became desperate. Early in 1929, when he was trying to work on *Axel's Castle,* he had a terrifying nervous breakdown. It took some time in coming and at first appeared to him something like the neurotic state of mind he had gotten into in the spring of 1917, when the United States had just entered the war and he could not make up his mind what to do. But these panics and depressions of the late twenties were deeper and more savage. Wilson was convinced that he was going insane, and when he reflected that it was at just about this age that his father had experienced his first breakdown, he even considered suicide. The worst phase of the breakdown was not of long duration, but it was severe and Wilson spent some time in Clifton Springs Sanatorium in northern New York, where he managed to stay away from alcohol for a time but where he became instead addicted to paraldehyde, the influence of which was still harder to shake loose.

The origins of this breakdown were clear even to Wilson himself. His complex and unmanageable sex life caused the wild, almost manic-depressive mood swings. It was, he said, a condition of indecision, much like the one he experienced in 1917 that brought him to a state of psychological collapse. (Psychiatrists usually see indecision and instability in interpersonal relationships as the main causes of manic-depressive states and the various lesser conditions of similar nature, such as cyclothymia or swings of mood.) This time it was his indecision over relationships with numerous women: he had been divorced from Mary Blair but had a daughter by her and naturally a strong feeling of loyalty. He already thought he wanted to marry Margaret Canby but was involved with a number of other women, including a working-class girl named Anna. A complex relationship with a girl named Winifred was perhaps at the root of the nervous collapse and precipitated its most terrifying symptoms:

One day I got a letter from Winifred in Europe, about whom I felt very guilty, especially since I had been tight at the time I took her to bed and thought that, if I had been sober, I should have had sense enough not to. I think that it was just at that time Winifred wrote me she had had a miscarriage (which I afterwards understood was imaginary). At any rate, I had written her by then of my intention of marrying Margaret. I found that I couldn't sit down in the evening and work at my book. . . . I took to drinking. . . . At last, when I set out, at the end of one week, to go down, as usual, to Red Bank, I found myself seized with panic as soon as I got into the taxi. . . . I began to tremble violently, and I realized that I could not go down to my mother's. (*Twenties,* 492)

As Wilson quite correctly perceived, this crisis of nerves, or whatever name we choose to give it, was due to the unwieldy nature of his sexual relations. He wanted and needed the stimulation he could get from multiple relationships, but he could not bear up psychologically under the stresses that arose from them. They were, after all, tentative, experimental, uncertain. Mainly uncertain, for uncertainty of one's personal direction, one's immediate relationships with those close at hand brings about those conditions of nervous collapse—tremor, agitation, clammy skin, sometimes insomnia, sometimes recourse to uncontrollably large doses of alcohol to bring the manic episodes to a debilitating conclusion.

Still, even if Wilson's sexual exploits were damaging, he remains one of the most sexually interesting men in American literature. He was strongly drawn to women, and they to him. Women were obviously not inspired by Wilson's physical appearance—even in his youth he was rotund and puffy, hardly handsome. Nor were they drawn to the awkward trappings of power—since he was not yet a famous writer—but to something tentative and ambiguous; something half formed and elusive. Clearly he had sex appeal that was powerful and, in a scholarly type, inexplicable. Wilson was drawn to women with an equal intensity. It may well be the manner and style of his sexual drive that accounted for his appeal to the women he knew. Wilson liked women but obviously not in that self-centered way that annoys so many women, not in the way that accepts sexual favors without involvement. What makes Wilson such an interesting writer about women must have been what made him attractive to women. He cared how they looked and how they behaved in bed but also about how they thought. Their sexuality was in their total environment—in their work, in their desires and longings. Sex was not something to be isolated from life as in the absurd mechanism of a pornographic movie; the only interesting sex is that which comes out of people's dreams, out of their historical background, out of their life-style. Wilson always seemed to have approached women in the totality of their beings, to have relished them for the complexity of their personalities, and doubtless that was a substantial part of his appeal to them.

Wilson was curiously drawn to women of the working class, or of an educational and cultural background different from his own. Perhaps he was able to appreciate in such women a coarser texture not found in women of his own class or of similar educational background. Perhaps for some strange reason he felt freer or less inhibited in their presence. Perhaps they could inspire in him a devil-may-care attitude—toward getting drunk, for example—that was beyond the capacity of his better-bred and more refined female acquaintances. But even the most earthy of the women he writes about are treated with great dignity in his diaries. They are in no sense lesser mortals but are immediately realized in the roundness of their being. For example, here is a description of his first meeting with Marie, the girl from Brooklyn with whom he was to have an extended affair and who immediately takes on an ethnic richness and a corresponding sexual ripeness:

I picked her up somewhere in the Forties or Fifties coming out of a hotel. We just looked at one another and began to talk. Looking out into the hot, the smothered summer night, the dark greenery of the park (Washington Square Park), its benches loaded with slowed and muted swarms of human beings, hundreds of them stupidly swarming in the night so close to my spacious empty room, my comparatively so much cooler apartment, just across the street, dirty, sweaty, giving out the sounds of life, but obscured by the darkness and restrained and keyed down by the heat. —When I first saw her on the street, I thought her whore-broken, hard-boiled—her dissatisfied, disagreeable look, as if she smelled a bad smell: but when I came to talk to her, I learned that her father was supposed to have come from Barcelona, and saw that her hands were strong, broad and thick, her fingers blunt and large. She had a simplicity and feminine gentleness under her hard-boiled New York manner.— When she came to the apartment, I was amazed to see how much younger she looked and how much handsomer. She had the large soft tragic eyes (with the "nose all over my face" and the thick red sensual lips which she worked into vulgar grimaces as she talked) of the Italian whores and peasant women of whom the Renaissance painters made madonnas. She told me about her brother in jail in Brooklyn, falsely accused of rape—this kid who had him indicted hadn't yet appeared for a trial, the boy she had been going with and who had been jealous of Marie's brother who had made all the trouble—she had retained a lawyer who was supposed to be very good, having got somebody off in some well-known case (well-known in the tabloid dailies)—she had given him everything she had, $350 (her tactful way of asking for money). (Ibid., 310-11)

New York was very much a melting pot in the 1920s, and women newly arrived from the Mediterranean countries were still unassimilated, reaching out to belong to the new world but not yet quite of it. Many half-assimilated Americans shared this kind of vulnerability, this social awkwardness; in Marie, Wilson molded it into a distinct kind of feminine charm and force. She had a hardness bred of the streets—and having come from Brooklyn said "bersterous" for boisterous—yet her crudity was not at the center of her being, but off to one side, like some shabby ornament or article of clothing.

Marie had been married at fifteen to a man who treated her cruelly; she only stayed with him three months. She had been brought up in a convent. Father James used to kiss her every morning when she opened the gate for him—an awfully passionate kiss, too. "Finally one day, she said, 'Father James, don't you know that that's a sin?' He stunned her with some technicality that she didn't understand." Her opportunities were slim. To escape the fate of having to stay on at the convent to be a servant she become a model and later part-time call girl. As a model she worked for Neysa McMein, "I saw in her then," said Wilson, "the 100 percent Americanized gypsy and Indian girls that Neysa McMein had been doing for magazine covers." She also worked as a model for a wholesale dress manufacturer but complained that it was always her luck in such cases to get somebody who was either married or engaged. "Then I get the bum's air, huh?"

Always, though, and relentlessly, Wilson went after the essential nature of the woman's charm, seeing her physical attractiveness as an integral part of her personality. Of Marie—"She had the large opaque glassy black eyes and curving overhanging brows of a grimacing Japanese mask when she glared (as she ordinarily did in public); but was capable of being appealed to through amiability, so as to melt into a delightful cunning good-natured smile of the eyes." So, too, with Wilson's erotic detail.

She was broad and had olive skin when she took off her bandeau, disclosed large full breasts of which the nipples were spread from pregnancy—she was marked all the way down from the navel to the pubes with a long straight dent which gave her bronze and anatomical look of Dürer's women—her cunt, however, seemed to be small. She would not, the first time, respond very heartily, but, the second, would wet herself and bite my tongue, and when I had finished, I could feel her vagina throbbing powerfully. —Thrust naked cock up into those obscure and meaty regions. Afterwards, she lay with the cover pulled over her up to the breasts, which were thus left bare. (315-17)

Certainly the best-remembered and most fully detailed of Wilson's amours was that with another working-class girl, later restored and presented in full detail in *Memoirs of Hecate County* under the name of Anna. Wilson met Anna at the Tango Gardens, a cheap dance hall on Fourteenth Street in New York. Wilson was deeply infatuated with Anna and sexually magnetized, but, again, the sexual attraction (as with Marie) was rooted in his sensitivity to her environment. Marie and Anna both came from crude and unhappy home environments; both were striking out for something seemingly just beyond their grasp. Both had a kind of inner refinement that seemed gratuitous to their station and social environment. In a typically American pattern they had a finesse and an ambition that were based more on hope than on circumstance.

Anna lived in Brooklyn with her mother and step-father. She had been married at seventeen. Lost a child. Her mother was Ukrainian. Her family lived in very confining tenement conditions. The stepfather sometimes tried to get in bed with her. "They made her do all the cooking, sleep in the basement—mother brought stepfather breakfast in bed—never did that for her when she had been pregnant." She felt estranged from her child who was with her husband's family in Oswego. Later the child was put in a home—"she cried about it, thought how she had hit her and knocked her down—if she could only get her back, she'd never do that again."

Above all, Anna was hemmed in by work, by the banal and the humdrum—and this seems to have held an endless fascination for Wilson. As so often in his writing the details of his amorous encounters, Wilson merges sexual details with those of work, of the trials and tribulations of everyday life.

Anna. Working at Schrafft's at $1 a day with tips—$20 a week. The skilled girls could make $50 a week. She looked as if she had been working, eyes protruding as if hard-taxed and face a little hardened. She left the baby at the nursery in the morning and had to be back by six to get her. Terrifically hot day in mid-July—I had waked up with rivulets of sweat rolling off my forehead on the pillow. She was wearing almost nothing—she showed me her little thighs bare all the way up—she had on, under her pink shirtwaist, only a little chemise.

She was wearing a pink shirtwaist, and white pleated skirt with some kind of yellow flower on it and nice white stockings with her old blunt black shoes. The mother had left her stepfather—and he had turned the place into a regular speakeasy with girls and everything—"they pulled down all the blinds at ten o'clock and I don't know what they do." I asked if the girls were terrible and she answered "Yes, they're terrible—what I mean—terrible!" One of them had explained to her that she got $3 a man ($6 an hour—she thought)—Anna was so foolish, you know, to work when she could do the way *she* did (here, as she went on, I saw Anna's nice fine humor begin to come out from under her hardened unfortunate surface, the result of having got up early in the morning, come to see me and gone to work) in order to earn her $15 in a couple of hours every night. I asked if the girls had been pretty—"I'm telling you, each one is worse than the other." One night they had a big fuss—the man gave one of the girls $5 and tried to get back $2 change—they had a big rumpus and threw the girl out.—Anna complained of her heart, which she said hurt her awful sometimes—I suppose she had to be on her feet too much at Schrafft's. (450)

Always, in these working-class women, there seems for Wilson to be the feeling of defenselessness, the feeling of vulnerability to the world that simultaneously heightens femininity and intensifies sexual passion. Anna loved not only passionately but with a sort of exuberant eroticism that Wilson catches to perfection:

Her pale little passionate face in the half light with that mouth moist, and always ready, more like a sexual organ than a mouth, felt the tongue plunging into it almost like intercourse—liked to cuddle up at night—cuddled up with her mother when she slept with her—her mother would push her away—I don't know what I do to her.—Responds so easily with that rhythmic movement—quickly catches rhythm to any stimulation. (410)

What makes Wilson's ethnic and lower-class girl friends so interesting is that they seem to mirror dramatically the condition of American women generally during the 1920s. They enjoy the new freedom and lack of restraint but still do not quite know what they want. They want "to do their own thing," to use the vernacular of a later generation, yet they have pulling at them not just one but several kinds of social compulsions, none of which can be resolved into a coherent and meaningful life-style.

The young men of Wilson's generation had been in the war and had come back disillusioned. Many were prepared to settle back into the normalcy that President Harding had planned for them. The women of the same age and of the next generation drifted to a different fate. They were now liberated, franchised, equalized by the Constitution of the United States. In larger and larger numbers they were being educated. Above all, in the swift urbanization of America, it had become obvious that there was no longer the need for the traditional female virtues, no longer any necessity to be tied to the kitchen stove, no longer any useful purpose in making butter or putting up preserves. What, then, was there for women? Where could they turn? The time had not yet come when large numbers of females could seek traditional male vocations, so women in the 1920s were in something of a quandary. They were liberated *from* something, but liberated *to* what? Forward or back, up or down, where could they go?

For the ethnic women so poignantly described in Wilson's diaries the dilemma was heightened by the fact that the shifting social scene was aggravated by their own lack of identity with American values. They had to make peace not only with the new conventions of youth but with their non-English speaking homes, their church, and all sorts of lingering folk traditions and conventions. In the lives of Marie and Anna there was a kind of touching alienation or confusion, a lack of direction that, for Wilson, added to the force of their elemental human charm. But what is especially instructive is that the greater complexity and confusion of social life led to more than a paper liberation of American women. Indeed it is questionable whether the paper liberation was very important. What was important was that the American woman became in the course of only one generation supercharged with interest and complexity. No longer tied to the stove and the hearth, even untutored lower-class women like Marie and Anna were thrown into circumstances where they could develop rich emotional lives, tender sensibilities that a generation or so before would have had to have been boxed up or destroyed in all but the very rare individual.

When we look around at the decade of the 1920s, we see that the age was a propitious time for the American woman, that there was something of a burst of creative energy in literature and the arts. A large number of women came to the fore as leading intellectuals, artists, writers, even scientists. In view of the fact that women in the 1960s and 1970s were expressing the belief that creative women were previously the rare exception, it is surprising to find that in the

1920s women were taking hold very rapidly and that the woman
writer (for example), far from being a *rara avis,* was a common and
respected figure. Before the decade of the 1920s was over it would
probably be possible to say that no country in the history of the world
had produced more sensitive and intelligent women writers in such
a short span of time. Some of the best are neglected today, which is
to be regretted, but Wilson did not neglect them in the twenties, or
in the later years of his career. Many of his essays from the twenties
are devoted to literary and biographical studies of women writers
who came suddenly to prominence after World War I—women as
distinct and varied as Edna St. Vincent Millay, Elinor Wylie, and
Dorothy Parker. Wilson had grown up in the same generation as
these women, yet he understood that in many ways they had gotten
a head start over their male contemporaries who had had to undergo
the trauma and nihilism of military service—at the very least several
years of spiritual inertia. Wilson clearly admired these literary
women, who were his contemporaries, and in his writings of the
twenties he made strenuous efforts to understand how their artistic
powers had grown so rapidly out of the shifting environment of the
new America.

Edna St. Vincent Millay was a forceful presence in Edmund
Wilson's life, and he in hers. For a short while they were lovers,
although sex seems not to have been the dominating motive in their
long relationship. Even at their most intense Wilson and Millay
seemed mainly to be drawing on one another's deepest creative and
intellectual reserves. It could be that we have so little from Wilson
about his intimate encounters with Millay because his respect for a
great poet prevented him from committing such details to paper;
more plausibly he did not do so because from the start his relationship with Millay was only peripherally sexual, his youthful passion for
sex being more comfortably focused on proletarian females like Anna
or Marie. Too, the character of Rita in his first novel, *I Thought of
Daisy,* that was thought to be partially based on Millay is clearly
muted and dulled in order to allow Wilson to get on paper the kind
of woman who charmed him most, his ideal American woman—"the
real, vital Pittsburgh: frank, vulgar, humorous, human."

Still, if in certain ways Wilson never allowed himself to become
enmeshed in Millay's life and was not among her more prominent
lovers, in the end he gave her his fullest understanding and some of

his best writing. The long piece that he composed shortly after her death and that serves as the epilogue of *The Shores of Light* shows just how deeply he loved Millay and how perfectly he grasped her essence. It is one of Wilson's best essays, and far and away the best biographical sketch ever written about Edna St. Vincent Millay. If he could never bring himself to write about the short but intense period when he knew Millay intimately, if he could never perfectly explain the nineteen-year period when he did not see her at all, in the end he was able to devote a passionate understanding to her work.

Not at all strangely it took Wilson many years to summon up all his talents for a full-scale evaluation of Millay as a poet and personality. He recognized her talents very early—long before he had met her—and wrote about her critically during the 1920s when she was at the height of her popularity. But Wilson was always a historical critic who had to allow a writer to be seen in the broadest possible context before he could get the kind of portrait he wanted and could do so well. The epilogue to *The Shores of Light* is Wilsonian historical criticism at its best, threading together social, biographical, psychological, and aesthetic materials to create a marvelously rich tapestry of biographical and literary analysis; it is also Millay after being mulled over, marinated, loved by Wilson for nearly thirty years and seen in her richness as a woman, a poet, and an inseparable part of the American scene.

In his survey of the American literary scene in 1926, "The All-Star Literary Vaudeville," Wilson gave a tentative evaluation of Millay, whom he then believed to be the most promising of the younger lyric poets. He had also judged that of the lyrical poets of the time he found the women to be more rewarding than the men: "Their emotion is likely to be more genuine and their instinct surer." Of these women he mentioned Lizette Woodworth Reese, Elinor Wylie, Louise Bogan, and Millay. Millay he declared to be the most important of the group "and perhaps one of the most important of our poets." And with the remarkably precise judgment for which he was already noted, Wilson offered a neat capsule summary of Millay's poetic talents: "With little color, meager ornament and images often commonplace, she is yet mistress of deeply moving rhythms, of a music which makes up for the ear what her page seems to lack for the eye; and, above all, she has that singular boldness, which she shares with the greatest poets and which consists in taking just that one step beyond where one's fellows stop that, by making a new contact with moral reality, has the effect of causing other productions to take on an aspect of literary convention." (*Shores of Light,* 242-43)

But if Millay's singularity, her share of poetic greatness, consisted largely of her boldness, in a new and startling contact with moral reality, we can only explain her work by understanding it in its fullest dimension as the work of a person rooted in a certain historical environment, in a certain moral climate. Thus we must do what Wilson finally undertook to do a quarter century later, namely, provide the psychological and historical setting that alone makes the poetry of Edna St. Vincent Millay meaningful, that alone makes the poet herself believable.

In his best historical fashion Wilson began his extraordinary portrait of Millay autobiographically, pointing out that he had admired Millay's work even before he had met her personally. A cousin of his had given him a copy of the *Vassar Miscellany Monthly* in which he took special note of a dramatic dialogue in blank verse by Millay entitled "The Suicide." Later the same year, his cousin sent him a copy of *A Book of Vassar Verse* that contained other poems by Millay and that he plugged in the *New York Evening Sun.* But it was not until after the war that Wilson got to meet Millay. She had been living for several years in Greenwich Village by this time and acting with the Provincetown Players as well as writing poetry. At a party to which both Wilson and John Peale Bishop were invited, Millay read some of her poetry.

She was, of course, a charismatic personality and read magnificently. "She pronounced every syllable distinctly; she gave every sound its value," said Wilson, who thought her to have been influenced by the English tradition in New England, perhaps to have been taught to read Shakespeare by a college or school elocutionist. And to the youthful Wilson her feminine charms were irresistible: "She was one of those women whose features are not perfect and who in their moments of dimness may not even seem pretty, but who, excited by the blood or the spirit, become almost supernaturally beautiful. She was small, but her figure was full, though she did not appear plump. She had a lovely and very long throat that gave her the look of a muse." (Ibid., 749)

In connection with his job on *Vanity Fair* Wilson was able to further cultivate Millay's acquaintance since *Vanity Fair* was publishing a good deal of her poetry and Frank Crowninshield was alert to her talents—indeed, he, more than anyone else, can be credited with getting Millay a large public. In deepening his acquaintanceship, Wilson, like his good friend John Peale Bishop, fell hopelessly in love with her. Of his closer and more intimate relationship with Millay, Wilson says little, although he leaves no doubt that his passion was real and intense. However, in view of Millay's well-publicized amours of the early twenties, Wilson's general comment on her effect on people is most instructive. She had, he said, a tremendous magnetism for people of both sexes, small children, even birds. At the same time he felt that her relations with her admirers had "a disarming impartiality." Although she reacted to the personality of the men she knew or to other traits such as a voice or a manner, she did not give the impression that personality much mattered for her except as subjects for poems. When she came to write about her lovers she gave them so little individuality that it was often impossible to tell which man she was writing about. The faces of the lads in "What lips my lips have kissed," are indistinct and unremembered:

> Yours is a face of which I can forget
> The color and the features every one,
> The words not ever, and the smiles not yet.

She could be very amusing in company but she was never a social person. She did not gossip; she did not like talking personalities. She was, said Wilson "sometimes rather a strain, because nothing could be casual for her; I do not think I ever saw her relaxed, even when she was tired or ill." She was never tyrannical, fatuous, or vain; "she was either like the most condensed literature or music, the demands of which one cannot meet protractedly, or like a serious nervous case—though this side of her was more in evidence later—whom one finds that one cannot soothe." (756-57)

Wilson then plunges into the kind of psychological/social analysis of which, during the 1920s, he became a master. The clue to the strain, the fierce intensity of Millay, and her great strength of character was "something as different as possible from the legend of her Greenwich Village reputation, something austere and grim." She had been born on the rock-ribbed coast of Maine and grew up in small and isolated Maine towns. Her mother and father had not lived together since the three Millay daughters were very young, and Wilson remembered hearing Edna speak of her father only once. The family lived a sort of hand-to-mouth existence with the mother working as a district nurse. But she was also a serious musician— trained as a singer—who conducted the local orchestra. The three Millay sisters were brought up in an atmosphere of music and poetry. Perhaps this was all they had, for they were poor and cut off from the world of affairs.

Edna did not go to college until she was twenty-one, and there would not have been funds even then had it not been for the fact that her very remarkable and precocious poem "Renascence" (written when she was nineteen) had attracted the attention of a summer visitor to Maine, Miss Caroline B. Dow, head of the National Training School of the Y.W.C.A., who raised the money to send her to Vassar. This very poem, "Renascence," which so impressed Miss Dow, gives us the clue to Millay's power and frenetic intensity. A study of claustrophobia as well as a great affirmation of the human spirit, it is the product of Millay's severely restricted early home life, of a small Maine town that offered few triumphs, little release for the emotions except in the life of the mind, in the release of art and poetry. In "Renascence" we have the girl "hemmed in between the mountains and the sea of Camden on Penobscot Bay. The girl is beginning to suffocate; she looks up, and the sky seems to offer escape, but when she puts her hand up, she screams, for she finds it so low that she can touch it, and Infinity settles down on her." She begins to feel all human guilt, all human suffering. She sinks down six feet in the ground and rain begins to fall. She prays to God for the rain to wash away the grave and a storm to set her free to the beauties of the world she has longed for. But she now knows that the sky will cave in on those whose soul is flat.

This poem gives the central theme of Edna Millay's whole work: she is alone; she is afraid that the world will crush her; she must summon the strength to assert herself, to draw herself up to her full stature, to embrace the world with love; and the storm—which stands evidently for sexual love—comes to effect a liberation. Her real sexual experience, which came rather late, was to play in her poetry the role of this storm, for it gives her the world to embrace, yet it always leaves her alone again, alone and afraid of death. Withdrawal is her natural condition; she was always ... extremely shy of meeting people; and she was terrified of New York, of which I do not think she saw much, for she would not cross a street alone. She feels that she is "caught beneath great buildings," and she longs to be back in Maine— though the Maine she is homesick for is never in the least idealized, but, on the contrary, a meager country with threadbare interiors, wizened apples and weedy mussels on rotting hulls. (759)

Millay's poems on love, her well-publicized love life, and her tendencies as a free and independent woman got her a large public audience in the twenties, although we can see from Wilson's analysis that almost everything popularly believed about Millay was a kind of half-truth. She was a highly complex woman torn between a succession of poles, none of which provided her with rest and contentment. She lived life with such a passionate intensity that she was always in danger of drifting into insanity, or physical and emotional deterioration. For long periods during her life she could write nothing and suffered from migraine headaches and alcoholism. Characteristically she wrote once to Wilson "I am at present under the influence of hashish, gin, bad poetry, love, morphine and hunger—otherwise I could not be writing you even this." For years Wilson refused to see her because her intensity was nerve-racking, and when he saw her again after nineteen years, he found her "more fatiguing than she had been in her younger years" and that he had to assert his middle-aged indifference to keep from getting involved in an unwanted whirlwind of passion.

Millay's sex appeal was undeniable, although perhaps because of his own early involvement (and disappointment) Wilson was unable to express it well in words. Her strong appeal to men was probably a blend of feminine fragility and masculine toughness, of fierce independence and a playful, even perverse, sense of humor and prankishness. The feminine side was exemplified in her inability to get around in New York without help, her perpetual impracticality, and her dependence on men to manage her affairs. Yet her independence of spirit asserted itself early. As a freshman at Vassar she had little but contempt for daisy chains and literary teas, and wrote with untypical female contempt for the conventions and proprieties of the place:

I hate this pink-and-gray college. If there had been a college in Alice-in-Wonderland it would be this college. Every morning when I awake I swear, I say "Damn this pink-and-gray college! . . . They treat us like an orphan asylum. . . . They trust us with everything but men—and they let us see it, so that it's worse than not trusting us at all. We can go into the candy-kitchen and take what we like and pay or not and nobody is there to know. But a man is forbidden as if he were an apple.*

At Vassar she was known for pranks and shenanigans of a singularly contemptuous sort. She cut classes and smoked in the cemetery since smoking was banned in class. Her graduation was nearly canceled when she stayed out all night; though this was punishable by suspension, President MacCracken vetoed the suspension on the ground that it would keep her from graduating. Her excuses at Vassar always had a neat offhand touch to them. One of her excuses for

*Norman A. Brittin, *Edna St. Vincent Millay* (New York: Twayne, 1967), 29. This was a letter to Arthur Davison Ficke.

missing chapel was, "It was raining and I was afraid the red on the pew would fade on my new dress."

The pungent offhand remark became something of a Millay trademark. She once wrote to Edmund Wilson: "I'm going to be thirty in a few minutes," and later, to one of her former lovers, Walter Brynner, who proposed to visit her at her country home, Steepletop, in 1935, "Can you come to Steepletop sometime in May. Can you do it without bringing your mother? I know she's grand and all that . . . but I'm going to die in a few days, and I have no time left except for people I'm crazy about." She had a blunt impetuosity that seemed charming and disarming to all who knew her. When she was getting started as a poet and still out-at-pocket she wrote to Harriet Monroe, editor of *Poetry,* "I am *awfully* broke. Would you mind paying me a lot." There was never in Edna so much as a jot of role playing or deceit.

Wilson accounted for Edna's playful and independent spirit by referring to a visit he paid to Edna on Cape Cod in the summer of 1920. It was the time he proposed to her. He had never before met Edna's mother and two sisters—a family that maintained a powerful solidarity in the face of the hardship and deprivation of their austere life in Maine. "I had never seen anything like this household, nor have I ever seen anything like it since. Edna tried to reassure me by telling me that I musn't be overpowered by all those girls, and one of the others added, 'And *what* girls.' " The three girls entertained him with humorous songs that they had concocted in their girlhood in Maine. They sang parts very well together: Kathleen, the youngest sang soprano, Vincent, baritone, and Norma, the middle sister, tenor.

Wilson proposed to Millay while swatting mosquitoes on a swing on the front porch, the only place he could take Edna to be alone. "She did not reject my proposal but said that she would think about it. I am not sure that she actually said, 'That might be the solution,' but it haunts me that she conveyed that idea." And in one of his rare but magnificent flashes of humor, Wilson observed: "In any case it was plain to me that proposals of marriage were not a source of great excitement."

If all three Millay daughters were enticing and extremely pretty, the mother seemed to provide the divine spark to the whole family. Certainly she provided the clue to Edna's springy nature. "She was a little old woman with spectacles, who although she had evidently been through a great deal, had managed to remain very brisk and bright. She sat up straight and smoked cigarettes and quizzically followed the conversation. She looked not unlike a New England schoolteacher, yet there was something almost raffish about her. She had anticipated the Bohemianism of her daughters; and she sometimes made remarks that were startling from the lips of an old lady. But there was nothing sordid about her: you felt even more than with Edna that she had passed beyond good and evil, beyond the power of hardship to worry her, and that she had attained there a certain gaiety." (*Shores of Light,* 760)

There was about these Millay women the feel of down-eastern independence, of Yankee tartness and eccentricity, qualities that always show through in Edna's poetry. But the long-enforced isolation of the Maine coast, the regular closed-in company of her mother and sisters had, in another sense, made Edna anything but an independent woman. She was always reaching out, trying new lovers, new environments. This expansiveness can be looked on as a kind of footloose adventuring, but the truth is Millay's core retained a certain softness and dependence. She wanted to be independent, to keep ties to other people to a minimum, but she could not survive alone. She needed other people to get her sober, to get her to eat right, to see to her health, and so on. We have Wilson's testimony that though Millay loved the anonymity of Greenwich Village she could not get around very well by herself and actually had to be helped across the streets.

Millay's fragile personality and near-hysterical insecurity led her finally to give over her succession of lovers, her somewhat disorderly Greenwich Village existence, in favor of a traditional marriage in which she became completely dependent on a single man. After being proposed to by numerous men, including not a few artists and writers of note, in 1923 Millay celebrated an unexpected marriage with Eugen Boissevain, an immigrant from Holland who had at one time been a fairly well-to-do coffee importer. Any marriage would have been unlikely for Millay who had scorned domesticity and made fun of traditional marriage. But Boissevain, a businessman twelve years her senior, seemed to make the marriage even more inexplicable. Expressing incredulity, the Chicago *Times* ran a long article entitled "Has Happiness Come to Repay/Fair Edna St. Vincent Millay," and subtitled "She Married as She Lived—On a Moment's Impulse."

But though Millay moved into her marriage quickly, she could not have made a better choice. Boissevain was clearly what she needed—a man she could depend upon. Certainly he was a man of considerable solidity and strength of personality, and he completely took over Edna's life, becoming her guardian, lover, father confessor, nurse, and manager. After a good five years of burning the candle at both ends Edna must have realized that she had to have somebody to see that she got medical care, to manage her affairs, and doubtless to stem the tide of a nerve-racking procession of lovers. As family friends and observers testified, Boissevain did everything.

Not only did he draw her bath and rub her back, he also assumed most of the household tasks because he felt that Millay should not be bothered by housework, which she hated, and because they had difficulty keeping servants at Steepletop, Boissevain cooked, washed, directed the household and estate, dictated letters, managed the business affairs, charmingly dismissed unwelcome guests, and finally was forced to post a sign: "Visitors received only by appointment."*

When Wilson visited Edna and Eugen Boissevain at their home, Steepletop, in Austerlitz, New York, near the Berkshires some twenty-five years after the marriage, Boissevain came out of the house in his working clothes, saying, "I'll go and get my child," indicating that he had been accustomed to babying her and catering to her for years—that this had become habitual and enervating. On the other hand, Boissevain probably made her later creative life possible, for without his strong support and talent for domestic management she probably would have burned herself out in the late 1920s. Boissevain probably had no significant literary influence on Millay's life, and if her work lost much of its spontaneous instinctual quality and took on a meditative or philosophical cast, her marriage probably had little to do with it. But Boissevain's careful attention to the details of her life probably made it possible for her to survive at all.

Edmund Wilson's final judgment on Millay is painted in full and precise detail. In middle age he could not seem to muster much patience for her neuroticism and inability to get hold of herself, or for her complete and childlike dependence on Boissevain. Yet he continued to find her a remarkable poet. Unfashionable as it now was, he held Edna Millay "one of the only poets writing in English in our time who have attained to anything like the stature of great literary figures in an age in which prose has predominated." It would be hard to know how to compare her to Eliot or Auden or Yeats— still harder to compare her to Pound. Since Wilson believed that "there is always a certain incommensurability between men and

*Anne Cheney, *Millay in Greenwich Village* (University: Univ. of Alabama Press, 1975), 12.

women writers," perhaps many kinds of usual comparisons are meaningless. But she does have in common with Eliot, Auden, and Yeats that

in giving supreme expression to profoundly felt personal experience, she was able to identify herself with more general human experience and stand forth as a spokesman for the human spirit, announcing its predicaments, its vicissitudes, but, as a matter of human expression, by a splendor of expression itself, putting herself beyond common embarrassments, common oppressions and panics. This is man who surveys himself and the world in which he moves, not the beast that scurries and suffers; and the name of the poet comes no longer to indicate a mere individual with a birthplace and a legal residence, but to figure as one of the pseudonyms assumed by that spirit itself. (*Shores of Light*, 752)

But if Millay were such a universal artist she was also clearly an American original. If the poet in the end is not a mere individual with a birthplace and legal residence, he is so at first; his concreteness and individuality make his universality possible. Edna Millay's personality had a distinctive quality and charisma that is hard to forget; in her strange and only partially explicable Greenwich Village odyssey she resembled a Sherwood Anderson character—certainly, on a more sublime scale she was much the same kind of restless and rootless Village resident that Wilson described in his Greenwich Village sketches. She was also somehow a perfect rendering of the American sexual predicament in which one embraces the notion of license and freedom without knowing where it will lead, without being able to control the results. Somehow, despite her universality, one cannot help feeling that Millay spoke to Americans as few of our poets have done, and that she got on paper some of the verities of American life with force and precision.

Dorothy Parker was another literary figure of the twenties with whom Wilson was closely acquainted, and her name frequently crops up in his writings of the period. Indeed there are more references to Dorothy Parker in Wilson's dairy of the twenties than to any other important literary female except Millay. Perhaps her frequent appearance in the pages of Wilson's diary was due to his close association with her at *Vanity Fair;* on the other hand Wilson strongly admired her as a writer and had occasion to praise her work numerous times over the years. He also found Parker an attractive woman, but he was somewhat wary of her brittle, even lethal, manner, which covered deep anxieties and personal insecurities.

Today, Dorothy Parker clearly stands apart from many of the literary characters of the Algonquin Round Table with whom her name was long associated—Alexander Woollcott, Robert Benchley, "F.P.A." (Franklin P. Adams), and Heywood Broun. Her output as a writer was not great; except for the many collected drama reviews, casual essays for magazines and her work in film, she was the author of only three volumes of poetry, two of short stories. But some of her stories and poems are first-rate and make Wilson's views on Parker and her work more than items of passing interest.

Wilson first met Dorothy Parker when he went to work for *Vanity Fair* in 1920. Indeed, Parker was partially responsible for Wilson getting his job there. She was reading unsolicited manuscripts at the time and had called one of Wilson's pieces to Crowninshield's attention. But when Wilson started to work he found that both Dorothy Parker and Robert Benchley had resigned in protest over an incident involving Parker. Apparently Condé Nast, the publisher of *Vanity Fair,* insisted that Dorothy stop writing about the theater because she was offending big name actresses, and thereby their producers and monetary backers. "Benchley and Dorothy joked about my being a scab, but were kind about showing me the ropes and took me for the first time to the Algonquin." Dorothy was two years older than Wilson, and he recalls her as not at all unattractive. "When I first met Dorothy in the office, she had been, I thought, overperfumed, and the hand with which I had shaken hers kept the scent of her perfume all day. Although she was fairly pretty and although I needed a girl, what I considered the vulgarity of her too much perfume prevented me from paying her court." (*Twenties,* 33)

Dorothy Parker's biographer John Keats makes distinct references to this very evident perfume. Dorothy took to using it as a way of disguising her drinking, which became a serious problem very early in life. Her chosen scent was a matter of no small significance. "She ordered soaps and perfumes from Cyclax of London, and her favorite scent was tuberose," a scent used by undertakers to mask the reek of the corpse.* Dorothy Parker was a woman whose ready wit, acid humor, and inventive way with language were always at the edge of a precipice; she always seemed to be playing with death, trifling with extinction.

*John Keats, *You Might as Well Live: The Life and Times of Dorothy Parker* (New York: Simon and Schuster, 1970), 92.

Dorothy Parker was born to a wealthy New York family, but her father, J. Henry Rothschild, was not related to the great family of Jewish bankers. Her early life was anything but happy and serene. Her father was a tyrant who hammered her wrists with a spoon if she was late for breakfast. Her mother died during her childhood and was supplanted by a step-mother who was a Catholic and sent Dorothy to a Catholic convent school in New York. Dorothy was terrified of her father and always regarded her step-mother as stupid and banal. She got no love from either and had no outlet for her own affections. It is not at all unlikely that her youthful mind formed the notion that there could be no genuine affections, that no personal relationships were reliable and durable. She attended a swank and academically respectable finishing school in Morristown, New Jersey, but found this also to be emotionally unfulfilling and had no sympathy for the daughters of Wall Street bankers and millionaires. After graduating she chose not to go to college but lived in New York for a few years in genteel literary poverty—of necessity since she had completely cut herself off from her father. In 1917 she married a handsome young man of good family named Edwin Pond Parker II —to change her name, she jokingly told her friends. Most people who knew Dorothy Parker well insisted that her first husband was pleasing, good-looking but nondescript. He went away to the service, and when he came back his marriage with Dorothy petered out. In any case, though he was suave and sweet and cultivated, he would have been no match for Dorothy's wit, and he would have been battered to death by her cruel and sadistic tongue.

Anyway, by the early twenties Dorothy was already making it big in the sophisticated world of the New York literary establishment— perhaps we should say subliterary establishment—the smart set of the Algonquin Hotel. She had established herself as a prominent member of the so-called Round Table that would gather for lunch every afternoon, the members outdoing one another with their puns and verbal swordplay.

Dorothy was certainly the queen, darling, and girl-wonder of the group. She became its ace smartcracker, and when Dorothy Parker is remembered today it is largely for her jibes or wisecracks. In the twenties her latest witticism could always bring an audience to attention at a cocktail party. Everyone in New York remembers what she said when Calvin Coolidge died: "How did they know?" Many of the best of Dorothy's cracks got printed in "The Conning Tower" of F.P.A. in the *New York World.* Some had to be kept for more private occasions. There was the brilliant answer Dorothy reportedly gave

to Frank Crowninshield's messenger boy who was after some over-
due copy: "Tell him I'm too fucking busy—or vice versa." When it
came to word games around the table at the Algonquin, none could
match Dorothy. Challenged to use the word "horticulture" in a sentence, she replied without hesitation, "You can lead a horticulture,
but you can't make her think."

Edmund Wilson went to the Algonquin during his stint on
Vanity Fair, but he did not take too keenly to most of the members
of the Round Table. Dorothy Parker was, or became, an exception
in some respects. But Benchley, Woollcott, and Heywood Broun—
especially the last two—left him cold. "They all came from the suburbs and 'provinces,' and a sort of tone was set—mainly by Benchley,
I think—deriving from a provincial upbringing of people who had
been taught a certain kind of gentility who had played the same
games and who had read the same children's books—all of which
they were now able to mock from a level of New York sophistication.
I found this rather tiresome, since they never seemed to be able to
get above it." The various members had individual eccentricities that
made them unattractive to Wilson. Woollcott had had an early attack
of mumps that left him sterile and also impotent apparently, and this
gave him an "uncomfortable personality." (Woollcott had been born
in the Fourierist phalanx not far from Red Bank and had actually
been delivered by Wilson's grandfather, Dr. Kimball.) Heywood
Broun was a "big soft lazy man" and in a letter to Christian Gauss in
1923 Wilson identified him as typical of the literary establishment in
New York. One simply could not live in New York and write anything serious—certainly it was not easy. "The tendency was for all
writers to be driven the way of Heywood Broun—into an enormous
mass production of diluted intellectual goods." (*Letters,* 108-9)

Benchley had some possibilities. "Dorothy regarded him as a
kind of saint, and he did have some admirable qualities. . . . I used,
in the days I first knew him, to urge him to serious satire; but he
proved to be incapable of this." (*Twenties,* 47)

But he was capable of a sly and pixyish humor on a rather high
level that makes him comparable with Dorothy Parker, though he
could never match her as a satirist. Benchley's talents dwindled later
on. He did some wonderful comic shorts in Hollywood in the thirties
but by then was drinking very heavily and actually died of cirrhosis
of the liver.

Dorothy, however, was capable of serious and sustained satiric
writing, which set her apart from most of her colleagues of the Round
Table. Her career as a serious creative writer was brief. In the thir-

ties, like Benchley, she went to Hollywood, and she made big money there. But she hated the place and deteriorated spiritually. She continued writing into the 1950s and 1960s, drawing big retainers for a monthly book review column for *Esquire* that she delivered only irregularly. In her later years she duped publishers like Bennett Cerf into paying big advances for books she did not have the slightest intention of delivering. But she did manage to turn out a small body of work that was true literature, and most important, a solid testament to the twenties.

In 1944 the Viking Press put out a volume entitled *Dorothy Parker* in the Viking Portable Library series and Wilson reviewed it in the *New Yorker*—a kind of a retrospective of the sort he was to write for Edna Millay a few years later. Her poems he found to be a bit dated. "At their best, they are witty light verse, but when they try to be something more serious, they tend to become a dilution of A.E. Housman and Edna Millay." Her prose he found to be as alive and brilliant as ever. After the twenties had faded for fifteen years and he read Dorothy Parker again, he was ready to insist that what was so wonderful about the twenties was that the writers of the time —he specifically mentions Parker and Scott Fitzgerald—could write with a freedom and a wild abandon that no longer seemed possible after a grim depression and an equally grim war.

In the twenties they could love, they could travel, they could stay up late at night as extravagantly as they pleased; they could think or say or write whatever seemed to them amusing or interesting. There was a good deal of irresponsibility, and a lot of money and energy wasted, and the artistic activities of the time suffered from its general vices, but it was a much more favorable climate for writing than the period we are now in. The depression put a crimp in incomes, and people began to watch their pockets. Then they began to watch their politics. (*Classics and Commercials,* 168-69)

From the perspective of 1944, Wilson felt that somehow the great creative voices of the twenties had been stifled, all too abruptly. The literary movement of the twenties tended to "break down and peter out, which we never should have expected at the time, when it seemed to us that American writing had just had a brilliant rebirth." Scott Fitzgerald died suddenly just when it seemed as though he might fulfill his great promise. And the same was true of Dorothy Parker, who was still writing in 1944 but no longer in her top form. Like so many writers from the twenties she did not seem to have anything she could get a grip on. The depression years were fine for social reformers and indeed for all kinds of social thinkers.

The war seemed to be breeding nothing but imitative writers and imitation books. Dorothy had moved to Hollywood in the thirties, said Wilson, straying from her natural habitat of New York; but this did her art no good. Like so many writers who went to Hollywood she turned to smoky and ill-defined social causes and progressive organizations. "She ought," said Wilson, "to have been satirizing Hollywood and sticking pins into fellow travellers; but she had not, so far as I know, ever written a word about either." (Ibid.)

Parker's decline during her Hollywood period, which extended for more than twenty years, may have had numerous causes of which Wilson only mentions one. For most of the Hollywood period she was in a condition of nervous and bodily deterioration. She was not unlike Edna St. Vincent Millay during those same decades. Dorothy was a dangerously unstable and defensive person; she feared interpersonal contacts and never knew how to give love or take it. She drifted further and deeper into alcoholism and paranoid states of mind.

She was to marry one more time, to a handsome actor by the name of Alan Campbell. At the time of the marriage in 1933, Alan Campbell was twenty-nine and Dorothy was forty. Many of Dorothy's friends saw a strong resemblance between Campbell and Edwin Parker and wondered if despite his striking appearance and sweet nature he might be pushed into the background by Dorothy's force, withered by her acid tongue. And, as an earlier poem of Dorothy's suggested

> Into love and out again,
> Thus I went and thus I go.

She also had a tendency, like Millay, to respond to physical attractions that burned brightly for a moment and then lost their power. Her characteristics for the ideal man were also none too promising: "I require only three things of a man. He must be handsome, ruthless and stupid."

Alan Campbell was only the first of these things, for he was generally considered to be both easy-going and bright as well as handsome. Furthermore, he was totally devoted to Dorothy and had the makings of a model husband. Dorothy's biographer paints a picture of him that is not at all unlike that of Edna Millay's father-figure husband, Eugen Boissevain:

She badly needed someone to take her in charge and give some point to her days . . . he made a wonderful major domo. When they were living together in New York before their marriage, Alan had bought the food, done the cooking, done all the interior decorating in their apartment, painted all the insides of the bureau drawers, cleaned up after the dogs, washed and dried the dishes, made the beds, told Dorothy to wear her coat on cold days, shaken the cocktails, paid the bills, amused her, adored her, made love to her, got her to cut down on her drinking, otherwise created space and time for her to write, and taken her to parties." (Keats, 175-76)

But their marriage was a stormy one. There was a miscarriage, a divorce, later a remarriage, and in between lots of trouble. Dorothy grew fat and her drinking increased. Although she loved Alan she turned the full force of her hatred on him in a torrent of words. She called him names, even in the presence of friends. She told people he was a homosexual and called him "the wickedest woman in Paris." She called him "a farmer's ass" and told all kinds of stories to his detriment. "Alan can't even boil an egg," she said, though the real truth was that he did the cooking and she was the one who couldn't boil an egg.

Dorothy Parker and Alan Campbell went to Hollywood during the thirties and made a lot of money writing for the movies. (Dorothy continued writing for the *New Yorker* and brought in other money from points East also.) But as Edmund Wilson correctly pointed out she never really succeeded in coming to grips with Hollywood. She was never able to direct at that modern Babylon her strongest and best barbs. She could strike out at it in private, and her ejaculatory responses were as keen and deadly as usual, but she never made of them any systematic unity. Clearly she hated Hollywood folk and found few in the town with whom she could identify.

When Dorothy finally left Hollywood for good in 1953 and returned to the New York she loved, she condemned the movie capital in some of her most incisive prose. She told Ward Morehouse of the *New York World Telegram and Sun:* "Hollywood smells like a laundry. The beautiful vegetables taste as if they were raised in trunks, and at those wonderful supermarkets you find that the vegetables are all wax, the flowers out there smell like dirty old dollar bills. . . . Sure you make money writing on the coast, and God knows you earn it, but that money is like so much compressed snow. It goes so fast it melts in your hand." (Keats, 261)

As Edmund Wilson pointed out, Dorothy Parker's natural milieu was the New York of the 1920s. This was the world that gave her the stuff of her art. While this world lasted it gave her work universal applicability *and* something totally and completely American. Dorothy Parker's world was the world of the stupid and banal cocktail party, of the housewife's coffee klatch, of the summer hotel, of "dining out." She had a perfect and deadly ear for the conversation of the middle-class housewife as she discussed with her neighbor the servant problem, adultery, the Wednesday matinee, problems of the heart. Of the people of her customary reflection—usually those of the middle and upper classes—she can write with great vividness and with the force of truth. "Drunk or sober, angry or affectionate, stupid or inspired," wrote Mark Van Doren, "these people of Mrs. Parker's speak with an accent we immediately recognize and relish. . . . It is only Ring Lardner who can be compared with her in the manner of hatred for stupidity, cruelty and weakness."*

Some of Dorothy Parker's best stories are deeply sympathetic and keenly understanding of loneliness as we know it in the largely urban and impersonalized society of postindustrial America. A good example is "Such a Pretty Little Picture," which Mencken and Nathan ran in the *Smart Set* in 1922. It is a short vignette, almost seen from a window frame. A man is clipping his hedge on a typical suburban plot. The man is bored by his meaningless and uninspiring job in the city, equally bored with this stupid little plot of land and the hedge he is having to clip. His wife is vacuous and domineering; his daughter dull and mediocre. He would like to chuck the whole business, take off for somewhere else—anywhere to escape this empty world and the meaningless daily routine. At the very least he would like to be able to speak of his loneliness and isolation, to be able to share it with somebody. But there is nobody. His world consists only of business acquaintances and other suburbanites. None of these will share his dream of bolting, of getting away from it and cutting everything off—his past, his family, his dreary job. The ironic title of the story comes from the picture painted by two neighbors who see him at work. Such a pretty little picture, they think: a good and solid husband with wife and daughter watching him from the porch. An ideal of suburban success and felicity.

This is the kind of story that Dorothy Parker could execute more neatly and precisely than anyone else of her time. Above all its mood is one that she could feel more genuinely and more vividly than any American writers since. Thus she must remain for us a writer who addresses herself to life as it is lived in America. As Wilson put it in an article in the *New Republic* in 1927, "Her wit is the wit of her particular time and place, but it is often as cleanly economic at the same time that it is as flatly brutal as the wit of the age of Pope; and

*Mark Van Doren's original statement appeared in the *English Journal.* Cf. Keats, 181.

within its small scope, it is a criticism of life. It has its roots in contemporary reality." (*Shores of Light,* 206)

This gift, Wilson concluded in later years, seems to have died with the coming of the depression. The twenties was a time to love, to live recklessly, to really commit oneself to something. Thus it produced writers like Scott Fitzgerald and Dorothy Parker who were rooted in contemporary reality, who actually caught us as we were, and told us truths about ourselves. No better tribute to the writers of the twenties can be paid than that paid by Edmund Wilson in his wartime review of *The Viking Portable Dorothy Parker:*

This collected volume has a value derived from rarity—a rarity like that of steel penknives, good erasers and real canned sardines, articles of which the supply has almost given out and of which one is only now beginning to be aware of how excellent the quality was. It seems to me, though I shall name no names, that it has been one of the features of this later time that it produces imitation books. There are things of which one cannot really say that they are either good books or bad books; they are really not books at all. When one has bought them, one has only got paper and print. When one has bought Dorothy Parker, however, one has really got a book. She is not Emily Brontë or Jane Austen, but she has been at some pains to write well, and she has put into what she has written a voice, a state of mind, an era, a few moments of human experience that nobody else has conveyed. (*Classics and Commercials,* 171)

When the lights went out at the end of the twenties, an era in American literature came abruptly to an end, and some of our most authentic and original voices were stilled. Women writers, especially, went into eclipse, quite unhappily for the fate of American culture. They, more than the men, had been caught unawares by America's drift away from glittering prosperity. They had been called upon to do much during and after the war and they had responded spectacularly. They had been tough and courageous at a time when it was needed, for which they paid a high personal price as the American they helped to explain wandered away. They gave us much to remember them by.

4

The Crumbling
Moral Order

Edmund Wilson had a curiously ambivalent attitude toward the 1920s. It was an era of youthful vitality, of social upheaval: it was a great time to be alive, especially for young writers and artists for whom it had become easy to declare independence from the stale world of prewar America. On the other hand, as the decade wore on, Wilson became increasingly skeptical of the possibility that writers, artists, and intellectuals would be able to do anything to create a healthy society out of the tumultuous, unhappy, and ambiguous conditions that pertained in twentieth-century urban America.

Many of Wilson's journalistic pieces of the late twenties suggest a mood of watchful waiting, as if it were possible to see, to hear, to feel, but not to know. A piece that Wilson wrote for the *New Republic* in 1926, "Thoughts on Leaving New York for New Orleans," seems to capture Wilson's prevailing mood in the years before the stock market crash. This evocative and discomforting document consists of nothing but a series of individual and seemingly unrelated observations about New York. Here are a few of them:

The Brevoort and the Lafayette are being unattractively renovated in the style of the lavatory of Pennsylvania Station.

In drug-stores, miscellaneous women, as they wait to use the telephone booths, are buying banana-nut sundaes and listening to phonograph records of Ukulele Ike.

At the Grand Central Palace there is a big Bathroom Fixture Exhibition.

Highbrow theatres are straining every nerve to discover another Michael Arlen.

Antique stores on Madison Avenue are selling fake china dogs for sixty-five dollars apiece.

On Park Avenue, above the Grand Central, many people—at very high cost—believe they are living in high style.

Detectives and tarts in collusion are framing victims in the upper Forties.

Smart bookstores on the side streets in the Forties are disposing of first editions of Joseph Hergesheimer for seven dollars apiece.

The art galleries are lined with carpets, like Campbell's Funeral Church.

People suffering from exhaustion, despondency and acute self-dissatisfaction are being treated by expensive specialists for dental trouble, mastoiditis, astigmatism, inflammatory rheumatism, ophthalmic goiter and fallen arches, then finally turned over to analysts.

Corner drug-stores will supply bad gin to people who are well enough known to them.

Students at Columbia University are electing courses in Collective Bargaining, The History of Modern Thought and Problems of Abnormal Psychology. (*American Earthquake*, 121, 123)

The humorous, sometimes sardonic, mood of these passages might have made them as suitable for the "Americana" section of Mencken's *American Mercury* as for the *New Republic*. But their scope and range leave no doubt about the impression Wilson was attempting to implant. It was not just the banality and superficiality of the Coolidge prosperity that was being questioned, but the incoherence, the fragmentary quality of American life. What do these disjointed items add up to? They are expressive of a social life, of a people not moving in any firm direction. America was full of activity—going, going, but pointing nowhere. Oh, indeed, there was freedom to move, to express oneself. There may even have been, as Coolidge promised, a chicken in every pot and a car in every garage, but what good does it do to be well fed, well housed, if you do not have a civilization, a nation? "Thoughts on Leaving New York for New Orleans," like so many of Wilson's essays of the period, calls into question the American's inability to develop a sense of community, to fabricate any kind of network of shared meaningful relationships.

For the average American citizen, life in the twenties was just too gay, too prosperous, too free. With a chicken in every pot and a car in every garage, it was easy to forget that a new gas station was ruining the end of the block; it was easy to overlook the polluted river that ran beside the brand new skyscraper of steel and glass. If there were failures in interpersonal life one could go right out and consult an expensive psychiatrist, an experience that could even be fun and worth gossiping about. Or one could turn everything off with bad gin and worry about things another day. If there was a certain vague and uneasy apprehension in the twenties it could always be put off for another day. The world was exciting; one could only hope it would remain so.

But 1929 was another matter. America was brought up with a start. The great bull market of the 1920s was dead, and although all the ramifications were not immediately evident, by 1931 no American could fail to see that the American system, and thereby the American "way," was far from perfect. Strange as it may seem, therefore, Wilson saw the stock market crash and the depression that ensued as a not altogether gloomy development. After all, the disaster was a dramatic one; it called for action. It also seemed to call for a national reassessment of priorities. Wilson hoped it would influence Americans to question once again their own nation and destiny, to question the mindless abuses and excesses of capitalism and ask if there were some better body politic, something more suitable for a society of free men and women.

These are a few of the reasons why Wilson's writing entered a new and vigorous phase during the darkest years of the depression. Some of his best writing comes from this period. *Axel's Castle* appeared in 1931, but Wilson did not follow this up with further efforts in the realm of aesthetic criticism as might have been expected; rather he returned to active journalism and in the next few years produced some of the most moving and brilliantly written journalistic pieces of his career. These pieces, later collected in *The American Jitters* and *The American Earthquake,* are also surely among the best examples of American journalistic writing and are today sadly neglected by students of American literature and history; they are vivid and poignant recollections of the coming of the Great Depression with its spiritual malaise, its gruesome realization of great hopes lost, of America brought to self-consciousness with a jolt.

Wilson begins his book, *The American Jitters,* with a sketch entitled "Dwight Morrow in New Jersey." Dwight Morrow, formerly a partner of the banking firm of J.P. Morgan, formerly ambassador to Mexico, now father-in-law of Colonel Charles A. Lindbergh, was running for senator from the state of New Jersey in 1930. He was even being pushed for the presidency by the *New York Morning World.* Unfortunately, and this point was not mentioned in Wilson's essay, neither Morrow nor the *New York Morning World* would live to see the 1932 elections; Morrow served only a few months of his term as senator.

What sort of a man was Morrow? He was, thought Wilson, "a sound old-fashioned American; the son of a schoolmaster and brought up in a home of old-fashioned plain living and high thinking, he has made his way by the traditional American road of shrewdness, perseverance, industry and thrift." He was a rich man, but his daughter, Anne Morrow Lindbergh, said later that she thought he would have been happier being a professor of history in some small college. His English biographer, Harold Nicholson, while admiring Morrow's many sterling qualities, said off the record in later years that Morrow was also an unhappy man who drank himself to death.

Still, clearly Morrow was a cut above the average politician. He was a gifted man, probably an honest man. The depression had not yet deepened; there was still light on the horizon. His campaign was dull, cautious. He supported Hoover's watchful waiting. As for the depression, he felt sure that confidence would pull the country through. He even suspected that a little depression might be a good thing. "There is something about too much prosperity that ruins the fiber of the people. The men and women that built this country, that founded it, were people that were reared in adversity." A compelling argument, but somehow it doesn't hold. Wilson's cynical response may not even fully reveal the inadequacy of the analogy. "It is a reassuring thought," he remarks, "in cold weather, that the emaciated men in the bread lines, the men and women beggars in the streets, and the children dependent on them, are all having their fibre hardened" (*American Jitters,* 3).

The heart of this essay is not so much what it says about the depression, or America's economic failure, admittedly not as obvious as it was to be a year later, but the failure of America's stalwart men of affairs to open their eyes to what was going on. They seemed to be enmeshed in the machinery of the capitalistic system out of which they grew. Their human qualities had been short-circuited, so they could not empathize with the problems of the man on the street. This thought is captured by Wilson with a stunning metaphor, a picture of Morrow at Krueger Hall in Newark, his voice being mechanically piped to the outside so that it can be picked up as easily by those milling around the building as those sitting in the auditorium inside.

A brilliant piece of reportage, quite characteristic of Wilson's best writing at this time.

> As you approach Krueger Hall in Newark, where Mr. Morrow is opening his campaign, you hear a gigantic mechanical voice, as bleak and unappealing as the Newark streets, which fills the air in front of the auditorium and makes it as easy to listen to the speaker outside as in. And even when you have gone inside and caught a glimpse of the little man in eyeglasses almost hidden behind the microphone, his earnest gestures and the movement of his lips still seem entirely unconnected with the great loud and hollow voice declaiming from the amplifiers on either side of the proscenium arch. What it declaims is a dull political speech, as padded and banal as any, and relying as much as any on meaningless catchwords and exhortations.

> Dwight Morrow is a sound old-fashioned American. . . . But his ideas about the present economic chaos do not, apparently, transcend the conviction that there is still an opportunity in this society for everyone to do as he has done and that, if everybody did, we should come round. And the giant ventriloquial voice which emanates from the nice little man is merely the voice of American capitalism. (5)

The voice of capitalism everywhere had thus become dehumanized; it could not transcend a tinny unreal sound; its utterances were nothing but meaningless political platitudes and catchwords. The great capitalist leaders are not corpulent brutes, taking the whiplash to production line workers (the vision always lovingly developed by the Marxists in Russia), but, as seen in greater complexity and subtlety by Wilson, men caught up in the drift of circumstances, unable to shake themselves loose from ideals that had once worked but now were useless and hollow.

In the longer and even more penetrating piece, "Detroit Motors," Wilson makes these same points again in rich detail. "Detroit Motors" is a description and analysis of Henry Ford's career seen against the background, the sights and sounds, of the great Ford River Rouge plant, and it moves toward the conclusion that the machinery of American capitalism on all levels had for too long been unwieldy and estranged from human purposes and ideals. The depression here is seen merely as a dramatic heightening of a failure or weakness that had been darkening the grain for a long time.

The first half of the essay is a description of the working conditions at River Rouge, fortified by well-selected interviews with Ford workers, many of whom had been with the company for years. The second part of the essay is devoted to Henry Ford himself: one-man owner and entrepreneur, president, and sole guiding light of the

Ford Motor Company. The essay is not the usual socialist/Marxist tract, where the lordly and villainous Ford is played off against the downtrodden but virtuous workers; no, the truth seems to be that the complexity and mysteriousness of the system consort to defeat everyone's efforts to set things right.

Admittedly, the Ford plant had become a sweatshop by the early 1930s; wages were better than elsewhere in Detroit but everything else was worse. One of the workers (an Englishman) told Wilson, "Ye get the wages, but ye sell your soul at Ford's—ye're worked like a slave all day and when ye get out ye're too tired to do anything—ye go to sleep in the car coming home." As far as wages are concerned, all the world knows that Ford made history in 1914 by declaring a five-dollar daily wage—unheard of in production line work in that year. Ford tried to ride for many years on this nifty little public relations gimmick, but the reality for workers was something else again. The cost of living nearly doubled in Detroit between 1914 and 1927, and though Ford raised the rate to six dollars in 1919, workers soon found themselves less well off than they were in the period before 1914. The rate was not raised to seven dollars until December 1929.

Even worse, technological improvements had made it possible to speed up production lines and get by with fewer workers. In 1925 Ford had been employing 200,000 men at six dollars a day, at a cost of $300,000,000 a year. By the fall of 1929 there were only 145,000 men working at Ford who, when the seven-dollar-a-day wage went into effect, would cost the company only $253,750,000 per year. With the coming of the seven-dollar wage (announced spectacularly at the White House in December 1929 as a shot of adrenalin to counter the adverse conditions on the stock market), Ford "was able to recruit the quickest and most vigorous workers at the expense of the less able ones" and was able to push all his workers harder.

Ford was not much loved by his neighbors and workers in Detroit, however revered he was throughout the rest of America. His factory was a cruel place of implacable energy; hours were long, breaks were few and short. Lunch, for which workers were allowed fifteen minutes, was served from a lunch wagon. Ford moved his plant out of the city of Detroit, building River Rouge so he could keep from having to pay any kind of welfare bills in the city. All in all, there was little evidence that Ford really cared about his workers or their community.

On the other hand, there was much to admire in Ford, and Wilson was the first to admit it. Clearly he was a mechanical and industrial genius. He was never motivated chiefly by hope of personal gain. "There is no evidence that Ford cares much about money for its own sake or for the things it can buy." He was known, of course, for having said that "history is bunk," and also for having remarked, "I don't like to read books. They muss up my mind." Yet by 1930 it had become obvious that Ford was not really a modern man of management. He was as suspicious of his own underlings as he was a decade earlier of the Wall Street bankers who were trying to euchre him out of his one-man control of the corporation. He surrounded himself by yes-men and mercilessly fired all those who seemed to arrogate responsibility. John Kenneth Galbraith explained Ford's decline during the 1930s and 1940s in terms of old Henry's refusal to admit the necessity of the large corporation being controlled by the technostructure, that is, a group of men sharing specialized information.*

Certainly, though, in attempting to maintain total authority, Ford accepted an almost intolerable burden as his company grew. Wilson is at pains to quote several Ford biographers who point to the psychological volatility and unhappiness of the man. There was always the simple country boy and tinker buried deep inside the business executive. At the same time, business pumped the spirit out of Henry Ford. This was noticed as early as 1923 by Ford's own pastor, Samuel S. Marquis, in a book called *Henry Ford, an Interpretation.* Reverend Marquis described Ford as a man of moods. One day he will seem "erect, lithe, agile, full of life, happy as a child." But the next day "he will have the appearance of a man shrunken by long illness." Louis P. Lockner, a former employee of Ford's, wrote in *Henry Ford: An American Don Quixote:* "In no other person have I observed so pronounced a dual nature as in my former chief. There seems to be a constant struggle for control on the part of these two natures. The natural Henry Ford is the warm, impulsive, idealistic, 'Old Man.' . . . The other Henry Ford has been imposed by the artificialities of modern civilization, by his environment, his business associates, his responsibilities to the huge Ford interests" (*American Jitters,* 77-78).

Although Wilson does not make this comparison explicitly he does so dramatically and forcefully nonetheless: Henry Ford was every bit as trapped in circumstances beyond his control as were his workers who were forced into more and more pressing production

*John Kenneth Galbraith, *The New Industrial State* (Boston: Houghton Mifflin, 1967), 88-91.

lines of Chaplinesque proportions. Ford was not a man of bad will; he had no desire to be an exploiter of his fellow man. He was overwhelmed by a complex economic network beyond his control. Sadly and ironically he got in over his head; things got beyond his control just as he was making a fetish of keeping control. Henry Ford was a great business leader, but he had been forced into a position where no kind of real social or moral leadership was possible. He was, furthermore, living proof that we have been able to grow no natural aristocracy out of the capitalist system in America. "The Leaders of Industry," said Carlyle of Victorian England, "if Industry is ever to be led, are virtually the Captains of the World! If there be no nobleness in them, there will never be an Aristocracy more." But it was Wilson's feeling that in American capitalism the leader has no chance to develop *noblesse oblige* or aristocratic independence; he is caught up in an environment in which he cannot bring his own best traits into play. And with the coming of the depression Ford was as cruelly beset as any of his workers; his company drifted idly; he himself floundered, pathetically unenlightened about the turn of events.

Another essay reprinted in *American Jitters,* "The First of May," also superbly illustrates this quality of American economic life, namely, the lack of control people have over things, the wayward and unplanned direction of current events. (Later reprinted in *American Earthquake* this was retitled: "May First: The Empire State Building; Life on the Passaic River.") Like the piece on Henry Ford it is divided into two distinct parts, each of which clearly foreshadows the other. Here we are introduced to the Empire State Building, the tallest building in the world in 1931 (and for more than thirty years thereafter), which, with its silver-bright chrome and steel, casts its light not only over the inferior edifices of Manhattan but over the industrial marshlands of New Jersey to the west, the grim habitations of Long Island to the east.

That the Empire State Building is a magnificent product of capitalistic America would be hard to deny. But it may seem rather gruesome that the building was built just as the depression was deepening, as were so many other art deco skyscrapers with their rich ornamentation and lavish foyers. Even as commercial America was gagging, many of these giants pierced the sky, the building laborers waiting only for the moment of completion to meet up with their final paychecks and almost certain unemployment.

Obviously, it is a thing of beauty. "In a warm afternoon glow the building is rose-bisque with delicate nickle lines; the gray air of rainy weather makes a harmony with bright pale facings on dull pale gray;

a chilly late afternoon shows the mast like a bright piece of silver-
ware, an old salt-cellar elegantly chased." The public rooms and
appointments are ostentatious. "The entrance hall of the Empire
State Building is four stories high and made of a strange specially
imported marble with an effect of crushed strawberries smeared into
gray. On the far illuminated ceiling are gold and silver suns and stars
and circles—conventionalized geometrical patterns supposed to be
devised from snowflake shapes. . . . The elevator doors are black with
somber silver lines: they suggest entrances to Egyptian tombs. The
halls are full of uniformed guards with guns in holsters" (132-33,
134-35).

The building was formally opened May 1, 1931, by former governor Al Smith, president of the owning company. It cost $32,000,000,
contained 10,000,000 bricks, weighed 600,000,000 pounds, and included 6,400 windows and 67 elevators. But Wilson does not fail to
point out a most devastating irony. The building was rushed to completion in less than one year, and forty-eight men were killed in the
process. (At one point the builders used telephoto to send for certain
materials that needed to be rushed in from Cleveland.) Yet for all this
rush, there really was no immediate need for the building. "Business
is extremely bad and even the office buildings already erected are full
of untenanted space. Of the offices in the Empire State Building only
a quarter so far have been rented, and in moving into it, most of the
tenants will merely be leaving more vacancies elsewhere." In all of
its sparkling newness the Empire State Building is a living monument to American failure.

If you look out of the top windows, or from the observation tower
on the eighty-sixth floor, the evidences of failure and decay are even
more obvious. Look out to Brooklyn, Long Island City, The Bronx,
Hoboken, all places that may catch the reflections of the Empire
State's steel and glass on a sunny afternoon. All contrast so sharply,
so grimly with the prize monument to commercial daring. Look out,
then, at Brooklyn, or over to New Jersey:

Straight streets, square walls, crowded bulks, regular rectangular windows—more than ten million people sucked into that vast ever-expanding
barracks, with scarcely a garden, scarcely a park, scarcely an open square,
whose distances in all directions are blotted out in pale slate-gray. And here
is the pile of stone, brick, nickel and steel, the shell of offices, shafts, windows
and steps, that outmultiplies and outstacks them all—that, most purposeless
and superfluous of all, is being advertised as a triumph in the hour when the
planless competitive society, the dehumanized urban community of which
it represents the culmination, is bankrupt. (136)

Out there in that other world we find the subject of the other half of Wilson's essay. In the vile New Jersey industrial marsh, near the Passaic River, and almost within the shadow of the Empire State Building, we find a Yugoslavian immigrant named John Dravic and his family. Dravic has been laid off from his job in a car shop and, seeking to make use of his time, borrows 300 dollars to open a cigar and candy store. He is a good family man, and in this sterile neighborhood flowers and vegetables flourish in his small yard. He loves music and has two violins, a cello, and a guitar. His two older boys have learned to play. But the store, which is not well located, fails, and one night Dravic shoots his children, including a baby, and then himself.

The Dravic story might even be looked upon as the other end of the spectrum of the Henry Ford story—but in 1931, so much more common. Everywhere there are people with nothing but the best of will who are caught up in a system that is beyond their control. It is not, after all, that poverty is all-pervasive, for just beyond we see the glittering nickel surfaces of the Empire State Building. No, the system is not yet a total failure when looked at in economic terms. But it is a failure when looked at in human and moral terms. If we can identify a single message from *The American Jitters,* it is that we ought to take the dramatic evidence thus presented to us and see that the depression is firm proof of the necessity of a national reevaluation of priorities. Wilson was as close as he would ever come to being a pamphleteering socialist at this time; since extravaganzas like the Empire State Building held little weight with him in comparison to human life and dignity, he could only conclude that the capitalist order had fallen into a shambles and needed to be replaced—if not precisely by Russian communism, then by something not very much different from it.

The American Jitters provides a vast and sometimes kaleidoscopic treatment of social conditions in America in 1931 and 1932. As a reporter Wilson toured the whole country trying to observe the grim drift of things, trying to track the hand of fate in the most characteristic environments of the land. He wrote to Christian Gauss from New Mexico, "I came out here by way of Virginia, West Virginia, Tennessee and Missouri, stopping off for various stories—and America certainly seemed a wonderful country. Its present sour situation is ridiculous." From West Virginia Wilson reports on the conditions of the miners in the company town of Ward—workers now almost reduced to serfdom ("Frank Keeney's Coal Diggers"). He reports on "Cousin Charles," the Tennessee tobacco farmer ("Tennessee Agrarians"). There is an Indian corn dance in New Mexico, a

Fourth of July in Colorado; a rich and variegated essay on Los Ange-
les, California ("The City of Our Lady the Queen of the Angels");
there are scenes and comments on America both urban and rural. At
the end of the book Wilson is back in the East, in Lawrence, Massachusetts: "The winter wage-cuts have begun; and the streets of Lawrence this October are as bleak as those of Newark last fall when
Dwight Morrow was running for senator." Lawrence is a textile
town: 23,000 workers are on strike. Poverty is ubiquitous though the
textile industry is not as badly hit as some. The workers had been
making less than twenty dollars a week before the cut. The women
make all the clothes and do all the cooking; they never get a chance
to leave the house. Many of the children have no shoes. "Some of the
families buy stale bread in bags" (274).

On the other hand, this book, a little gem of reporting, is not
mainly a political treatise. If there are Marxist overtones they are
always kept strictly to the side; above all Wilson never intrudes any
"this is the time to take up arms" kind of material. Instead he attempts to present a warm and human portrait of America at the
depths of the depression, following Dos Passos in the attempt "to
study all the aspects of America and to take account of all its elements, to compose them into a picture which makes some general
sense." The word *general* is precisely what is important for Wilson;
it refers as always to basic human concerns. The goal is to produce
a living portrait with which the average general reader can sympathize—a goal always evident in Wilson's writing.

The late twenties and early thirties were fertile years for Wilson,
not only because of the sheer amount of writing he did in that period
but because he was seemingly able to work in so many different
dimensions at the same time. It is nothing short of startling that the
author of *Axel's Castle,* a work of delicate and precise literary criticism, could turn around almost immediately and engage in a national
reporting campaign that involved strenuous investigative trips to
coal mines, labor camps, and pool halls, and that he managed to do
both with equal finesse. On the other hand, the diversity of Wilson's
work at this time is not at all unusual when we remember that he
always regarded himself as a general or historical critic. He did not
regard literature and daily social life as being locked into separate
compartments with the literary critic being the one who kept his

nose clean of things political, his eyes shut to what was going on right down the street.

A literary critic who neither knew nor cared that people were starving within the sight of the Empire State Building would be an anemic, empty, and bloodless critic, his opinions about literature probably without enduring value. On the other hand, a social reporter or social reformer who limited himself to grievances, political platforms, and the injustices of the moment would not be in a position to say anything of permanent and lasting value about history or the progress of civilization. Thus it was, while so many American intellectuals were mindlessly singing the praises of Russian communism in the depression, Wilson was embarking on ambitious plans to travel to Russia, to survey the breadth of Russian culture, and to see if it were really true that we had something to learn from our Russian neighbors. Because of this Wilson found himself almost immediately veering off from the standard intellectual line of the thirties, penetrating ever more deeply into the mysteries of national existence on two continents, and trying to figure out what kind of life, what kind of civilization, was possible in the twentieth century with airplanes flying overhead, production lines grinding workers into oblivion, and Hitler and Mussolini snarling just offstage.

Wilson was never given to writing pure literary criticism, pure history, pure reporting, or pure anything else. Admixtures, blends, and the whole fabric of human experience were what he wanted to get down on paper. Consider, for example, *Axel's Castle,* the book that won for Wilson a great national literary reputation—a book still regarded by some as his finest achievement in literary criticism. The book is not in any sense an essay in pure or aesthetic criticism. Like all of Wilson's later works on literature it attempts to ask large questions about the place of literature in the scheme of things, about the moral value and significance of works of art. There is poetry. But what does poetry say to Hitler? There is drama. But does Hoover watch drama? Is there any form of literature that appeals to the masses or that grows spontaneously and truthfully from the masses? Are our most revered arts dying on the vine?

Such questions swirl around in *Axel's Castle* even when the book seems to be fastened so securely to the dimension of the aesthetic. Outwardly the book traces the development of the symbolist movement and contains essays on Yeats, Valéry, Eliot, Proust, Joyce, Gertrude Stein, and Rimbaud. But it ends by questioning the relevance of some of these symbolists to modern life and to the problems that impinge on our present existence.

The New
REPUBLIC

Published Weekly

Wednesday May 11, 1932

Gov. James Rolph, Jr.

The Man Who Keeps Mooney in Jail

by ERNEST JEROME HOPKINS

Edmund Wilson
and the American Mind

Newton Arvin on Brooks's Emerson

The Death of Hart Crane

FIFTEEN CENTS A COPY

FIVE DOLLARS A YEAR

VOL. LXX. NO. 910

Most of the essays in *Axel's Castle* discuss artists who are in retreat, who want to escape from the world. Of all the symbolist poets discussed in this volume, only Yeats, Wilson's favorite, really came to grips with the modern world and made some attempt to create a stable order out of the disorder—and lost none of his creative power in doing so. Most of the others represent one or another kind of withdrawal from the world—either in the style of Axel, the hero of Villiers de l'Isle-Adam's poem of that name who made an escape by removing himself from the real world to a world of high aestheticism, or in the style of Rimbaud, who escaped into a cult of the primitive. The former tendency can be seen in the heroes of Pater, Mallarmé, and Eliot. The latter tendency can be seen in novelists as diverse as D. H. Lawrence and Ernest Hemingway. Artists of this kind seek to put off their contact with life, seek to escape from the larger fabric of the social world either by geographical separation (Lawrence's Mexican interlude) or by the adoption of curious and isolated pastimes (Hemingway's bullfights and safaris).

Wilson, of course, does not deny that there is some justification for the escapist tendency in twentieth-century literature. The *fin-de-siècle* poets withdrew from the general life of their time because art no longer seemed relevant to that life. In Gautier's time, the bourgeois had been identified as the enemy, and the poet or novelist "took a lively satisfaction in fighting him." But by the end of the century, the bourgeois world had so completely inundated the world of art that there was no way for the poet to resist—except by going into hiding. "The artistic heroes of Thomas Mann with their abject 'inferiority complex' " and inability to stand up to the down-to-earth force of the German burgher are typical of the end of the century. But after this period there was little that the writer could hope to gain by the development of this kind of realism, or by satire of middle-class life. True, certain writers, like H.G. Wells and Bernard Shaw, tried to spin ideas out of the social sciences that would combat the bourgeois world, but this trend did not become sufficiently powerful to serve as a guide to the mainstream of literature. So "if one had no sociological interest and no satirical bent and so no way of turning society to account, one did not try to struggle with it: one simply did one's best to ignore it, to keep one's imagination free of it altogether" (268).

Now this does not force us to the conclusion that the withdrawal literatures of either tendency—that of Axel with its private fantasies or manias taken for realities, or that of Rimbaud with its abandonment of the twentieth century for some primitive place—have not provided us with much moving, refined, and sensitive literature. In 1931 Wilson was of the opinion that "though we shall continue to admire" the symbolists as masters, they "will no longer serve us as guides." A sudden disquiet convinced him that the masterpieces of the early twentieth century will not be enough, that we cannot continue to get sustenance from the private imaginings of Axel's castle, or from any of the current repetitions of Rimbaud's style of retreat—"by occupying ourselves exclusively with prize fighters or with thugs or by simply remaining drunk or making love all the time." It appeared to Wilson, as the depression moved toward its darkest hour, that these kinds of literature will not be able to nourish us in any way. "The question begins to press us again as to whether it is possible to make a practical success of human society, and whether, if we fail, a few masterpieces, however profound and noble, will be able to make life worth living even for the few people in a position to enjoy them" (293).

So again we return to the thesis that literature must address itself directly to one's time, that the artist must engage himself directly with the problems of his age—not, of course, merely as a social reformer taking up this or that already well-delineated cause, but as a barometer of the most subtle, disguised, and as yet uncomprehended changes in the environment. Above all, at the beginning of the depression, it was already obvious that none of the escapist forms of literature, however rewarding they had been, could speak to American problems, could get around the failure of nerve that had come over American society, could obscure (or cure) the impending economic disaster that seemed about to bring down in shambles everything people had come to rely upon since the Civil War. Wilson's feeling at the time of writing *Axel's Castle* was that literature in America would have to discover new forms if it were to survive. Perhaps literature would become more akin to journalism (Wilson himself was experimenting along these lines), or perhaps the literary imagination could devote itself to some of the newer art forms—radio, television, moving pictures. Perhaps, in the face of science, particularly the social sciences, literature would not be able to survive at all. But always there was the feeling that if literature were to survive it would have to grow organically out of the rich soil of American experience.

Wilson's work as a literary critic took some strange but not entirely unpredictable turns during the 1930s. After the publication of *Axel's Castle* he made no immediate attempt to embark on another full-scale work of literary criticism. During those early and cruel years of the depression he was involved in general national reporting for the *New Republic*. Later on he was to make the travels to Russia that would result in *Travels in Two Democracies*, and begin the scholarly activity that would result in *To the Finland Station*. But it was not to be until the 1940s that Wilson got back into the mainstream of American literature and the American historical tradition. He was not, strictly speaking, able to follow up the philosophy expressed in *Axel's Castle*, namely, that the writer must find out new ways to address his own generation with new forms of artistic expression.

A look at Wilson's literary pieces written from the beginning of the depression through the late 1930s will show that he was continuing to cultivate his broadly cultural and international interests. Wilson's collection of essays from the 1930s, *The Shores of Light*, contains essays entitled "André Malraux," "C.L. Dodgson: The Poet Logician," "Lytton Strachey," "The Satire of Samuel Butler," and "Gertrude Stein Old and Young." But the subjects of Wilson's essays during the final half of the thirties predominately concerned the economic upheaval and the possibility of finding answers for America's troubles abroad, new ways to look at our social and cultural disorders. Thus we find as typical of this period essays entitled, "The Literary Consequences of the Crash," "The Economic Interpretation of Wilder," "An Appeal to Progressives," "The Literary Class War," "The Classics of the Soviet Stage," "American Critics, Left and Right."

The period between 1930 and 1935 was one of obvious political and social concern for Wilson. On the other hand, though his views were sympathetic to those of the intelligentsia of the period, they were always also eccentric and untypical. Like most writers of the period, Wilson was moving to the left, and he was assuming that all honest writers would be doing so also; but other than this general tendency—which path, which way?

Wilson had started moving left earlier in the twenties than his colleagues on the *New Republic*, including editor Herbert Croly. In "The Literary Consequences of the Crash," he writes that even in 1927, at the time of the execution of Sacco and Vanzetti, he was aware "that we liberals of *The New Republic* were not taking certain recent happenings as seriously as we should" (*Shores of Light*, 496).

The 1920s were not particularly good years for the liberalism of the style of Herbert Croly. Croly's book, *The Promise of American Life*, published in 1909, represented a kind of progressive idealism that no longer meant too much by the 1920s, with its nervous frenetic environment and the predominance of a Tory political outlook in the manner of H.L. Mencken. On the other hand, the *New Republic* style of liberalism would not exactly be able to come into its own in the depression either since now the swing was *too* far to the left. Up to his death in 1930, Croly firmly rejected Marxism and refused to entertain the idea that there was or could be any kind of real class conflict in the United States.*

Croly's liberalism, to which Wilson was morally sympathetic, grew up with Theodore Roosevelt progressivism. It was an attempted revival of Hamiltonian public policy, built on a faith that a large and active government composed of responsible citizen-leaders could become a reliable organ of the people. Such a government need not attack large corporations but rather could control and direct them in the national interest. Thus a civilized and responsible government could be a true expression of the nation's will.

But even the prosperous years of the 1920s were making clear that the kind of liberalism dreamed of by Croly in 1909 was not taking hold in America. There was the Teapot Dome scandal, proof that men of the moneyed classes were not beneficent aristocrats who looked upon government as a place for disinterested service. It was obvious, too, that the political system did not pick the best for the highest, that the Theodore Roosevelts were not the norm. Looking for the norm we find Hardings and Coolidges. Not far below them were the Falls, Sinclairs, and Doheneys who in the full glare of reality were a far cry from what Croly had in mind as disinterested public officials recruited from the commercial classes.

By the time Croly died in 1930 there was very little for the old-style progressive liberal to have faith in. True—and here Wilson differed from the newly popular far left—the American capitalist and the American politician were not bad men; they were not evil or ill intentioned. This was the main point of the essay on Dwight Morrow that opened *American Jitters.* In America the capitalist and his political functionaries are removed from human reality, separated from what is going on in actual experience. "The capitalist Americans of

---

*There is a great deal in Wilson's writings of the 1930s about *New Republic* liberalism. See, for example, "The Literary Consequences of the Crash," "H.C." (Herbert Croly), "The Literary Class War." Apparently Wilson never read Croly's *The Promise of American Life* until after Croly's death in 1930, though he was drawn to Croly personally in an idealistic way. But as soon as the depression came along Wilson was strongly motivated to ask if there was any way that the Croly style of progressive liberalism could be brought back to life. He concluded almost immediately that there was not. On Croly, see also Wilson's letter to Arthur Schlesinger, Jr., in *Letters,* 197-98.

the twentieth century are certainly more kindly and democratic than the landlords of the feudal age; but, on the other hand, the capitalist system makes it very much easier for people not to realize what they are doing, not to know about the danger and the hardship, the despair and the humiliation, that their way of life implies for others. The feudal lord might flog or kill his serfs, but he was dealing directly with the human realities as the stockholder or banker is not" (*Shores of Light,* 522). What the capitalist economy has spawned is not the wonderful sense of community Croly and other progressives dreamed of in 1910 but a kind of alienation and spiritual emptiness.

And this became dramatically evident with the coming of the depression since the vacuity and sterility of the life under capitalism could no longer be disguised as it was, garishly and blatantly, under Coolidge. In an essay written in 1931, "An Appeal to Progressives," Wilson made the point that the crash immediately punctured the great American dream that there was some glamour about a poor boy becoming a millionaire or taking a seat on the stock exchange. Nor was there much to the myth about the blessings of prosperity. Here is a characteristic Wilsonian blast at capitalistic culture that is really only an intensification of what he had already been saying in the twenties:

The Buicks and Cadillacs, the bad gin and Scotch, the radio concerts interrupted by advertizing talks, the golf and bridge of the suburban household, which the bond salesman can get for his money, can hardly compensate him for daily work of a kind in which it is utterly impossible to imagine a normal human being taking satisfaction or pride—and the bond salesman is the type of the whole urban office class. The brokers and bankers who are shooting themselves and jumping out of windows have been disheartened by the precariousness of their profession—but would they be killing themselves if they loved it? Who today, in fact, in the United States, can really love our meaningless life, where the manufacturer raises the workers' wages only in order to create a demand for the gadgets which for better or worse he happens to have an interest in selling them, while agriculture goes hang, and science and art are left to be exploited by the commercial laboratories. (Ibid., 527)

Wilson was thus thoroughly convinced by 1930, and probably long before, that progressive style optimism and liberalism had led to a *cul-de-sac;* there was nowhere the liberals could go and nothing they could do, at least along traditional lines. What was there, then, for the young American writer? What options remained open? Croly-style liberalism led to a blind alley; the cultural conservatism of a Mencken also seemed inappropriate and unseemly for a time when people were starving. The path that seemed most logical, perhaps inevitable, was the one heading toward socialism or communism. Such was the path now being taken by Michael Gold in the *New Masses,* and shortly after by many of the young writers who became members of the Communist party during the 1930s. At a time when American liberalism might conveniently be expected to come into its own, at least as some kind of moral force, it was met by a swing to the left so strong and so sudden that the liberal found himself a rare, curious, and superannuated bird.

Wilson was one of those who immediately perceived (and here he differed from his colleagues on the *New Republic*) that the political and economic system in America was in a shambles and that what it needed was a complete overhaul. Between 1930 and 1935 he believed that we ought to see what kind of inspiration could be had from socialism, that we ought at least to be learning something about what was going on in Russia, and that we ought to be learning something about the history of European social thought, including Marxism and communism. In this he differed at first from his colleagues of the *New Republic* who, as John Dos Passos wrote to Wilson, "are all so neurotic about Communists" (ibid., 498). On the other hand, as we can see from Wilson's essays of the period, "An Appeal to Progressives," "The Literary Class War," and "The Economic Interpretation of Wilder," Wilson was never particularly interested in swallowing communism in one gulp. He was no ideologue. He had no appetite for brassbound dogma or for simpleminded tractarianism, which kept him manifestly separate and distinct from hard-line leftists like Gold and Granville Hicks. As it happened, Wilson was one of the first American liberals to turn away from the actual system of communism in Russia; indeed, he was denouncing it just about the time his colleagues on the *New Republic* were becoming enchanted with it!

Still, Wilson's interest in the origins of European social thought in general and socialism in particular was a dominant one in the thirties. Indeed he blames that interest for a falling off in his literary activities, and in later years wrote almost apologetically of his neglect of literary events during the thirties. In a brief note appended to the end of "An Appeal to Progressives," he wrote: "From the fall of 1930 to the spring of 1934, I spent a good deal of time reporting political and industrial events, and thereafter, till 1940, writing a study of Marxism and the Russian Revolution, so that I did not give the literary events of these years as much attention as I had given to those

of the twenties or as I was afterwards to give those of the forties"
(ibid., 533).

As early as 1932 Wilson was urging his friends and literary acquaintances to give serious thought to Marxism as a possible replace-
ment for the obviously bankrupt and seemingly unreformable
capitalist system. He was not urging, however, the one-dimensional
sloganeering of the *New Masses* or the *Daily Worker*, but rather, as
was always his way, a penetrating historical analysis of the great
Marxist thinkers. Even as he was writing detailed, specific, and vivid
news stories from the coal fields of West Virginia, the industrial
marshes of New Jersey, or the orange groves of California, he was
urging his friends to become readers of history, social thinkers but
not yet social activists and revolutionaries. Late in the summer of
1932 we find him writing his old friend John Peale Bishop, warning
him against the slick generalities of the moment in favor of close
study of the major thinkers:

As for Marxism, etc., it seems to me that like most people who haven't looked
into it, you don't really understand the point of view, and I strongly recom-
mend to you the works of Marx himself, Lenin and Trotsky. I can assure you
that you'll find them good reading. Be sure to read Trotsky's *Literature and
Revolution,* an extraordinary and unique piece of literary criticism. A good
way to begin is probably with the *Communist Manifesto* and Marx's *Eighteenth Brumaire of Louis Bonaparte.* If you can't swallow the abstract parts
of *Das Kapital* (there is an excellent new translation in Everyman's), at least
read the historical. The point is that the literature of Marxism is not really
a body of dogma (you know that Marx said he was no Marxist and that
Trotsky's writings have been suppressed by Stalin), though Communism
itself—the Third International, that is—has some of the characteristics of a
secular church: it corresponds more or less to the literature of the Enlighten-
ment before the French and American Revolutions, and people of our own
time can no more afford to be ignorant of it than people of the eighteenth
century could of Voltaire and Montesquieu and Rousseau. (*Letters,* 227)

During the 1930s Wilson, with his usual tendency toward con-
trariness and independence, refused to keep step with his fellow
writers on the *New Republic* and with the younger generation of
writers generally. Naturally, like they, he was intrigued by Marxism,
but he did not expect to import Marxism as a political doctrine
already fit for use. He wanted to follow it to its roots, to find out what
it had done and could do for European culture and, by implication,
for our own. He was determined to read all of the relevant books, to

delve into the biographies of the principal Marxist thinkers, and the studies that he engaged in as the result of this work resulted a few years later in the publication of one of his most popular and successful books, *To the Finland Station*.

On the other hand, it might be argued that Wilson, like most of the young writers and intellectuals of the depression years, had rather too easily given up on the American system. At the time of the writing of *American Jitters*, Wilson had reached the rather facile conclusion that American capitalism was finished; and so too the American style of government. Later on he would have to admit that he was wrong. Yet, the deflection of interest away from the American scene—even though Wilson could fairly insist that his long European interlude was to bring new and fresh ideas to the American shore—resulted in the neglect of the American political and social system as it stood and kept him from other ideas that might have better occupied his time. What the American system needed in the thirties but did not get from the young writers and intellectuals of the time, including Wilson, was a thorough study of the American government and of the verities of its economic system. Except for those few intellectuals directly involved in the political arena through the New Deal, there seemed to be a kind of ready acceptance of the belief that everything was falling apart and that nothing could be done within the social order then in existence.

So Wilson lost a great deal of valuable time in the thirties studying European political history, when he might have done better to look in greater depth at the kinds of problems that he tackled in *American Jitters*. How much better it would have been for Wilson to further develop the kind of material found in essays like "Dwight Morrow in New Jersey," which in fact he was eminently qualified to do.

Unfortunately, though, Wilson never really learned much about economics (he showed no interest in the subject when he was a student at Princeton and never made any attempts to master it in later years). While the New Dealers were having to hurl themselves against the hard reality of American existence during the depression years, Wilson was perhaps too easily taking the escape route of the ivory tower. Believing that all was lost and that what was going on in Washington was mere application of salves and ointments to a dying body, Wilson never really made the effort to find out how the American economy operates and why it had gotten in trouble. Nor did he explore the latent possibilities for the future using the institutions already in place.

A lack of knowledge of economics and of the intricacies of American politics in fact dogged Wilson's footsteps throughout his days. In the Eisenhower and Kennedy years his critics would point out that Wilson really did not know much about what was going on in Washington, that all he knew was that he did not like what he saw. He remained, like H.L. Mencken, a debunker of the political carnival; he believed that politics was an unsavory game, not practiced by either gentlemen or humanists. This is not necessarily a grievous defect in a cultural critic, of course, and Wilson's aloof attitudes are worth listening to precisely because most of us Americans cannot stand back and view with detachment a system in which we are daily entangled. Wilson's stubborn insistence on standing aside and his refusal to engage in the nitty gritty of American politics may well have given him a privileged vantage point that outweighed his Tory disdain for the stale airs of politics.

It is not quite accurate, then, to describe Wilson's Russian travels, his readings in European socialism, as deflected purpose, personal failure—for Wilson was always a general historical critic, not a political scientist. His concerns were predominately moral and humanistic. He responded to the cruelties of the depression in ways that might be expected of a committed humanistic writer. Believing that post-Civil War industrial America had crumbled, along with the moral structure that was spun out of it, Wilson looked for an escape. As was already evident in *Axel's Castle,* there could be no salvation in aestheticism. Our broader native literary and intellectual traditions were still healthy and could possibly provide some nourishment but not in 1932-1933 when people were starving. As a literary critic and Americanist Wilson therefore slackened his pace for a while as the thirties drifted on. At this time the moralist and general critic had few avenues open to him, and Wilson did about as well as might be expected. There were fertile possibilities that he missed, but he would start picking up on them as the decade of the thirties drew to a close.

5

Two Ailing Democracies

In the middle 1930s, having taken at least partial leave of his reporting duties on the *New Republic,* Wilson embarked on a phase of his
career that resulted in two books that add luster to his credentials as
a critic of culture. One of these, *To the Finland Station,* has always
been among his best-known works; the other, *Travels in Two Democracies,* although much less popular today, is nonetheless of considerable interest. In the usual pattern of Wilson's travel books, it is clearly
and forcefully directed to his fellow countrymen.

In 1934, nurturing a belief that American society was in a state
of collapse and that no amount of delving into coal mines, mortgaged
farms, or boarded-up factories would yield anything new about the
nature of our problems, Wilson began a scholarly study of the origins
of European socialism that eventually led to the publication of *To the
Finland Station.* In the following year, from May to October 1935,
he visited Russia so that he could reinforce from firsthand experience
a vision that he had of a new social order along Marxist lines. This
vision was never clear and well defined, which Wilson was to discover, and when he found that Marxism was not really working in
Russia it seemed even more doubtful that it could be made to work
in the United States. After this discovery he backed off and started
working in another direction. While American left-wing intellectuals
were still casting around for excuses for the ruthlessness of Stalin,
generally impervious to the totalitarianism that was sweeping all of
Europe in the 1930s, Wilson was returning to literary criticism. His
next book, *The Triple Thinkers,* was a clear retreat from sociological

criticism and brought new perspectives to bear on the land of his birth.

But the sojourn into Marxism was a necessity for Wilson just as it was for most writers of his day. As a writer, he had been forced into reflective social consciousness. He had had to become an abstract thinker. Gone was the possibility of being a *bon vivant* or a literary drunk in the Greenwich Village style. Wilson put this well in a piece he wrote in 1944 for the *Princeton University Chronicle* entitled "Thoughts on Being Bibliographed." Writers of the thirties had no choice but to be different from writers of the twenties:

There was suddenly very little money around, and the literary delirium seemed clearing. The sexual taboos of the age before had been dismissed both from books and from life, and there was no need to be feverish about them; liquor was legal again, and the stock market lay gasping its last. The new "classes" of intellectuals—it was a feature of the post-Boom period that they tended to think of themselves as "intellectuals" rather than "writers" —were in general sober and poor, and they applied the analysis of Marxism to the scene of wreckage they faced. This at least offered a discipline for the mind, gave a coherent picture of history, and promised not only employment but the triumph of the constructive intellect.*

To the Finland Station is Wilson's effort to become part of this new surge of intellectual activity, to provide discipline and substance for the mind as well as a coherent view of history. The book, subtitled *A Study in the Writing and Acting of History,* offers a panorama of European social thought. It is not intended as a complete history of Marxism or the ideas that led up to it. Rather, like so many of Wilson's books, it is a personal reading of history, an attempt to engage the reader and involve him in the excitement and moral force of history.

Sherman Paul, Wilson's first biographer, rightly points out that "an accurate subtitle for *To the Finland Station* would be 'On Heroes, Hero Worship and the Heroic in History,'" for the book is a series of portraits of figures—all oversized intellectual figures—who had an impact on history.† It was Wilson's attempt to prove that by thinking and acting man can move against the dead institutions of society, against the inertness of matter, against the cruelty of nature.

---

*This appeared in *Princeton University Library Chronicle* in February 1944, accompanying a bibliography of Wilson's work. Reprinted in *Classics and Commercials,* 107-8.

†Sherman Paul, *Edmund Wilson: A Study of Literary Vocation in Our Time* (Urbana: Univ. of Illinois Press, 1967), 139.

The men in this book refused to ride along on the back of a wave but believed that the course of history could be changed if they rose up, took some violent hand in the course of events. *To the Finland Station* is, as Meyer Schapiro said in the *Partisan Review,* a study in "the revolutionary personality" (Paul, 127), a testament to what man can attain working alone and in opposition to the mainstream of the social order.

There was Vico. An impoverished scholar, an obscure professor of rhetoric, standing outside the mainstream of European philosophy, who through a sheer burst of imaginative activity cast off the stale metaphysics of scholasticism and the nonhumanistic mathematical philosophy of Descartes and found a new direction for science by basing it on an intimate investigation of human society. Wilson's book begins with Michelet's rediscovery of Vico's *Scienza Nuova* (1725) in 1824. The twentieth-century reader can understand Michelet's excitement about the discovery of this creative mind that came awake "amid the dusts of a provincial school of jurisprudence." A wholly new approach to human society appears as if at one bold stroke. "Here, before the steady rays of Vico's insight—almost as if we were looking out on the landscape of the Mediterranean itself— we see the fogs that obscure the horizons of the remote reaches of time recede, the cloud-shapes of legend lift." As the monsters and gods recede, "what we see now are men as we know them alone on the earth we know. The myths that have made us wonder are projections of a human imagination like our own" (2).*

An even bigger hero to Wilson was Michelet himself, who saw history as "the war of man against nature, of spirit against matter, of liberty against fatality," and who believed that the human world had an organic character. According to Michelet, the historian's responsibility is to reconstitute the past not only to allow people to enjoy it but so they may profit from its full complexity, its ability to help us with our own environment. History is not inert or dead material but living activity—much like writing. History is not past but activity for the present; we might say with Benedetto Croce that "all history is contemporary history." That is, its purpose is to speak only to things in the contemporary world.

The great hero of the book is, of course, Lenin, whose triumph in 1917 supplied the title of the book. (Wilson wrote to Christian Gauss in 1934: "I thought that *To the Finland Station* was a good title

*The edition of *To the Finland Station* referred to in this chapter is the Anchor Books edition of 1953, which contains a concluding essay not in the first edition.

because the Finland Station in St. Petersburg was where Lenin arrived when he got back from exile. . . . It marked dramatically the first time a trained Marxist had been able to come in and take hold of a major crisis.") And Lenin is the showcase figure *par excellence* for Wilson because he demonstrates so forcefully that the historical idealist, the revolutionary mind, can rise up and take hold of things, influence the course of history.

Wilson can identify with Lenin, as perhaps he cannot with Marx, because Lenin is so thoroughly a middle-class figure. He is not strange, not exotic; his background was not that of some wild bomb-throwing terrorist—his was a comfortable, smug, almost American upbringing. This is what Wilson wanted his typical American to know —that the man who brought the revolution, who sought to change the world, was from a conventional, orderly, and civilized background. We are given an extensive description of the house where Lenin grew up:

Going inside, the American visitor finds himself in the presence of something so perfectly comprehensible and familiar that he can hardly believe he has traveled so far from Concord and Boston, that he is back in tsarist Russia. And it is surprising to find in Soviet Russia an interior so clean and so definite, so devoid of the messiness characteristic of more pretentious places. The furniture is mostly mahogany, and almost exactly the sort of thing you would find in your grandmother's house. In the living-room, low-ceilinged and simple, there is a long old-fashioned grand piano, on whose music rack rests the score of Bellini's blameless *I Puritani*, with dried ferns pressed between the pages. . . . This was evidently also a place where people read, studied their lessons and played chess. There are chessmen, a map on the wall, a little sewing-machine. Elsewhere there are book-cases and book-shelves: Zola, Daudet and Victor Hugo, Heine, Schiller and Goethe, as well as the Russian classics; and many maps and globes: Russia and Asia, the two hemispheres, the world. (353-54)

This could, of course, be the home of Wilson's own grandparents for there is a striking similarity betwen the selection of details and those poured out in such biographical works as "At Laurelwood," *A Prelude,* and *A Piece of My Mind.*

Wilson's admiration of Lenin was deep at the time, although his later discoveries revealed it to be unjustified. The important thing is that Wilson in 1934 hoped to show the American reader how the revolutionary mentality, far from being the work of some undisciplined wild men, was the product of deeply passionate, feeling individuals, born more often than not to genteel surroundings—with books, music in the home, just as we might find in Boston or Philadelphia. Such men work from the heart and the intellect, and if they want to turn over the social order we are familiar with, it is only one aspect of it, that which is dead, that which will no longer work. They do it precisely to preserve human dignity, civility, culture, and fraternity.

At least this was Wilson's view in the mid-1930s at the height of his faith in socialistic revolution, at the height of his belief that any society in trouble, and especially our own, might be made over, and that this work could safely be left up to visionary historians, idealists, maybe even our own native intellects—if we would but give them free reign.

Wilson, however, never wanted to rest his case on ideology, on any kind of purely intellectual apparatus, and his infatuation with Lenin and the socialist experiment in Russia led him to plan an extensive tour of the Soviet Union in 1935, which gave birth to another book of a more leisurely character. *Travels in Two Democracies* contains occasional essays about America not included in the *American Jitters* and a series of sketches from his immediate Russian experiences. These Russian sketches are not primarily concerned with politics or with the deepening of Russian totalitarianism but with the Russian people, the life and culture of Russia as seen through an American traveler's eyes in 1935. Here Wilson not only shies away from Stalinism but forcefully denounces it, seeing clearly that the ideals of 1917 had collapsed. He presses his search for a bond between Russia and the United States deeper and deeper into the human substratum, tentatively abandoning the hope that any kind of ideological apparatus will be of any use.

Wilson was clearly fond of the Russian people and seemed to reach the conclusion that when you stripped away all ideological considerations, all the vast political and historical differences of the two peoples, the Russians had more in common with Americans than they did with the people of the rest of Europe. They are a friendly, informal people. "It is much easier to establish friendly relations with Russians than with the people of any other country I know. When you smile at them, they always smile back." (*Travels,* 183) They are never stiff, and they never insist on standing on ceremony.

An American coming to Russia from England discovers not without surprise that in certain fundamental respects he has more in common with the Russians than with the English. The people in Europe who speak his language are in some ways the furthest removed from him. The English, with their antiquated social system, cannot forgive a branch of their own race who have scrapped that system and prospered. On the other hand, the Soviet Union is certainly the European country which has most in common with ours. When we travel from London to Leningrad, we realize, however pessimistic we may have been before we left the United States in regard to the operation of capitalism in producing class differences and antagonisms, that American democracy means more than we thought. Our period of pioneering was more like the present period in Russia which is preoccupied with settling new country, constructing new industrial plants and developing natural resources, than like anything else that has happened in Europe; and the American and the Russian, who have both left the old system behind, feel a natural sympathy with one another. . . . I felt far closer to the young engineers in my cabin with whom I could hardly exchange a word than with the English people with whom I ate. (161-62)

The Russian segment of *Travels in Two Democracies* consists of a series of daily impressions that seem to show that the Russian people, liberated from the czar in 1917, were living a euphoric life of newly discovered freedom—almost oblivious of the totalitarianism that was growing up around them. As a travelogue the book is constantly discovering the amiability of the Russian people. They are warm; they mix well with everyone, even foreigners; they love literature, science, all aspects of culture. "In no country I have been in, even France, has literature such prestige as in Russia; in no country, even in Germany of the day before yesterday, has science commanded such respect. Books at the present time are hardly less necessary to the Russians than food and clothing themselves. Even the factories have their bookstores." (211-12) Writers from America and elsewhere are lionized in almost dizzying ways. The Russians, Wilson discovers, are not very keen on practical amenities: "Latches on bathroom and toilet doors and plugs for washbasins and bathtubs hardly exist in Russia. When I reached for the roller towel, it immediately came off the roller, and I fell against the hot-water pipes and burned my elbow severely" (157). (A long hospital stay later in Wilson's journey revealed Russian medicine to be funny, quixotic, and antiquated but still warm and personal.)

In one striking historical passage Wilson explains the vitality of the Russian people by pointing out that they are like children waking up to life. They are, after all, a people whose "great grandfathers and grandfathers were exchanged for pigs and dogs." Before the revolution, 80 percent of Russians were illiterate. As a result "they are taking most seriously their new duties of citizenship." They have an almost religious belief in what "the people" can do. Naturally they want the revolution to succeed because they identify the revolution—even Marxism-Leninism—with themselves. There was no hasty willingness to see the system of government as something imposed from above. As late as 1935 communism was almost universally believed to be a free expression of popular will.

In a reflective chapter, Wilson is willing to admit that an obvious defect in Russian society is the absence of long-standing democratic institutions. Despite the feeling of hopelessness and dreariness of his homeland in the early depression years, Russia convinces him that America had a great many things worth keeping. "I feel convinced, since I have been in Russia, that American republican institutions, disastrously as they have always been abused, have some permanent and absolute value. I don't believe that they will necessarily be destroyed in the course of the transformation of society." But he continues to maintain that some form of socialism will have to be overlaid on existing American institutions. Although Wilson found the Russian system imperfect, he notes that, "We shall be in no position to reprove the Russians till we shall be able to show them an American socialism which is free from the Russian defects." In the meantime, he argues, until Americans do find something better, we must in some way acknowledge the superiority of what the Russians have. "You feel in the Soviet Union that you are at the top of the world where the light never really goes out, just as you know in the Gulf of Finland, where the summer day never ends, that you are close to the geographical top" (321).

The 1935 trip to Russia was to be the pinnacle of Wilson's infatuation with Russian socialism, and long before 1940 he was to become much more skeptical of the idea that we had a great deal to learn about government from the Soviet Union. Even as early as 1935, he probably should have been more keenly aware of the questionable practice of linking the spiritual force of a people with any kind of political ideology. Russia may have been a rejuvenating experience for someone who had spent the early thirties investigating the coal fields of West Virginia or the tarpaper shacks of Hudson County, New Jersey. Because of their newfound freedom there may have been strong and fresh currents in the Russian atmosphere—a feeling of being at the moral summit of the world. But whether this had anything to do either with political ideology or with the moral force of political thinkers was an altogether different matter.

On leaving Russia, and on reading about the cruel intensification of Stalinist dictatorship during the mid- and late 1930s, indeed, the flowering of dictatorships throughout Europe, Wilson reassessed his views of socialism; by the late thirties he was much less optimistic that socialism had something to teach us in America. In 1940 he wrote a brief summary of the subject that was later included in *The Shores of Light* and the 1953 paperback edition of *To the Finland Station*. Here he freely admits that Marxism is in relative eclipse and that the original ideals have been broken. He continued to believe that Marx was a visionary of first importance. The original Marxism was a mixture of "old-fashioned Judaism, eighteenth-century Rousseauism and early nineteenth-century utopianism." Marx was an idealist reacting to the cruelty of unbridled capitalism; his goals were humanitarian and compassionate. "Marx assumed that capitalist society had corrupted the human race by compelling it to abandon spiritual values for the satisfaction of owning things" (*Finland Station*, 475). But Marx and, after him, Engels tended to be visionaries —their historical and philosophical ideas were loose, soft, and wayward, naturally vulnerable to exploitation and misinterpretation.

That Wilson had never been strongly drawn to the apparatus of the Marxist dialectic comes out in some strictly imaginative literary works of the late 1930s. In "Karl Marx: A Prolet-Play," which was included in the first edition of *To the Finland Station* (but not the later Anchor edition), Wilson bitterly attacks the dialectic and suggests that Marx himself would not be above taking up a dictatorial role. In the play, Marx exterminates his colleagues after the Revolution of 1848, removes his beard to reveal "the smiling face of Comrade Stalin," and concludes with the words, "Forward to socialist inequality and democracy."

But Lenin, the great hero of *To the Finland Station*, takes an even bigger fall in Wilson's 1940 estimation. Indeed it is a tribute to Wilson's intellectual honesty that he admits that his middle-class hero had feet of clay and that not only did Lenin get caught up in an unsuccessful communist apparatus, but he had a great deal to do with its bogus and dishonest character. The idealistic Lenin wanted to do good, but in the end he wanted other things more.

Lenin's aims were of course humanitarian, democratic and anti-bureaucratic; but the logic of the whole situation was too strong for Lenin's aims. His trained band of revolutionists, the Party, turned into a tyrannical machine which perpetuated, as heads of a government, the intolerance, the deviousness, the secrecy, the ruthlessness with political dissidents, which they had had to learn as hunted outlaws. Instead of getting a classless society out of the old illiterate feudal Russia, they encouraged the rise and the domination of a new controlling and privileged class, who were soon exploiting the workers almost as callously as the Tsarist industrialists had done, and subjecting them to an espionage that was probably worse than anything under the Tsar. (480-81)

This is certainly a fair and judicious reevaluation by any standards of honesty. Some later critics of Lenin, such as the libertarian Solzhenitsyn, were even more harsh in their judgment. Solzhenitsyn portrays Lenin as having an almost eagerly totalitarian mind and in his *Gulag Archipelago* undermines the long-fashionable idea that the Soviet regime started out as freedom loving and only later turned dictatorial under Stalin. As early as 1917, according to Solzhenitsyn, Lenin called for "the merciless suppression of attempts at anarchy on the part of drunkards, hooligans, counterrevolutionaries, and other persons."* Only a year later, in an essay entitled "How to Organize the Competition," he proclaimed the necessity of "purging the land of all kinds of harmful insects." With great suddenness, everywhere there appeared insects who needed stamping out. Phrased with characteristic Solzhenitsyn irony: "The people in the local zemstvo self-governing bodies were, of course, *insects*. People in the cooperative movement were also insects, as were all owners of their own homes. There were not a few insects among the teachers in the gymnasiums. The church parish councils were made up almost exclusively of insects, and it was insects of course who sang in church choirs. All priests were insects—and monks and nuns even more so" (28).

Whether we accept Solzhenitsyn's more extreme stance, which is that Lenin was an evil and devious man, or Wilson's undoubtedly more generous view that Lenin was forced into a totalitarian habit of mind by the rush of events and a cruel weight of circumstances beyond his control, there can be no denying that Lenin turned out to be a disastrous failure as a democrat and humanitarian. The Russians most certainly did not wait for Stalin to lose their liberties as some later Soviet historians liked to say.

Reading *To the Finland Station* after several decades one still feels the great surge of power and discovery in the work. Wilson's faith in some kind of humanitarian socialism is as appealing and convincing as the day it was written. In another sense, however, *To the Finland Station* is a *cul-de-sac*. It is a hymn of praise to a kind of idealism that could not take root in the soil of twentieth-century American society. Wilson hoped to find something in European intellectual history and in postrevolution Russian experience to revivify what had been lost in American life. He lived with Russians for almost a year and was sparked by their innocence and charm. He believed them to be the light at the top of the world and hoped he

---

*Quoted in Aleksandr Solzhenitsyn, *The Gulag Archipelago, 1918-1956*, trans. Thomas P. Whitney (New York: Harper and Row, 1974), 27.

could bring some of that light back to America to shine on dark factory towns. But cultural importations of this kind have seldom been accomplished, and by the late 1930s it was clear that the light of Russia was being methodically snuffed out while the United States, for some inexplicable reason, was somehow managing to muddle through.

᷾

Wilson was to carry his interest in Russia throughout his life. He learned Russian and he read Russian works of literature in the original. He carried on an extensive correspondence with other writers about Russian life and letters, occasionally involving himself in issues of precise and intricate scholarship. But his later delvings into Russian culture were almost entirely nonpolitical. He finally settled back to do what he could do best—read with a sensitive eye the great Russian writers. In a later collection of his writing, *A Window on Russia,* published the year of his death, there is not a single chapter on politics or socialism, or what happened to the great dream of the liberal thirties. There are two essays on the Russian language. There are discussions of Solzhenitsyn and of Svetlana Stalin, both very little concerned with matters political. The bulk of the book is devoted to Russian writers: Chekhov, Turgenev, Tolstoy, Pushkin, Gogol, all in the idiosyncratic personal style for which Wilson was to become known in his later years. Political ideology as a way of saving the world had seemingly vanished for Wilson.

The 1930s marked a great turning point in Wilson's career. By the late thirties he was no longer involved in investigative journalism, and such intellectual history as he was later to pursue was usually cast in the mold later adopted in works like *Patriotic Gore* and *Apologies to the Iroquois.* During this time, Wilson was returning to purer forms of literary criticism, striking out in several directions in books as different as *The Triple Thinkers* (1938) and *The Wound and the Bow* (1941).

Wilson's multiple shifts of direction in the 1930s are most remarkable for their total honesty and rightness. Although he never announced to the world the realization that his excursions into European socialism had led to a *cul-de-sac,* the realization was clearly there. *To the Finland Station* is a work of some power and nobility, yet it must be seen today as a work of minor importance for Wilson. It does not contain the kind of writing that he could do best and is not the kind of work he should have spent long years doing. Still,

American intellectuals had to stab out blindly for something solid in the darkest years of the depression, and few came up with books possessing the moral force of *To the Finland Station*.

So the 1930s came to an end. During the forties Wilson was to return to a more personal style of criticism. And he was to return in full force to his old vocation as an Americanist—"critic of things American" Van Wyck Brooks once called it. Before long he would dig in again with American literature, taking the measure of its whole range from Hawthorne to "the boys in the back room." He produced an anthology of American literature (*The Shock of Recognition*) in 1943, and his finest work of fiction and a peculiarly American achievement in 1946 *(Memoirs of Hecate County)*.

In 1932 Wilson felt that American society had lost its moral foundations; that it was a failure. On the other hand, he had not found it a success in the twenties, even though it was interesting, variegated, and—for the artist—instructive. Perhaps no social order in the history of the world has been successful, and perhaps people have been led to expect too much from the American experiment. On the other hand, if Wilson ever had one vocation, he was a historical critic, a writer who believed that the only resource a writer has is the depth of his own life's experience. After his brief romp as an ideologue Wilson must have seen that the United States was still the center of focus, that there was only one stance he could have as a writer, and that was the stance he had developed since childhood. Wilson was still to travel many roads, but now, more clearly than ever, they all led home.

6

Back to the
Native Ground

Following his disillusionment with Marxism and spurred by a growing doubt that his own destinies as a writer could be perfectly realized in the political realm, Wilson once again began to direct his
energies toward the literature and culture of his native land. Not that
he sought escape in a more ethereal realm of *belles lettres,* or that
he returned to the kind of literary criticism he so nearly perfected
in *Axel's Castle;* rather, by the late thirties he seems to have reached
the conclusion that the creative writer can make a contribution that
is not necessarily political. Wilson's superb essay on John Jay Chapman, published in the *Atlantic Monthly* in 1937, foreshadows the
path of Wilson's literary vocation over the next several decades—
indeed for the rest of his life. Recalling how Chapman perceived the
futility of his more zealous commitments in the era of genteel, reform club politics and how he was "thrown back on individual con-
science" as an escape from political and social activism, Wilson
perceives that he, too, has been wasting time as a political gadfly and
has a moral obligation to return to a role where his talents could be
pure and forceful and true.

By the late thirties, Wilson was convinced that a writer need not
be an active participant in day-to-day politics and need not be a
hard-line theorist with ready cures for all the sorrows of the world.
The writer's mission is not one of activism but of self-discovery; an
act of rendering the world as he himself encounters it. Although such
self-knowledgeable creativity may not pay immediate dividends, it

is a moral force that may have a greater overall effect on human experience than the writing of tracts and manifestos.

In another crucial essay, "Marxism and Literature" (like "John Jay Chapman" reprinted in 1938 in *The Triple Thinkers*), Wilson firmly castigates the sociological style of criticism that had become so prevalent in the depression years. He insists that the literary critic should avoid the Marxist entanglement because it commits him to a rigid and stereotyped theory of literature and because it renders him incapable of doing justice to the finer spirit of literature. The only aim of criticism should be to explain and appreciate the subtleties and complexities of the literary art.

The man who tries to apply Marxist principles without real understanding of literature is liable to go horribly wrong. For one thing, it is usually true in works of the highest order that the purport is not a simple message, but a complex vision of things, which itself is not explicit but implicit; and the reader who does not grasp them artistically, but is merely looking for simple social morals, is certain to be hopelessly confused. (278)

For Wilson, there always had to be artistic understanding and insight accompanying and standing behind any social interpretation of literature. He believed that the best of the early Marxists knew this. Frederick Engels, for example, in a letter to Margaret Harkness, expressed the notion that the more the novelist keeps his political ideas hidden, the better it is for his art. In Engels's opinion, Balzac, with his reactionary notions, was worth a thousand Zolas with democratic reformed ones. Balzac thought himself to be a defender of the status quo and deplored the decline of high society; but actually "his irony is never more bitter, his satire never more trenchant, than when he is showing us these aristocrats ... for whom he felt so profound a sympathy."

Many of our modern leftist critics, however, are deficient in such literary sensitivity, and this is the basis for Wilson's lack of sympathy for the literary left during the thirties. One of the favored practices of the leftist critics was to offer specific formulas for the construction of ideal Marxist books. Wilson cites the example of Granville Hicks, who, in an article entitled "The Crisis in Criticism" that appeared in the *New Masses* in 1933, actually drew up a list of requirements to which every Marxist work of literature should aspire. According to Hicks, every work must be directed to the proletarian reader and make him see his role in the class struggle. For this reason, literature must "directly or indirectly show the effects of the class struggle"; it must "be able to make the reader feel that he is participating in the lives described"; and finally, the author's viewpoint must "be that of the vanguard of the proletariat; he should be, or should try to make himself, a member of the proletariat" (281). Unfortunately, in Hicks's opinion, no novel yet written perfectly conforms to all these standards.

The trouble is, said Wilson, none ever will. In scorning the Marxist critics' attempt to find one, he drew a comparison between their ideas and those of the "new humanists" who had dominated American criticism in the previous generation. Both the Marxists and the new humanists set standards for literature that no writer could possibly meet. "The Humanists knew down to the last comma what they wanted a work of literature to be, but they never . . . were able to find any contemporary work which fitted their specifications." Nor could the Marxists find any for theirs. So both the humanists and Marxists had to provide imaginary versions of what the supposed great writer would be like. "The Humanists had Sophocles and Shakespeare; the socialist realists had Tolstoy. Yet it is certain that if Tolstoy had had to live up to the objectives and prohibitions which the socialist realists proposed he could never have written a chapter, and that if Babbitt and More had been able to enforce against Shakespeare their moral and esthetic injunctions he would never have written a line" (282).

What this all comes down to is that the job of the literary critic is more subtle, more personal, more intricate than that allowed by the various forms of socio-economic criticism. In a later essay from *The Triple Thinkers,* entitled "The Historical Interpretation of Literature," Wilson develops an aesthetic theory that clearly breaks with all kinds of doctrinal sociological criticism. In doing so however, he does not banish all his old heroes of *To the Finland Station,* for he continues to believe that the best approach to literature is through humanistic and historical synthesis.

Once again, as in *To the Finland Station,* Wilson traces the modern pursuit of a historical (as opposed to either metaphysical or scientific) ideal to *La Scienza Nuova* of Giambattista Vico in the eighteenth century. The philosophy of Vico made possible a way of putting the study of literature in a completely new setting. The "new science," as opposed to the "old science," started from the presupposition that in the histories of all nations, poetry appears as the first and primary mode of expression, as the vehicle of a people's first articulate life, and expresses, "not the peripheral, the pleasurable, or even the commodious dimensions of life, but the most intimate, stern and fundamental necessities of the life of the people, that is, their laws, their wisdom, their religious rites, their sacred formulas of birth, marriage and death, of imitation, of war and peace, and their rude speculations on the cosmos."*

Vico's view of history is the first strictly humanistic theory to arise in the modern world. Its happy news was that you could take humanity exactly as you encountered it, that you did not need to look beyond it for some ultimate truth or unrealizable ideal. It is a doctrine of man understanding himself. Vico held the idea that at the dawn of human civilization man was mostly a poet, his language not full of practical truths and expositions, but vivid representations, images, similes, comparisons, metaphors, circumlocutions—phrases explaining the natural properties of things, all expressed in ways that in comparison with modern speech must have been robustious, emotional, evocative. And if such was man's origin, such is his nature, his essence. The search for man must first and forever involve the search for his poetic consciousness. And poetic consciousness always grows out of intimate moments of life and death.

The student of literature, the critic, and the philosopher of art must thus begin their intellectual journeys with an intimate and personal reading of some historical people, perhaps a close examination of their own national history—a conviction of Vico's later shared by Hegel, Herder, Taine, and Sainte-Beuve. The critic must know with full intensity some indigenous culture, and he must have some poetic outlook on it.

Here it was that Wilson's study of European thought was to pay dividends in his own work. If the Europeans at first directed Wilson to Marxism, they eventually directed him back to his homeland. They led him to see that the true vocation for the humanist critic is loving attention to his own civilization. Of course this had been Wilson's belief since his youth. During the 1920s he had been a dedicated and assiduous Americanist, and even his internationalism during the 1930s could be seen in retrospect as nothing less than a desperate search for ideas that could work in America.

None of this should suggest that Wilson's strong pull toward Americanism around 1940 became immediately apparent to the reading public. In fact, it would probably be fair to say that it was around this time Wilson began to acquire a reputation for himself as a wide-ranging man of letters. Wilson's collections of criticism now seemed to be moving in so many directions, touching so many di-

*Summarized in A. Robert Caponigri, *Time and Idea: The Theory of History in Giambattista Vico* (London: Routledge and Kegan Paul, 1953), 83.

verse topics, that his fellow intellectuals found it difficult to determine where he was heading. Americanism and historicism would probably not have been the first thing brought to mind.

A book like *The Triple Thinkers* is an excellent example. This book, subtitled *Twelve Essays on Literary Subjects,* has no major unifying force besides Wilson's own personality and focus of interest. In addition to the essay on John Jay Chapman, there are others on Paul Elmer More, Pushkin, George Bernard Shaw, and A.E. Housman. There is an essay on "The Politics of Flaubert" and another, "The Ambiguity of Henry James." There is an essay on Wilson's old teacher at the Hill School, "Mr. Rolfe." And there are three essays on the theory of literature: "Is Verse a Dying Technique?" "Marxism and Literature," and "The Historical Interpretation of Literature," the latter being a defense of the historical approach to literature as opposed to both Marxist and formalist criticism.

Not that all of Wilson's books in the next few years were as loosely assembled as this. *The Boys in the Back Room: Notes on the California Novelists,* a short book published in 1941 and then collected in *Classics and Commercials,* has a very clear-cut unity in that it clusters a group of writers, mostly from California, who in a characteristic manner failed to live up to their talents. In his next, and much more important work, *The Wound and the Bow* (1941), the cohering unity was Wilson's long-standing fascination for the psychic wound to which the genius of art is somehow related. There are studies developed at varying levels of complexity dealing with the psychologically traumatic youths of Dickens, Kipling, Casanova, Wharton, Hemingway, and Joyce. The theory lurking in the background was not narrowly Freudian and had no hard-and-fast psychological doctrine behind it that bound Wilson to a lifetime of toil as a "psychological critic." Indeed so pragmatic and eclectic was Wilson's theory that it could never be confused with the many European imports of similar stripe. Yet though Wilson continued to set some store by this approach to literature (there were strong traces of it in *Patriotic Gore*), he was never to use it again on this same scale.

During the period between 1943 and 1948, when he was literary editor of the *New Yorker,* a tremendous range of topics was forced on Wilson by the demands of weekly reviewing. There were no further collections of his criticism during this period, but his most important work of fiction, *Memoirs of Hecate County,* appeared in 1946, and an interesting postwar travel book (*Europe without Baedeker*) appeared in 1947. All of this confirmed Wilson's reputation as an eclectic man of letters.

Nonetheless, despite this apparent diversity, and despite the heavy demands of regular reviewing, Wilson's work during this period clearly and unambiguously demonstrates a regrowth of his infatuation with America, particularly with the American literary scene. He spent a long time reading and rereading the American classics in the early 1940s, and this prompted him to put together his superlative anthology, *The Shock of Recognition,* which is "mostly a collection of American critical documents written by first-rate figures: Emerson on Thoreau, Henry James on Hawthorne, Santayana on William James, etc." Unlike the typical literature anthology, this anthology has the advantage of allowing one writer to mirror the genius of another. (The title of the book came from a sentence in Melville's essay on Hawthorne: "For genius, all over the world, stands hand in hand, and one shock of recognition runs the whole circle round.") As such, the work reflects Wilson's renewed interest in historical criticism and the distinctly American past. Here American authors are not seen in their singularity but in the round, hand in hand, taking spiritual sustenance from their environment and giving sustenance in return.

In the course of his regular reviewing duties during the midforties Wilson turned out a great deal of criticism, much of which has not been reprinted, but his collection of literary pieces from the 1940s entitled *Classics and Commercials,* published in 1950, gives a clear idea of Wilson's main interests at that time. Again there was Wilson's diversity and seeming eccentricity—there are essays on such offbeat topics as "The Poetry of Angelica Balabanoff," "The Musical Glasses of Peacock," "George Grosz in the United States," "John Mulholland and the Art of Illusion," and "Glenway Wescott's War Work." There are excursions into English and European literature: " 'Never Apologize, Never Explain', The Art of Evelyn Waugh," "A Guide to *Finnegans Wake,*" "A Long Talk about Jane Austen," "Reexamining Dr. Johnson," "Vladimir Nabokov on Gogol," "A Dissenting Opinion on Kafka," "The Original of Tolstoy's Natasha," and numerous others.

Still, the majority of the essays are on American topics; some are purely literary, others deal with minor matters of special interest to Wilson. American concerns are clearly in the forefront in: "Alexander Woollcott of the Phalanx," "A Toast and a Tear for Dorothy Parker," "Katherine Anne Porter," "William Saroyan and His Darling Old Providence," "Books of Etiquette and Emily Post," "Edith Wharton: A Memoir by an English Friend," "William Faulkner's Reply to the Civil-Rights Program."

It is especially interesting to note that in selecting his work from the 1940s for *Classics and Commercials,* there is not one but three essays on the work of Van Wyck Brooks—no other writer, American or European, received anywhere near this amount of attention. In the beginning of the book there is a study entitled "Van Wyck Brooks's Second Phase"; in the middle, another entitled "A Picture to Hang in the Library: Brooks's Age of Living"; and at the end we find "Van Wyck Brooks on the Civil War Period." Over the years Wilson was one of the strongest supporters of Brooks as a literary historian, and Wilson's attraction to Brooks doubtless says a great deal about Wilson's own ideals of criticism and historical writing. Brooks was never popular among academic literary critics and historians who occasionally admired his tough-minded early work such as *America's Coming of Age* and *The Wine of the Puritans* but could see little of value in his tender-minded *Makers and Finders* series, a large project of leisurely, genteel, and old-fashioned literary history that Brooks turned out in the quarter century between 1930 and 1955. These mellow histories were handled roughly by the critics when they first appeared and have generally been underrated ever since. A characteristic attitude about the later Brooks was expressed by Howard Mumford Jones in his *Theory of American Literature.* "Brooks," said Jones, has "charm and insight," but his volumes "have been received with more enthusiasm by newspaper reviewers and other tasters of literary wares than they have been by professional scholars." The reason for this is not hard to find. William Van O'Connor, in *The Age of Criticism,* says that Brooks's later works are "hardly criticism at all. They are genteelly chauvinistic histories in which the American past is presented in a delicate amber haze."

Wilson did not share this view, and it is obvious that there was something in the later Brooks that penetrated to the heart of his own historical method. Wilson freely admits that Brooks was not really a literary critic in the narrow sense and was "not particularly sensitive to form and style in themselves." On the other hand, Brooks's contribution is unique, for he has mastered a historical-biographical narrative form that depends on highly imaginative synthetic powers—"an art which has its special difficulties unknown to the teller of invented fables."

Brooks's later historical series was not precisely a literary history. Neither was it a history of ideas, even though, in his first volume, he professed to be writing "a history of the New England mind." Like Wilson, Brooks spun his imaginings in the interstices of the web of conventional scholarship. His historical imagination was unique: "He is a master, our only real master since the death of Vernon Parrington, of the social interpretation of literature inside the national frame."

This was a valuable contribution. We Americans have a short history and one that is easy to grasp in its outer and public dimensions, but we never seem to know our history in an inward and intimate way. Literary history seems to be a perfect example of this poverty. Even professionally trained literary scholars are acquainted with the large and well-painted highway signs of literature, but they are unfamiliar with the byways, the curious inner physiology. Brooks has a feel for the intimate dimensions of literary history and makes an effort to supplement the intellectual's starvation diet of conventional literary history. In a review of Brooks's *Flowering of New England* and *New England Indian Summer,* Wilson gives us a clear explanation for his admiration of these unique historical works. To read *New England Indian Summer* (1865-1915) he says, is

for an American old enough to have been young in the period described, a constantly fascinating and surprising revelation. You will find out in this new book of Mr. Brooks why people went abroad every spring, and why they sometimes went and never came back. See the chapter called "The Post-War Years," in which he tells how the commercial development that followed the Civil War extinguished the old enthusiasm for culture along with the republican ideals and made cultivated people in general ashamed of the United States—a chapter which perhaps provides the most satisfactory analysis that has yet been made of this situation and which may well become the classical account of it. In the same chapter, you will find out why the ladies in your childhood read the English Kipling and Conan Doyle, and why you were told that Mark Twain was "vulgar." (*Classics and Commericals,* 17)

Brooks's literary histories, though often offensive to those looking for ironclad intellectual documents, answer a crying need on the American cultural scene. We have not had any deep and imaginative treatments of literary history. The field is as barren as that of political history is rich. Americans are cut from their great literary figures and find them alien and removed. We may be taught that Emerson and Whitman are great figures but it is hard for the American of the twentieth century to warm up to them, to get inside of them.

Again the comparison with political history is apt. Americans have a craving for knowledge about their major political figures— there are tens of thousands of Americans who have an intimate knowledge of Lincoln's administration of the Civil War, who know the names of his cabinet members, or who retain a full complement of Lincoln anecdotes, and one suspects that there are a great many Americans who even have a fair knowledge about Warren G. Harding and his cronies. But it is hard to imagine more than a small number of people knowing anything at all about Whitman and his times, much less anything about William Dean Howells in the context of his social and literary relations. Our literary figures are, for reasons not fully understandable, somewhat unreal to our minds and unrealizable to our imaginations. They are not sufficiently a part of our mental landscape.

The visitor to London somehow has little difficulty conjuring up Dr. Johnson stepping into a neighborhood pub—even a pub in the most modern hotel. The spirit of Dr. Johnson seems to surround one in London, if only we choose to invoke it. But strain as hard as we like, we find it impossible to bring Washington Irving back to the streets of New York. Not only are the tie-wig and velveteen breeches gone, but of Washington Irving there is nothing left in the urban atmosphere. A great pity, too, since Washington Irving was once as much the spirit of New York as Dr. Johnson was the spirit of London. In short, it seems an undeniable truth that there is no way we can bring back our past literary culture with the snap of the fingers; it is doggedly resistant to the modern American mind; it requires a monumental effort, talent and knowledge that even most literary scholars do not possess.

Nor can we bring back the physical environment and ambiance of our writers with any degree of ease. A visit to Cambridge, Massachusetts, with its encroaching slums, and all the bustle connected with defense contracts at MIT or Harvard, with the comings and goings of the present-day college student, hardly gives us the wherewithal to bring Longfellow back to his house nearby. A visit to Concord provokes no feelings of closeness to Emerson. Emerson's Boston and Concord resist familiarity and intimacy on the part of his present-day countrymen to whom he has supposedly contributed so much. The fact is that the average scholarly monograph is not very helpful in this regard either. We can find out a great deal about how Emerson's thought was related to this or that philosophical movement in England, or to Hegelian idealism, but the largest determining factors in the man's makeup—his own conditions of life, the nature of his own personal culture—are denied us. We know little about how he related to or was affected by his friends, what his life-style was like; we know little about his house and land, his agricultural pursuits, his cultural interests, the flavor of life in Concord—for all of these things are no longer our property and cannot easily be retrieved in an examination of the surface of Emerson's thought. Above all, it is not enough to know, on an intellectual level, what Emerson's doctrines were all about, or what form his poetry took, for the essential Emerson still has a good chance of eluding us, especially as anything other than intellectual cold storage pablum. Indeed we must know what it was like for Emerson to preach Unitarianism at the beginning of the nineteenth century, to have a wife who could not understand what Unitarianism was all about, to keep a cow out in the back (and the twentieth-century American can no more imagine Emerson having a cow than he can imagine his college professor having one), to plant a garden, to entertain visitors from abroad.

For Brooks it was not enough to skim from point to point across the New England cranium as in an autopsy room. He had to produce a living being and was not satisfied until he had done so. This was the great virtue of his work. He set himself the task of bringing America's literary past to some facsimile of living being, to get inside literary culture and recreate it in loving detail so that it is not estranged from us and, in the end, so that it will have some of the fullness of meaning that textual criticism alone cannot provide.

The importance of this to Wilson is not so much that Wilson perceived in Brooks's historical method a direction for his later work, for even *Patriotic Gore,* the work of Wilson's that could be most closely compared to the *Makers and Finders* volumes, is a markedly different sort of work in style and content. In another way, though, as can be seen in the three separate essays on Brooks in *Classics and Commercials,* Brooks's skill as a historical writer must certainly have evoked admiration in Wilson and reinforced his own belief in the value of historical criticism. What Wilson learned from Brooks was that our national literature had been too long abandoned either to the pedants or to the specialized intellect. What American letters need are not the services of the scholar or the standardized problem solver but the imaginative writer with his own eccentric and characteristic vision of things.

Undoubtedly Wilson's interest in writers like Brooks and Parrington around the time he put together *The Shock of Recognition* solidified his own career as an Americanist. By the time he was being hounded for back taxes in the mid-1950s, and his lawyer half-seriously suggested he take asylum in another country, Wilson knew positively what he might not have known in the twenties—that he was a dedicated American critic. He was spiritually tied to the American scene in such a way that he could imagine being tied to nothing else. The United States was his spiritual home, his vocation.

૨૭

Edmund Wilson wrote no sustained and comprehensive treatise on the United States, though his homeland was in the forefront of his thinking during every stage of his career. The closest he came to an orderly exposition of the subject was an essay entitled "The United States," which he wrote in the early 1950s and which appeared in *A Piece of My Mind: Reflections at Sixty* (1956). A collection of somewhat disjointed reflections, "The United States" is nonetheless a revealing essay and manages to provide a unity to what Wilson was writing in the 1940s and 1950s. More important, we can also see in it some fully developed ideas that had been among the intellectual equipment he inherited from his father whose upbringing had been in the traditions of the old Republic.

Wilson's lofty patrician outlook prompts him to begin by pointing out that "the United States is not a nation in the sense that England or France is. It is a society, a political system, which is still in a somewhat experimental state" (21). The United States has yet to develop much of a feeling of permanency and fixedness, though civilization here goes back for over four hundred years.

Not a nation in the European sense, we are therefore subject to panics and upheavals of various kinds. In earlier times there was a fear of subversion by foreign powers. No sooner had our government been formed than fear of the Directory brought about the passage of the Alien and Sedition Acts. Shortly thereafter the Napoleonic conquests brought unease to the administration of Francophile president Thomas Jefferson.

Later, large-scale immigration from non-English Europe brought another kind of panic. The great immigrations from Ireland and Germany in the middle of the nineteenth century gave rise to the Know-Nothing movement and other expressions of true-blue Americanism. The arrival of European Catholics raised the specter of domination by the Catholic Church, of popish plots to undermine traditional Protestantism. At the end of the First World War "we had the first spasm of 'Red' hysteria," and after the second, another such spasm in the McCarthy purges.

There have also been other kinds of panics, perhaps even more widely feared. From the very beginning ours was an open country that gave rise to wild speculation in land, banking, and industry. This speculation, when allowed to rage unrestrained, led to bankruptcies, financial panics, and breakdowns in the money market. If it were only the economic system that was at stake here, this situation would

be disturbing enough. But the political system and our national ideals
have always been on the line. In building the country—its industry
and financial institutions—we have always had to compromise between our faith in the libertarian beliefs of the founding fathers and
the aggrandizing practices of the moneyed interests that plundered
the people and robbed them of their liberty.

In short, America was forced early in its history to follow a path
that the drafters of the Declaration of Independence would not have
approved, mainly because the country evolved in a direction they
could not have foreseen. Eighteenth-century reformers, like Condor-
cet or Jefferson, formulated an ideal of "the career open to the talents," in which everyone would be free, to the extent of his abilities,
to get an education, to hold office, to work for the common good.
"They could not imagine that a race would arise who would exploit
the opportunities of freedom at the expense of the common good,
simply to enrich themselves." Jefferson had planned for a nation that
would grow without people "cashing in," and there was no way you
could reconcile the ideals of republican responsibility with the mentality of "cashing in."

The result of the whole situation was that you had, on the one hand, the
millionaire insisting on his right to freedom to do as well for himself as he
could, and, on the other, the unfortunate citizen—squeezed out by the rich
man's monopoly, left penniless by the failure of his banks, compelled to work
in his factories or reduced to a bare subsistence by his money-lending tricks
and the prices he charged for the necessaries of life—complaining that conditions in the United States were depriving him of the right to life, liberty
and the pursuit of happiness. Since both sides are claiming this right, these
crises have to be met with compromise. (22-23)

On this question of the effectiveness or satisfactoriness of compromise in the political sphere Wilson says nothing. Of course, by
definition compromise means picking something that is not completely satisfactory to either party concerned; it means a forced abandonment of ideals, and above all, further psychological traumas to
add to those already present. Most Americans have been taught to
revere political compromise in all things, completely forgetting the
sinister dividends in moral agitation and upheaval.

Wilson believed there was some telling significance in the fact
that we have had two sorts of presidents in the United States—the
"public spirited idealist," who has the good of the country at heart,
and, in later years at least, may be called to office precisely in order

to save the nation from its excesses. The presidents of the early Republic were such, said Wilson, and so were Lincoln, Theodore Roosevelt, Woodrow Wilson, and Franklin Roosevelt. On the other hand, this type is likely to be followed by another type, perhaps the small party politician (Harding, Truman), or the captive of special interests (Grant). Wilson does find borderline cases such as Grover Cleveland and William Howard Taft. But those from the inferior end of the scale, who are in office most of the time, "ha[ve] no conception of what the other half has been up to." They are either the products of the party machine and have had their whole existences circumscribed by party politics or are military men or other specialists (engineers, perhaps, like Hoover) and largely ignorant of politics or economics. Most important, as Wilson saw it, the process was largely one of mountains and valleys, ups and downs—there was never any stability or common vision.

Wilson's discussion of presidential types suggests that this distinction is not limited to the political sphere—it runs through all American life. But it is important to see that it has little in common with any pattern found in Europe: nothing depends on rank or class. Whether of poor or patrician background there seem to be these two types of Americans, those who "have a stake in the success of our system . . . so that . . . they share the responsibility to carry on its institutions . . . find expression for its new point of view . . . give it dignity . . . make it work," or those who have no interest in American ideals, who have no sense of America's role or destiny. These people "are merely concerned with making a living or a fortune, with practicing some profession or mastering some technical skill, as they would in any other country" (26).

Wilson believed that the schism between these two types may have been wider, more threatening, in the early years of the twentieth century than in the 1950s. While at Princeton in the era of conspicuous consumption—millionaires' mansions and luxurious country clubs—the sons of serious, idealistic republicans (spelled with a small letter *r*) stood clearly apart from "the debonair young men who were planning to be bond salesmen and brokers as almost belonging to a different race." Still, money, class, geography, ethnic background seemed to have nothing to do with it.

This was not merely a matter of education or of coming from the Eastern seaboard: The Middle Western countryman Lincoln had this sense as highly developed as any New Englander from Harvard. Nor was it a matter of

blood—Anglo-Saxon or Dutch—or of ancestry—a family from the seven-
teenth century: Jacob Riis and Carl Schurz had it as much as Theodore
Roosevelt or any of the Adamses or Lodges. (26)

The theory expressed here by Wilson is a curious one. Perhaps
it is mysterious because it affords no logical explanation for the rise
of these two types of individuals. The theory in a rudimentary form
is not a new one. In the early Republic the threat of a class of individuals who would prefer to enjoy the fruits of liberty without assuming
the responsibility for them troubled the founding fathers deeply and
persistently. Men as different in political convictions as Jefferson and
Hamilton took pains to plan and justify a social order that would
prevent the rise of irresponsible leadership. All had firm ideas of
where the irresponsible leaders would come from and how the com-
monwealth could be spared their plunders. The same was true of a
number of writers of the nineteenth century, from James Fenimore
Cooper to Henry Adams. Nearly all of them had clear-cut theories of
where the idealistic, responsible American citizen would come from.
Cooper, for example, was able to identify a wide variety of idealistic
types and give a good account of their moral underpinnings. He
explained and justified the moral roots of Indians and noble savages,
of certain kinds of frontiersmen, of the landed aristocracy of the
Hudson River valley, but he brought damnation upon the head of
shiftless Yankees, small-potato lawyers, and despoilers of the land,
like Aaron Thousandacres and generated systematic explanations in
historical terms for these variant behaviors.

In his essay "The United States," Wilson never really explains
how it is that of two young men at Princeton, each coming from the
same social class, the same geographical area ("Hecate County," shall
we say, or Red Bank, New Jersey), one becomes a sacrificing idealist
willing to lay down his life for the American dream, while the other
craves nothing but to be a bond salesman, accumulate his private
hoard, build up his estate. He speaks of them as two separate strains,
two breeds, so different in the Princeton of 1915 that they could
almost be identified as two separate animals. But for all his psychological insight it is a pity that Wilson did not delve into this phenomenon
more deeply.

Too, Wilson's gallery of American types is open to question on a
number of other grounds. First, and perhaps most obviously, there
is the rigidity of the classifications. Human nature is such that people
are not cast in iron at an early age. One can be an idealist at the age
of twenty and a self-centered bigot at fifty—and of course, vice versa.

It is perfectly possible that the hell-bent-for-millions bond salesman will mature into a dedicated partisan of the common good; it is equally possible that the youthful social reformer will fall into some stagnant backwash of his own making.

Wilson's vision of the social order leaves much to be desired for other reasons. He has a too-easy tendency to cut off the commercial and professional classes from any form of grace. Although it is true that the idealistic politician, the poet, and the literary critic may give their all, so, too, do the lawyer, the doctor, and the journeyman. There are times when one gets the idea that Wilson tries so hard to refute the idea that man can live by bread alone that he goes to the opposite extreme of suggesting that man can live by the spirit alone. No society in the past has done so, and in this the United States is not unique. The United States is certainly not more materialistic than any other nation of history: perhaps it is only that we have found new ways to dramatize materialism.

Furthermore, it is doubtful that Wilson's dichotomy of two types —the idealistic visionary on the one hand, the seemingly mindless struggler for the almighty dollar on the other—really have very much to do with the dynamism of America. William Graham Sumner, the well-known nineteenth-century social scientist, believed that America's strength was neither due precisely to the idealist or the go-getter but to what he called "the forgotten man." For Sumner, the forgotten man is the very one who nobody notices; he excites neither the emotions nor the sentiments. "He is the clean, quiet, virtuous, domestic citizen, who pays his debts and taxes and is never heard of out of his little circle." To a greater extent than any previous civilization, America has been the creation of its middle class, not the product of any kind of heroic individuality; to dramatize the achievements, whether for good or ill of poet or millionaire, reformer or bond salesman, is probably to miss the decisive forces in American life. Wilson's Tory aloofness may have left him estranged from the middling masses and condemned him to look for heroes among uncommon and specialized types.

Another wrinkle in Wilson's essay shows up in his tendency to accept elitism in American life, though he regularly poses as the unflagging foe of elitism in all its forms. In this same essay on American types Wilson absolves Henry James of the responsibility of developing strong American feelings, because even though James was concerned with America and even felt a certain loyalty toward it, his primary stake "was in the art of imaginative literature, which was for him international." In a comparison between James and George

Santayana on the one hand and Justice Oliver Wendell Holmes on the other, Wilson was willing to admit no moral distinction between Holmes, who gave his full devotion to his homeland, and Santayana and James, for whom America was important but not central. The point is, if you can extend such courtesies to writers and philosophers you probably ought to be able to extend them to political and business leaders as well—especially in view of the fact that some of these have proven to be passionately devoted to American life in ways that have little to do with getting and spending.

There is in his essay "The United States" one further topic, not clearly related to this discussion. Again, unfortunately, Wilson does not go much beyond scratching the surface. The subject is "Americanism," by which is meant a love and partiality toward America, sometimes genial and benign, sometimes narrow and perverse. Wilson had earlier insisted that the United States was not a nation, that it lacked some kind of spiritual unity. Here, in counterpoint, he is discussing evidence for the idea that the cohering forces that we have experienced have not always been healthy.

Of course Americanism had a serious and rational meaning in the colonial period and later. We can understand and sympathize with an early usage of the term in a letter from Thomas Jefferson: "The parties here in debate continually charge each other . . . with being governed by an attachment to this or that belligerent nations, rather than the dictates of reason and pure Americanism" (32).* But in the nineteenth century, with the expansion of immigration and the arrival of large numbers of Roman Catholics from Germany and Ireland, there appeared a new and more unsavory form of Americanism, or nativism as it has sometimes been called. It was this new and more virulent form of Americanism that gave birth to the Know-Nothing party of the 1850s, to the strange spectacle of Americans just off the boat expressing active hatred for those still in passage ("Americer fer the Americans bejabers"), and still later such phenomena as the American Defense Society, the Ku Klux Klan, and, perhaps by extension, some of our later political witchhunts and purges. Wilson does not trace the history of these perverse uses of "Americanism," but he does conclude that the term is now in the shadows. "It may not be true that 'Americanism'—like Dr. Johnson's 'patriotism'—is invariably 'the last refuge of a scoundrel'; but it has

*Wilson offers this as the first quotation given in the *Dictionary of Americanisms* published by the University of Chicago Press. The letter was written in 1797.

been made to serve some very bad causes, and is now a word to avoid" (35).

Wilson might have done well to pursue this idea in some of its deeper ramifications. It may be, for example, that much of our political and social life is circumscribed by perverse forms of envy or jealousy—what Mencken called "puritanism," a suspicion and hatred of the activity of one's neighbors. It could be that fear and jealousy of other people because of their religion, their moral practices, their political beliefs, the clothes they wear, the house they live in, whether they give to the community chest, whether they keep their grass mowed, are among the defining characteristics of American life. Richard Hofstadter points out that although we have never been burdened by the worst aspects of class hatred (as has England, for example), we have not exactly freed ourselves from it either. American political life, said Hofstadter, "has served again and again as an arena for uncommonly angry minds."*

Wilson, unfortunately, does not get into these matters at any depth, at least in this essay. But we get a glimpse of the outline of his critique of American life: we have built a country but not a spiritual civilization; we started out as strong individualists but ended up with perverse and standardized manners and morals; we have spent too much of our time snooping into the affairs of our neighbors; we have thought too much about whether the present generation of politicians is "clean" and not enough about the cleanliness of the system itself. This essay again is an expression of the Tory side of Wilson, of his belief that you cannot have sensible politics until you have a sound civilization; that you cannot have decent social relations unless you have strong and independent individuals to engage in them.

Wilson's more determinedly philosophical reflections on America as found in his essay on "The United States" always raise more questions than they answer. But Wilson's great genius is due to the breadth and diversity of his questioning, to the wide casting of his net. If an essay like "The United States" was not wholly satisfactory in the tightness and rigor of its argument, it was because Wilson was engaged in bigger things. In the two decades after his "shock of recognition" in the early forties, he was to do his best work as an Americanist. In *Memoirs of Hecate County* he was to write one more work of fiction, easily his best. This, together with *Patriotic Gore* of the next decade, represents the pinnacle of Wilson's achievement as

The Paranoid Style in American Politics (New York: Vintage Books, 1967), 3.

an American writer and as a critic of American life. These two works, needless to say, represent two different sides of Wilson and arose from distinct moods. Obviously they have been valued differently by readers of divergent views and temperaments. But these two works reveal Wilson's greatest talents operating most brilliantly, and in tandem they give eloquent meaning to all he was trying to say about America during the prime of his life.

Edmund Wilson at the beginning of his career. *University of Illinois Library*

Edmund Wilson, Sr.
*New Jersey Historical
Society*

Christian Gauss,
Wilson's Princeton
mentor. *Princeton
University Library*

A Princeton classmate, F. Scott Fitzgerald.
Library of Congress

Another classmate and
lifelong friend, John Peale
Bishop. *University of Illinois
Library*

Wilson began his postwar career on Conde Nast's *Vanity Fair; right,* a cover by John Held, Jr. *University of Illinois Library*

Dorothy Parker, a colleague at *Vanity Fair. Eastman House*

Edmund Wilson in the 1940s. *Culver Pictures*

Van Wyck Brooks, whose work as a literary historian attracted Wilson's interest and support in the 1940s. *Elsevier-Dutton*

Edna St. Vincent Millay. *Vassar College*

The Hill School, decorated for a game with Hotchkiss;
below, the Old Stone House at Talcottville.
University of Illinois Library

Edmund Wilson in the 1960s. *F. Kurt Rolfes* (from Richard Hauer Costa, *Edmund Wilson, Our Neighbor from Talcottville*, Syracuse University Press)

7

The World of
Hecate County

Memoirs of Hecate County was Wilson's last major work of fiction
and by all standards the best. In a preface to a revised edition of the
work in 1959 Wilson said that "*Hecate County* is my favorite among
my books," a view he continued to maintain throughout his life. It
is a somewhat neglected work today, but it continues to hold interest
for anyone seeking an understanding of Wilson the Americanist.
Memoirs contains moods and reflections that had been many years
developing and it has deep roots in Wilson's experiences of the twenties and thirties. It is a book of shifting moods, so we have to be
careful not to conclude that here is the solid and permanent essence
of Wilson's America; still Wilson wrote the book "as a satire and
warning" (*Letters,* 486), and one cannot help believing that he had
intended the book to be an emphatic criticism of American society
in narrative form.

    Memoirs of Hecate County was first published in 1946 and con-
sists of six stories loosely related by a single narrator and by time and
locale. The action takes place roughly between 1915 and 1940, most
of it in the 1920s and 1930s. The locale is vaguely suburban, perhaps
more accurately, using a term made popular by A.C. Spectorsky,
exurban—locale suggestive, let us say, of Monmouth County, New
Jersey, or perhaps some other "far distant" and elegant suburb of
New York at the very end of the commuter's line—Suffolk County
on Long Island, Rockland or Putnam County, New York, Fairfield
County, Connecticut, or Bucks County, Pennsylvania. The ambiance
is as much rural and bucolic as it is suburban—the homes are set back

on large parcels of land and do not run in rows. In answer to an inquiry from Van Wyck Brooks, Wilson claimed that the model for the narrator's house was one near Stamford, Connecticut (*ibid.*, 544), but many of the scenes were doubtless drawn from numerous places in Wilson's past—Red Bank, perhaps even Cape Cod. The narrator divides his time between Hecate County and New York City, which suggests that geographical place is not of utmost importance—Hecate County is a state of mind, an ideal construct of the imagination.

When the book first appeared in print there was a good deal of speculation about this matter of locale. Some assumed the place to have had a specific historical location like Faulkner's Yoknapatawpha County, Mississippi. There was, however, even more speculation and disagreement on the point of whether the book was a novel, a series of stories, or something else. Because of the lack of a single narrative thread, few critics were drawn to think of the work as a novel; on the other hand, it was not exactly a collection of stories either. Among the reviewers Malcolm Cowley pointed out that "one physical and social and moral frame" unified the book and that it was a grouping of "novels." He also observed that there was nothing new about this in American literature; one thinks of Faulkner's *Go Down Moses* and Sherwood Anderson's *Winesburg, Ohio.**

Critical discussion of the work was not limited to this relatively trivial matter, however. The book is a depressing one, filled with dark moods—sometimes of ennui, sometimes of nausea, sometimes of the macabre and the diabolical. These depressing qualities did not endear the book to the critics—even the serious critics. In a review of *Memoirs* in the *Partisan Review* entitled "Le Misanthrope," Alfred Kazin, a long-time Wilson admirer and friend is troubled by the lack of human passion in the book and by the purely mechanical life of the narrator and other characters. Diana Trilling who, in the *Nation*, expressed the belief that as a writer "Wilson was the most torturedly alert to the social-moral disintegration of the last two decades," nonetheless objected that the author had a tendency to wallow in this disintegration, to take no action against it, that he had not managed to construct "some principle of private order from which a principle of general order could be induced." This belief that the artist/moralist in Wilson was flat, purged, and empty was also expressed by Malcolm Cowley in the *New Republic,* who found the book lacking

*For discussion of the critical reception of *Memoirs,* see Charles P. Frank, *Edmund Wilson* (New York: Twayne Publishers, 1970), 138.

in "moral faith," the stories held together "by a single mood of revulsion," which never lets up.*

The critical opinion was thus somewhat consistent but it did not seem to have been a crucial factor in the public reception of the book. The book received immediate recognition precisely because of the people who found in it passion and lifeblood—of the wrong kind. Almost immediately after its appearance the vivid eroticism of the central story, "Princess with the Golden Hair," brought *Memoirs of Hecate County* into direct confrontation with the last vestiges of comstockery in America: the book was banned in Boston in April 1946. A month later, acting on a complaint from the Society for the Suppression of Vice, the New York police raided local bookstores, and the New York Public Library removed the book from circulation in September. Worse was yet to come. The book involved its publishers in a long, complex, and expensive legal battle. In November the special sessions court of New York City found the book immoral and fined the publisher and its local bookshops $1,000, a fine that was later affirmed by the appellate court and, eventually, on October 26, 1948, by the Supreme Court of the United States. Except for the few who got their hands on the book right after it came out, *Memoirs of Hecate County* was immediately a scarce and forbidden item (Frank, 153-54).

But the heyday of the Sumners and Comstocks was nearing its end, and with the publication during the 1950s of *Lady Chatterley's Lover* to say nothing of *The Memoirs of Fanny Hill,* the rather stately eroticism of *Hecate County* must have seemed tame by comparison. Even though the New York State injunction was not broken, L.C. Page reissued the book in 1959, and this was followed by numerous paperback editions, all of which enjoyed a brisk sale. Wilson undoubtedly gained a great many readers from the spicy publicity generated by the legal battles over the book, although surely a great many were surprised to find the overall tone and character of the book to be quite different than they had been led to expect. No matter how appealing the erotic passages of "Princess" may be—and they have a very strong appeal—no serious or educated reader could help but see that they are embedded in a work of determined purpose and

*Alfred Kazin, *Partisan Review,* Summer 1946, 375-80; Diana Trilling, *Nation,* March 30, 1946, 379-81; Malcolm Cowley, *New Republic,* March 25, 1946. For a more complete list of reviews of *Memoirs* in each of its editions, see Richard David Ramsey, *Edmund Wilson: A Bibliography* (New York, David Lewis, 1971), 24-26.

moral force. Far from being frivolous or commercial, the author of
Memoirs of Hecate County was a social critic of lugubrious, almost
pathological seriousness. But the work was the product of shifting
moods and impressed itself on readers in strikingly different ways.

In retrospect, Wilson referred to *Memoirs of Hecate County* as
a "suburban inferno," but in describing the stories to Maxwell Perkins of Scribner's while they were being written, he stressed the
strong element of fantasy with only "a kind of odor of damnation."
Apparently Wilson was somewhat inconsistent about the intended
impact of the stories. Early on he planned to use on the title page a
quotation from Ovid's *Metamorphoses,* emphasizing that the overall
theme was "transformations" in society and in human life. For a
time, too, he was playing with the idea of giving the book a subtitle,
Bedtime Stories for the Middle Aged, but later abandoned this rather
ambiguous indicator (*Letters,* 435). In place of the quotation from
Ovid, Wilson finally settled for an epigraph from Gogol's *Viy,* clearly
emphasizing the diabolical and preparing the reader for that forceful
mood of the work:

Of a sudden . . . in the midst of the silence . . . the iron lid of the coffin burst
open with a crash, and the corpse of the dead girl sat up. Even more frightful
was she now than the first time. Frightfully her teeth rattled, convulsively
her lips twitched, wildly she screamed incantations. A whirlwind swept
through the church; the icons fell on their faces; the smashed panes flew out
the windows. The doors were torn from their hinges, and an innumerable
horde of horrors swept into the holy church. The whole place was filled with
a terrible sound of the scratching of claws and the swishing of wings. In a
flock, they swooped and wheeled, searching everywhere to find the philosopher.

When the book finally went to print the mood of diabolism came
clearly to the fore. Evil, witchcraft, and the actual presence of the
devil are felt throughout the book. We must not forget the title—
Memoirs of "Hecate" County, and we soon see that nearly all the
women in the book are witches. Nearly all the men are drained and
lifeless after having sold their souls to the devil.

Still *Memoirs* is about a number of things, not all of which are
precisely macabre. It is about middle age; it is about the flatness and
futility of the idle rich; it is about sexual neuroses; it is about the
silliness of cocktail parties and long weekends. What Wilson did was
assemble a great many of his personal experiences and compose what
he believed to be a proper warning to his fellow countrymen. This
is what happens to Americans—not just the affluent few, because

America is an affluent country and the prosperous middle class animates the spirit of the country. We are damned by our moral weakness and lack of purpose; we have created nothing around us that makes life worth living and so fall into a kind of agitated stupor.

The thread that holds *Memoirs* together is the consistent point of view of the narrator, a seemingly aimless and neurotic young man of good social and educational background—a character much like the diffident side of Wilson himself but without Wilson's genius and creative drive. One gets the feeling that the genesis of *Memoirs* was probably Wilson's nervous breakdown of 1929, that he spun at least the mood of the work from that unhappy year of increasingly meaningless and debilitating amorous encounters and personal upheavals. The narrator is in a state of near psychological collapse, and the book is a recitation of the sights, smells, and sounds of ennui and mental disorder.

Sherman Paul, Wilson's first biographer, believes that the model of the book is Flaubert's *L'Education Sentimentale.* Certainly Frederic Moreau, the hero of Flaubert's novel, bears a striking resemblance to Wilson's hero; he treads a similar path of damnation. Wilson had already made detailed reference to this character in *The Triple Thinkers,* remarking that Moreau "is a sensitive and intelligent young man equipped with a moderate income; but he has no stability of purpose and is capable of no emotional integrity. He becomes aimlessly, will-lessly, involved with love affairs with different types of women, and he is unable to make anything out of them; they simply get in each other's way till in the end he is left with nothing" (109).

Even more important, *L'Education Sentimentale* was a political novel as well as a psychological one. Moreau's aimlessness was the product of his class, a result of middle-class mediocrity. Moreau is in love from the beginning with the wife of a flashy business wheeler-dealer who both requites his love and holds him off with her various moral defenses (much like Imogene in "The Princess with the Golden Hair"). In the end Moreau is too weak, too ineffectual to take the unrooted wife away from the businessman. These two male characters are seen to suffer from the same basic defects. "Frederic and the vulgar husband at bottom represent the same thing: Frederic is only the more refined as well as the more incompetent side of the middle-class mediocrity of which the dubious promoter represents the more flashy and active aspect" (110).

This is a subtle truth that Wilson may have forgotten a few years later when he wrote his essay, "The United States," and contrasted the two types of Princeton graduates in 1916—the mindless broker and the clean-cut idealist. For with all of the examples of failures and breakdowns in his own family, Flaubert's point is one that Wilson had been pondering throughout his career; in the middle-class society the idealist, the man of feelings, often fails to find anything in life, fails to rise above the materialism against which he pits himself. In Flaubert's novel, Moreau turns out to be nothing but the undramatic and insipid counterpart of the flamboyant entrepreneur. So, too, in *Memoirs of Hecate County:* the unnamed hero firmly believes himself to be set apart from the society of the commercial rich around him, but his own moral values are corrupt. He involves himself in base personal entanglements and mind-wearying exercises that condemn him to flatness and stagnation.

To be sure, it was Wilson's belief, as it was Flaubert's, that the possibility of a higher culture is diminished by the existence of a powerful, dynamic business society. Neither puts any stock in the idea that the leisure that is bred of affluence can lead to social enrichment and to widespread artistic achievement. As Wilson says so accurately about Flauber's "political" novel, mirroring his own view of the disintegration of American society:

Flaubert's novel plants deep in our mind an idea which we never quite get rid of: the suspicion that our middle class society of manufacturers, businessmen and bankers, of people who live on or deal in investments, so far from being redeemed by its culture, has ended by cheapening and invalidating all the departments of culture, political, scientific, artistic and religious, as well as corrupting and weakening the ordinary human relations: love, friendship, and loyalty to cause—till the whole civilization seems to dwindle. (113)

Whether or not Flaubert's novel was in any important sense a model for *Memoirs of Hecate County,* there can be no doubt that the above statement was a guiding formulation of Wilson's own political views in *Memoirs.* There were many novels along similar lines in the twentieth century, especially in France, culminating perhaps in Jean-Paul Sartre's *La Nausèe* in which the hero becomes alienated from middle-class society and looks for some way out, some escape from the grim, even "nauseating" middle-class world with its utter staleness and rigidity. *Memoirs of Hecate County* may not be a great work of art in this genre, but it is a powerful work, in part because it relentlessly questions the survival of culture, of individuality, of human values in the commercial and material civilization that has been the United States for the past hundred years.

Although Edmund Wilson claimed that *Memoirs of Hecate County* was the favorite among all his works, critics never took

Wilson seriously as a fiction writer, probably because he never took fiction writing seriously himself. His own instincts as a scholar, historian, and critic always tended to get the upper hand and to control his imagination. Wilson had gifts as a storyteller, he had dramatic gifts, he had superlative abilities to recreate human situations, but he did not always have the desire to sustain any of his efforts. He could sustain scholarship doggedly, determinedly, but he could only sustain fictional ideas as long as they struck his fancy. Not surprisingly, the stories in *Memoirs of Hecate County* are of uneven quality. When all of Wilson's powers and interests are engaged, as they were in "The Princess with the Golden Hair," the writing and the observations are on a high plane. It is interesting to keep in mind, however, that "Princess" is the most autobiographical of all the stories; we find much of it intact in his diaries of the 1920s. Nonetheless, the direct observations are transferred with great artistic skill and with deep sympathy into a powerful human narrative.

The same may not be said, however, of a story like "The Milhollands and Their Damned Soul." Here one gets the feeling that Wilson has a number of pet peeves to get off his back, and he does this in an economical way, as if he were saying: "Look here, now, I've got to make fun of publishing techniques, or book clubs—get it all in and be done with it." Much to the detriment of his art, Wilson often writes this way. Still, Wilson is always historically interesting, and if some of the stories in *Memoirs* dry up as fiction, if they seem unsatisfactory as completed works of the imagination, each remains the work of a restless and penetrating critic of American life. As always, Wilson successfully combines his artistic sensibilities with a powerful historical vision. Although an artistic itensity is not sustained throughout, Wilson's moral authority and intellectual force never weaken.

The first story, "The Man Who Shot Snapping Turtles," raises many questions that recur throughout the book, since right from the start we are puzzled about the writer's stance. In his discussion of Flaubert's *L'Education Sentimentale,* Wilson complained of the ambiguous impression created by that work. "Is it a satire? The characters are too close to life, a little too well rounded, for satire. Yet they are not visualized enough, not quite responsive enough, to seem people of a straight novel. But we find that it sticks in our crop." The same may be said of "The Man Who Shot Snapping Turtles," a rather grotesque satire with implausible characters. Yet the story sticks in our crop because of a real but undefinable hideousness.

Asa M. Stryker is one of the narrator's neighbors in Hecate County. At one time he taught chemistry in some "snooty sounding college in Pennsylvania," but he now lives on a small inheritance and is, like so many in Hecate County, one of the idle rich. Stryker's chief topic of conversation when the narrator visits him is the wild ducks that live on a small pond on his place. He loves the beauty of these ducks and describes them to his neighbors in rich detail. Unfortunately his pond is also the residence of snapping turtles who catch hold of the ducklings and drag them under. The turtles, of course, are a clear-cut sign of evil in the universe—especially to Stryker, who sees the world in vivid black-and-white terms. The ducks and the turtles obviously represent the aesthetic and evil. Yet, from the beginning we are led to see the twisted sense of values in the mind of this denizen of Hecate County. Even his reasons for admiring the beauty of his favored ducks are distorted and perverse. Stryker is impressed by the ducks because there is "something princely about them—something which, as he used to say, Frick or Charlie Schwab couldn't buy." The moneyed classes of Hecate County know nice things, they have a feel for beauty, but in the end this sense of beauty is corrupt and meaningless. The contrast between the beautiful birds and the malignant creatures of the mud is seen against the backdrop of some larger universe of moral depravity.

Stryker goes to extreme lengths to rid himself of the hated turtles. He shoots them; he drains the pond; he hires workers to rake through the mud with giant rakes; he poisons the waters with chemicals; he puts up elaborate fences—all to no avail. Stryker develops a paranoia of a peculiarly Manichaean kind, seeing in the tenaciousness of the turtles a plot to take over the world. His neighbors believe he is unhinged.

One day Stryker explains his frustrating battle to Clarence Latouche, an advertising man of southern background. Latouche cannot see why Stryker continues to torture himself with this silly problem and suggests that down in the south these turtles make pretty good eating—certainly they make good soup. At first Stryker cannot seem to understand this attitude: "Right is right and wrong is wrong, and you have to choose between them." But Latouche is not much of a believer in moral absolutes and gets by in the world with "a low and pragmatical attitude." In time he brings about a reversal in Stryker's firm moral resolve, proving that like most things in Hecate County, firmness and resolve have little substance.

In contrast to the repugnant scenes of Stryker's fight against the turtles in the mud are the scenes in which Stryker is convinced that if he cannot destroy the turtles, at least they can be exploited as an object of commerce. Stryker becomes an entrepreneur, a manufacturer of turtle soup. He elicits Latouche's help—an advertising man's wild fancy whose flight of imagination brought out the best in Wilson's sardonic humor. No problem at all in writing advertising copy for snapper.

You know, the truth is that a great big proportion of the canned turtle soup that's sold is made out of snapping turtles, but that isn't the way they advertise it. If you advertize it frankly as snapper, it will look like something brand-new, and all you'll need is the snob appeal to put it over on the can-opening public. There's a man canning rattlesnakes in Florida, and it ought be a lot easier to sell snappers. All you've got to do up here in the North to persuade people to buy a product is to convince them that there's some kind of social prestige attached to it—and all you'd have to do with your snappers would be to create the impression that a good ole white-haired darky with a beaming smile used to serve turtle soup to Old Massa. All you need is a little smart advertising and you can have as many people eating snapper as are eating [he named a popular canned salmon], which isn't even nutritious like snapper is—they make it out of the sweepings from a tire factory.—I tell you what I'll do," he said, carried away by eloquence and whisky, "you organize a turtle farm and I'll write you some copy free. You can pay me when and if you make money." (11)

The story moves on to an unsignificant and unhelpful conclusion, but the two phases of the story, the mindless battle against the evil creatures of mud, and the silly exploitation of them for commercial purposes, pin down the style and substance of Hecate County. The people of Hecate County are loose in the world; the devil haunts them. They come from a background of some seeming substance and moral firmness, but everything they have relied on is weak and powerless; the ground they walk on is ready to shift. Stryker's original affection for the ducks was grounded in a shallow gentility that one associates with the idle rich; they like nice, pleasant things, everything as it should be—a well-ordered universe with no backing of genuine civilization. One might as well have the turtles as the ducks because there are no standards of good and evil, the beautiful and the ugly. Everything is phony and meretricious.

In *Memoirs of Hecate County,* then, Wilson is returning to some of the American themes that had been troubling him since childhood, his suspicion of the commercial classes, his doubts about the humanity of the mannered classes as they existed outside the walls of Laurelwood or Talcottville. Once more it is Wilson's commanding theme of the disintegration of old American values, values that fall into the muck and mire of a shifting pond bottom. For a while one can always sit on one's porch and enjoy, as did Stryker, the artificial, well-kept grounds, the aesthetic niceties maintained by the hired hands, but in the end the only thing that is real is the mud in which all values are equally corrupt.

The next story of the book, "Ellen Terhune," seems to follow logically from the first, as if the first were but a dramatic introduction to the disease of Hecate County in repellant satirical form and the second a more searching analysis of the problem in which the narrator attempts to go back in his own family history and that of "Ellen Terhune," his childhood friend, to examine more subtly, more searchingly, the interpersonal traumas of life in America.

Sherman Paul remarks that "Ellen Terhune" shows Wilson in the Jamesian mode just as "The Man Who Shot Snapping Turtles," shows him in the Hawthornesque. Perhaps this is the mood; the substance is not unlike Thomas Mann's *Buddenbrooks,* a tale of the inability of the delicate artistic temperament to exist in the commercial maelstrom.

In this story we get a closer look at the narrator's state of mind. Since Ellen Terhune comes from a similar background and is similarly afflicted, we must assume that the story is a fictionalized version of the accounts Wilson has given in his autobiographical essays of the mental decline and deterioration of the generation of his father and his uncles.

The narrator is having a breakdown; he suffers from hallucinations, drunken stupors, and severe states of depression. He pays several visits to the house of Ellen Terhune, each time seeing her as if in some earlier stage of her life. He sees her first in the 1920s after her marriage has broken up, later as a talented young musician around the turn of the century, then as a charming and precocious girl of about thirteen in the early 1890s, and finally as another young girl from about 1880 who may be Ellen's mother, pregnant with Ellen.

The narrator, who throughout *Memoirs* is an aloof and distant figure commenting on the denizens of Hecate County as an outsider, is closely involved with Ellen Terhune. The ambiance of her childhood home is described in some detail at the beginning and is redolent of Wilson's mother's home at Laurelwood. Ellen's grandfather, too, had been a doctor, and the house, unlike those of the new prosperous classes, was "humanistic," showed evidence of wider interests than now, and was "richly lined with the evidences of his pastimes, his studies and his travels." Clearly this world had nothing to sustain it in 1926 when the story begins and the personalities of the narrator and Ellen Terhune are disintegrating—reaching back frantically to this past that can no longer sustain them.

Ellen Terhune did have a certain success in music, becoming one of the most accomplished composers of her day. But the story is largely a chronicle of an artist's disharmony with the outside world —doubly difficult for a woman perhaps. It is a story Wilson had to tell because it was the story of the breakdown of the artistic personality that he had seen in his own family and, in the twenties, in himself. Ellen Terhune's struggle is seen against the historical backdrop of the years of Edmund Wilson, Sr.'s, crippling neurosis, and, as always, there is the social disintegration that parallels the psychological. The flashbacks to the earlier stages of Ellen Terhune's life are accomplished through the hallucinations of the narrator and enable Wilson to show the progressive disintegration not only of a life but of a social order.

Always there is the belief that the artistic personality is a delicate one, that it requires a certain harmony and tranquility in which to survive, and that this harmony has been absent or shattered in America in the years since the Civil War. Ellen's grandfather's generation, like that of Wilson's Grandfather Kimball, had held up. But Ellen's own parents were unsuited to one another. The father was a Wall Street man with a seat on the stock exchange. He was ruined in the crash of 1887 and after that had done badly. Later he took to drinking and, when Ellen was eleven, killed himself in a cheap little hotel in New York. But her mother and father had never had a pleasant relationship. They came from extremely different backgrounds. Her mother had once studied violin and had wanted a professional career. Ellen had never forgiven her father for forcing her mother to give this up. Ellen, too, as we find out, was wounded by the failure of both her parents to find what they wanted in life, and she carried into her own career, and her marriage to the conductor Sigismund Soblianski, a kind of rigidity and inadaptability of which she was quite aware but against which she was powerless. Her creative talents survived, but practically she was paralyzed by a psychic wound that held her fixed to times past, forced her to rehearse the failures and frustrations of her parents. Above all, she seemed, somehow, out of place in the world of the twentieth century with its cocktail parties, its endless chatter, its meaningless appliances.

Nothing sums up the story of Ellen Terhune as well as the contrast of the opening and the closing scenes—the description of the grandfather's home in 1926 and the description of Ellen's death in a hotel for musicians in New York. In contrast to the old doctor's genial surroundings—the high, green picket fence, the covered drive with big *porte cochère,* the gingerbread architecture with cupolas, "with foolscap tops, dormers with diamond cones, balconies with little white railings and porches with Ionic columns, all pointing in different directions," the matted honeysuckle outside, the books, statues, and private treasures inside—we have instead the mechanical and inhumane world of New York. Ellen Terhune died there alone, away from the place of her tranquil beginning.

She had gone to New York hoping to be able to compose. There was a piano in her room and for a few weeks she was able to play on it. Later she fell into a stupor and the management became aware that she was not eating or going out. A doctor was called but Ellen revived and started playing the piano again—but in pounding out the same things over and over again she made the hotel people fear that she was going insane. On the day of her death she wanted to go out and fumbled with her coat and keys and had to be helped by the maid. There was a certain telling poignancy in the manner of her going:

> She went out quickly and rang for the elevator. On the trip down, the elevator boy said, he had stopped and gone back up a floor to get a passenger who had rung after they passed, and Ellen had "bawled him out," telling him he must never go back once he had passed a floor. This sudden scolding had so flustered the boy, who was new and rather inexpert with the old-fashioned elevator, that he had made the situation worse by stopping below the door and then jerking the car up just as the passenger was stepping down. Then, in an effort to make up for his delay, on the assumption that Ellen was in a hurry, he had shot abruptly down, in a drop which the passenger who had just got in said afterwards had given him an unpleasant shock. It must have shocked Ellen, too, for she was pale when they reached the bottom, and leaned against the side of the elevator for a moment before she got out. The boy was worried and tried to help her; but she stepped out by herself into the lobby, and there she fell dead. It was said that she had had a bad heart. (72)

Wilbur Flick, the central character of the next story of *Memoirs,* is perhaps a more typical citizen of Hecate County than Ellen Terhune. In part, though, he is merely her male counterpart, a further extension of the same story about the weakness and unsteadiness of the twentieth-century leisured aristocracy. Wilbur Flick seems to be a composite character, perhaps partly fabricated of some of Wilson's own self-doubts and projections of failure.

Historically "Glimpses of Wilbur Flick" is a story of the 1930s and is bathed in the atmosphere of that time, giving Wilson numerous opportunities for satires of fascism, communism, the New Deal, the right wing, and other crosscurrents of the time. From a purely literary perspective, "Glimpses of Wilbur Flick" may not be one of the best stories in *Memoirs,* but it is interesting to students of Wilson's political and social ideas.

Wilbur Flick, like Edmund Wilson and the story's narrator, arrived in college as something of a lone wolf, an outsider. He was quite a bit wealthier than the youthful Wilson, however, having been the heir to a baking powder fortune. He was an only child and an orphan and had spent much of his youth traveling around Europe with a tutor. As such he never had any connection with the other rich boys in his college class, "because he had neither been to their schools nor belonged to their social circles." He was scornful of all college traditions, lived not on campus but in a fancy suite at the local inn. Seemingly college life meant nothing to him and he was something of an oddity to the other boys. He flunked out at the end of a year and moved to New York where he proceeded to live the life of a connoisseur and cocktail party host.

The narrator speaks of a number of meetings with Wilbur during the twenties. He attended some of his parties that "were among the jumpiest of the period." He followed Wilbur's career—or lack of it —with mild amusement and indifference and watched the progress of his first marriage, which ended in divorce. But the narrator's relationship with Wilbur was strengthened somewhat after the crash when Wilbur lost quite a bit of his fortune and came to live in Hecate County.

Wilbur's life seemed more settled in the thirties than in the twenties, partly due to his more stable second wife who gave a certain dignity to the Flick household. At the same time, as the depression wore on, Wilbur's role as a member of the idle rich became more shaky both psychologically and economically. Wilbur's hobbies and interests became annoying as well as eccentric to those who knew him, especially the narrator. He and his wife were both probably alcoholics and suffered from a lack of purpose; their lives drifted aimlessly, and with the hungry multitudes increasing steadily their position as coupon-clipping idlers became increasingly unsupportable.

One evening, after the New Deal was well under way, the narrator recounts the details of "a heavy economic conversation at Wilbur's place" where the topic turns to the masses of the unemployed who seem to be a drain on the nation's economy.

" 'You know how I'd handle the problem?' said Wilbur, in that bold and authoritative tone with which the rich like to announce their opinions. 'I'd take the whole lot of unemployed and I'd put 'em on an old steamer that had been condemned and I'd send 'em out somewhere in the middle of the Atlantic and I'd have the whole outfit sunk.' "

But the narrator has no intention of letting this slide, and he puts the sting on it with one of the most delicious ironies of *Memoirs of Hecate County.*

" 'We'd have to send you on that ship, Wilbur,' I said. 'What do you mean,' he asked, exhilarated by his eloquence. 'Well, you're unemployed.' 'Go to Hell!' he said. He pretended to accept it as a joke, but his further discussion of the subject flapped with a broken wing" (87).

In later discussions Wilbur attempts further justification of his idle-rich status on the grounds that the rich provide for the survival of the best, for the survival of civilization, but we can clearly see from what follows that Wilbur's position is unsupportable. The rest of the story chronicles Wilbur's chaotic attempts to make some kind of spiritual peace with a world in which he is manifestly a parasite—however "civilized." He is not lucky in this. He finds the country intolerable and he moves back to New York. He suffers from insomnia and becomes a habitual drug taker. For a while in the middle thirties he enters a sanatorium. Later he converts to Catholicism.

Throughout this period Wilbur's political views remain fractured, incoherent, essentially groundless. Once, in the late thirties, at the time of the Spanish Civil War, the narrator is invited to Wilbur's uptown apartment to a party that was supposedly raising money for loyalist Spain. He participates in a left-wing singing group and is now touting the *Daily Worker* as "a live wire—the only paper that told the truth about what was going on in the world." The narrator cannot understand this new turning to the left and finds it as absurd as his earlier right-wing stance.

I had wanted to ask him, at first, how he had reconciled his old ideal of government by the elite with his championship of Spanish republicanism; but, as I watched him among his new friends, I perfectly understood what had happened. The Communism of the later thirties, as instilled by his persistent wife, did not of course present itself to Wilbur as a democratic movement at all, but as a kind of exclusive club which was soon to dominate the world; and it had provided him at the moment he needed it with a role that both flattered his vanity and appeased his moral discontent; an occupation that was guaranteed always to remain entirely unreal and never to let him in for any final responsibility. And did it not also provide a revenge against a world in which he had found no place? (107)

Is Wilbur's faith in communism as a kind of exclusive club, or "the coming thing," simple naiveté? Is it insanity? No, it is quite clear that it is neither of these things. It is social unrealism of the sort Wilson found infecting everyone in the thirties. It represents what inevitably happens in a civilization whose ideals are short-circuited or washed out. But, above all, Wilbur, a typical Wilsonian character, is a member of a social class that is by nature purposeless and ineffectual. And this is why the corrupt, diabolical, perhaps even the damned in him takes the upperhand. What can become of the patrician classes in twentieth-century America? They can sometimes shake themselves loose and stand away from the mainstream like Wilson himself; they can plug hard at some commercial vocation and become a success (one thinks of Wilson's portrait of Dwight Morrow), or they can flounder around in a moral vacuum and ultimately become some kind of a weakling or moral pauper—like Wilbur Flick and Ellen Terhune. To a large extent America is a pageant of human misfortune, with the polished and refined members of the upper classes the most shining and dramatic examples.

The next story in *Memoirs,* and surely the best remembered by the book's readers, is "The Princess with the Golden Hair." The original readers of the book in 1946 were not aware how much of this story was autobiographical—this was found out only after the publication of Wilson's diaries from the twenties; but in 1946, hardly any readers—and this includes the readers of the Watch and Ward Societies—could fail to notice the extraordinary quality of the story, its uncompromising realism and stubborn honesty.

Of course it is the eroticism of this story that has kept *Memoirs* selling over the years. Everyone who reads the story is moved by the narrator's relationships with two vivid female characters, the well-born and pampered Imogen and the warm and earthy Anna from an immigrant neighborhood of Brooklyn, always oppressed, always buffeted about in her work and her family relationships.

In a recent tribute to Edmund Wilson's fiction, John Updike, fourteen years old in 1946 when *Memoirs* first came out, tells of the time he took the book out of the public library in Reading, Pennsylvania. In retrospect, he claims only an imperfect recollection of most of the other stories, but "Princess," which he "read, as they say avidly," gave him his "first and to this day most vivid glimpse of sex through the window of fiction." It is not, said Updike, that there were not any explicit sex scenes in the literature of 1946. One could find plenty of hot and juicy sex in Erskine Caldwell, John O'Hara, or the southern California detective fiction of James Cain and Raymond Chandler. But "the sex in these writers was not fortified by Wilson's conscious intention of bringing sexual realism into American fiction." The deadly human seriousness, the lack of snigger and smirk, was what made the sex of "Princess" so powerful.

There is a true whiff of Hell in Hecate County, less in the specific touches of supernatural diabolism with which this utter rationalist quaintly adorned his tales, but in the low ceilings and cheap underwear of the sex idyll, the clothes and neurosis of the copulators. America has always tolerated sex as a joke, as a night's prank in the burlesque theater or fairground tent; but not as a solemn item in life's work inventory. It was Wilson's deadly earnest, his unwinking naturalistic refusal to release us into farce, that made *Hecate County* in all its dignity and high intent the target of a (successful!) prosecution for obscenity. Earnest, but not Ernest Hemingway, who never in his fictional personae shows himself compromised, as this sweating, fumbling hero of Wilson's so often is; Hemingway's heroes make love without baring their bottoms, and the women as well as the men are falsified by a romantic severity, an exemption from the odors and awkwardness that Wilson, with the dogged selfless honesty of a bookworm, presses his own nose, and ours, into with such solemn satisfaction.*

Still, more important, according to Updike, Wilson's eroticism has the ring of truth because it is not spun out to excite himself or his readers. Its purpose is always to illuminate the social and psychological underpinnings of the two women and the narrator. Never separable from the erotic detail is Wilson's serious analysis of economic and political realities as they constantly interact with the basic conditions of American life.

In "Princess with the Golden Hair" the two strongly developed female characters are seen as enchanting, bewitching, or confusing the narrator while his life disintegrates into intellectual and spiritual confusion. He becomes embroiled with these women not merely because of their sexual charms but because they represent distinctly different social classes, neither of which the narrator can fully identify himself with. These women are interludes in the narrator's sex

*John Updike, "Edmund Wilson's Fiction," in *Edmund Wilson: The Man and His Work*, ed. John Wain (New York: New York Univ. Press, 1978), 165. This article, in a different form, appeared earlier in the *New Republic.*

life, since they replace his more or less permanent girl friend Jo Gates who appears in several stories of the book. But they are devastatingly destructive in their effects—as one might expect of the bewitching female—and the narrator's sexual triumphs seem to lead only to further indecision and nervous collapse.

The narrator's first infatuation is with Imogen Loomis, the wife of Ralph Loomis, an advertising man. The Loomises live in Hecate County, not in splendor but in extreme comfort. Imogen, long unattainable and resistant to the narrator's blandishments, is supplanted sporadically by Anna Lenihan, a dance-hall waitress of distinctly lower-class origins. But the narrator can never totally love or identify with either of these women because of his own lack of social stability. He uses each to feed his half-baked political ideas. He uses his ambiguous social position to attract both women—Imogen because he is an adventurer and bohemian who holds out promise of some undefined life-style transcending the blandness and superficiality of the advertising executive husband; Anna because he belongs to the neat, clean, and respectable upper-middle-class world.

Here we find out something for the first time about the hero's family and background. He has a small but adequate income from his mother's side of the family. His father had been an accountant and at one time hoped that the son would follow into business. At college he majored in economics, although as a young socialist he found himself at odds with the professors of economics "who were mainly apologists for the bankers on the board of trustees . . . people . . . who had a sympathetic interest in business without the competence to be businessmen." At one time he had thought he might teach, but his radicalism made him uncomfortable with the academic economists, hence, the teaching career never materialized. Neither did any other coherent and purposeful life-style. He went to Europe to go through the museums; he tried writing a bit; he read endless books on art and on society. All the time he was plagued with guilt that he had not accomplished anything. He settled in Hecate County because he could live there cheaply and get by with his small income. He did so in this prosperous territory by renting from friends of his relatives "a most remarkable place in the woods, situated on a charming little river, for considerably less than it was worth."

Here he covets his neighbor's wife and attempts to woo her by his superior culture, his sophisticated radicalism, his supposed superior taste and "brilliant" conversation. But always there is the guilt —never really moral in its origins (the narrator never seems to have given a second thought to adultery as such)—because he recognizes his limited achievement in society. "I was carping and sulking in my tent, I was shirking the dust and heat. . . . I was missing something very important: the real dignity and glory of life. After all, despite his limited intelligence, Ralph Loomis had in some sense earned Imogen." He had provided for her well—winters in New York, an Elizabethan house in the country, all the travel she wanted.

Unfortunately for the narrator's own sanity, his feelings of guilt point both ways: not only does he feel irresponsible in the eyes of his patrician family and neighbors, his own radicalism and progressive tendencies make him feel guilty that in his limited circumstances he can do nothing for the poor and underprivileged. Walking down Fourteenth Street in New York he reflects on the plight of the workers who made the shoes so nicely displayed in the window but were having to strike (this was 1929) because they did not have enough money to buy such shoes. "I had a vision of the economic system as a pitiful and disgusting fiasco."

Perhaps the perceptive reader of *Memoirs of Hecate County* will now have little difficulty understanding the title. The hero is literally haunted by these female spirits who keep popping up and down in his life—much like the witches of *Macbeth* perhaps. Each of them rises in turn from the mist, holding out a hand, some kind of promise, that can never be realized, or, if realized, only under cruel and deceptive circumstances like the coming of Birnum Wood to Dunsinane. Wilson's hero, like Macbeth, is clearly trapped in a murky environment, a forest of shadows and stale vapors from which he lacks the power and vision to extricate himself.

What should he have seen about these two women from the beginning? How is it that they are able to ensnare him in a web of social uncertainty and disharmony? The answer is, of course, that they are themselves out of joint with nature and with the harmony of the spheres. Like the other women encountered by the hero throughout the book they are in some very significant way displaced persons, spiritually unhoused, warped by cruel historical change.

Consider Imogen, the neurotic rich man's ornament, torn between the comfort and security of her husband's hearth and the vague promises from her lover that there is something more exciting in the world of art, bohemianism, and social reform. Since she has no firm ground to stand on herself, all she can do is lure her lover into her own unsure and treacherous waters.

Like Ellen Terhune, Imogen Loomis's childhood was outwardly prosperous and secure but inwardly injurious and traumatic. Her mother and father were unsuited to one another, their marriage a disaster. All this comes out one day when the narrator takes Imogen for a ride around Central Park in a victoria. She has never spoken of her family much before, but the presence of the horses reminds Imogen of her father who had been a horse fancier.

"I haven't seen him since I was seventeen. He treated my mother terribly—and he treated me terribly too." He was an Irishman, a great athlete in Ireland, a famous football player, very handsome. He had also been a war hero in the Sudan and had gotten all kinds of decorations. But after he returned from the war and came to America nothing seemed to go right for him. He had been lionized in his youth, but in America "he wasn't able to settle down to lead any ordinary life." He married Imogen's mother, a beauty of Swedish extraction, and tried to be a farmer because he had come from the country. "But he hadn't liked farming at home, and he could never put his heart into it when he tried to be a farmer." He took to drinking and did horrible things to both mother and daughter. The mother was of patrician background, although her family had lost its money before coming to Minnesota. Nevertheless she maintained the pretensions of aristocracy and did not mingle with the lower-class Swedes of Minnesota. In well-rendered and perfectly typical Wilsonian detail:

She had only a few Swedish friends—and the evenings when they came to see us, my mother and they used to carry out all the aristocratic Swedish drinking customs. You can't drink unless you ask somebody to drink with you, and the hostess invites everybody to drink in turn—and the gentlemen, when they lower their glasses, are supposed to hold them for a moment just opposite the third button of their uniforms or where the third button would be, and they look solemnly at the man that they're drinking with before they put them down on the table. But my father used to spoil it by getting drunk beforehand and drinking freely whenever he felt like it. (*Memoirs,* 171)

The daughter naturally sided with the genteel mother rather than the drunken father and made no attempt to contact the father in her adult life, though he continued to live in Minnesota. The result of this traumatic environment on Imogen is obvious. She reenacts and relives her mother's strained and attenuated gentility, but of course there is no way she can recapture the Swedish environment from which it sprang.

Imogen is not the queenly creature she believes herself to be. She fancies herself highly cultured and educated, but the conversations with which she beguiles the hero are superficial and trivial. Because he is as infatuated by her supposed beauty as an adolescent boy, he is perpetually reading great wisdom and subtlety into her coquettish remarks—probably because his mind is short-circuited by his frustrating attempts to bring her to bed. From the beginning of the story the two play games of deceptive flattery in which they assure each other that they are too good for their immediate environment. To escape the allegedly demeaning world of New York or Hecate County they spin out elaborate fantasies in which they imagine that they are moneyed and live in exotic places. Such fantasies only succeed in further maddening the hero who is getting nowhere with his burning quest to bed his great princess.

He is also held back for a long time by an obscure physical ailment she only hints at. This ailment turns out to be a bad back, for which she wears a tight and constricting brace. He goes to the library to look up something about spinal diseases and comes upon a book called *The Hysterical Element in Orthopedic Surgery* in which he discovers that "many of these so-called back ailments are nothing but neurotic shams." When after two years of torment he puts aside all of the fantasies and talks Imogen out of the back brace for a few hours, he finds sex to be both an excruciating triumph and a vast disappointment. Her body is perfection itself—no sign of any spinal curvature or any need for a brace—so perfect in fact that it seems only partially real. "I found that I was expressing admiration of her points as if she were some kind of museum piece." Her female fluids make "things easy for the entrant with a honeysweet sleek profusion," but this seems to have only the effect of desensitization. "She became, in fact, so smooth and open that after a moment I could hardly feel her. . . . The delight of the climax, when it came—even with her there in my arms—did not somehow connect with my vision" (251, 253).

After his sexual encounters with Imogen it becomes clear that he has been caught up in a game of deceptive counters, that all along there has been nothing—no substance, no solidity, no earth, no sex. Even before the final confrontation with Imogen the narrator clearly perceives that Anna is quite different. "The world of Anna was the real world, the base on which everything rested." He meets her at a dance hall on Fourteenth Street in New York and asks her for a date. She is slim and pretty, and when he talks to her he can see that she comes from the immigrant neighborhoods. Her name is Anna Lenihan and she comes from a Russian/Jewish background. Quite surprisingly the quality of her intelligence is good—there is nothing "common" about her. At least her desperate working class background has given her a solidity, a reality.

She had in a sense never even been Americanized—that is, she had never been vulgarized as many children of immigrants were, who, in adapting themselves to our cities, had acquired bad manners and a blatancy that, for some reason, seemed much more offensive than any mere peasant crudeness of their parents. She had a Brooklyn pronunciation of English—an accent worn down on the lips of the crowd as the long Brooklyn pavements had been by their feet; but she had somehow, in simplicity and humility, escaped this New World barbarization. I recognized her temperament as Russian—or, more specifically, I suppose, Ukrainian: for she had little of the Russian volatility, and the cadences that were sad in her voice expressed a deadening of resignation rather than the Russian complaint. She was naturally cheerful, well-balanced, amiable, considerate and sensual, as the Slavs of southern Europe are: and there had survived through so much that was degraded and harsh, so much that, it seemed to me, was nightmarish in her life, a clear little power of perception and a cool little faculty of judgment, a realistic sense of the way things were that had never become embittered, a sensitiveness of feeling that had never been dulled and a humor that had never been coarsened. (206)

Here, of course, the far finer and more discriminating voice of Edmund Wilson is drowning out that of his narrator. We can see why it is that the narrator's relationship with Anna is so much more real, the sex so much more earthy and meaningful. She instantly drags him out of his stale Hecate County environment and puts him in touch with what is real and human in his own existence.

She would chide me in her straight little way when I had done too much drinking and she always knew at once and was anxious when my nerves were under strain. I found I could talk to her about dissonances between members of my family and the fantastic behavior of my friends. Whenever it was a question of relationships, she seemed perfectly to understand. When I showed her pictures of paintings, she went directly to the figures as people, commenting on their physical characteristics and probable personalities. She appreciated things that amused me as few women of my acquaintance did. She always noticed very clearly herself what people did and how they talked. And on my side I was never bored by her stories about her family and their neighbors, which were told quietly and were never repetitious. (231-32)

There is a great deal of additional information about Anna in Wilson's diaries of the twenties, but it all points in the same direction. This more simple rudimentary character gave the narrator (and of course the young Wilson) his first breath of freedom from the artificial environments in which he had been reared—whether of high society, of scholarship, or of circumspect sexuality.

Unfortunately, none of this is enough for the narrator's salvation —whatever it may have been for Wilson. He has wandered through a wasteland, a sexual wilderness in which his search for any kind of meaningful relationship is frustrated and defeated at every turn. He himself and his two lovers stand on the kind of quicksand that had become so characteristic of life in America at that time—personalities that were too weak to stand up against new and more powerful environments, social backgrounds that were confusing and ambiguous or must operate in a foreign or incompatible context. "The Princess with the Golden Hair" is one more poignant rendering of Wilson's view of American social impermanence and moral indirection.

The last two stories in *Memoirs of Hecate County* are less interesting than those before them. "The Milhollands and Their Damned Soul," is a satire on business but, more specifically, the cocktail circuit of the publishing industry. It is amusing reading but seems to fit in rather mechanically as if it were *de rigueur* for Wilson—a moral lesson he felt he had to recite after a number of years of agitated exposure to the New York literary scene. The second of the two stories, "Mr. and Mrs. Blackburn at Home," would also be of little literary interest except that in a kind of wild crescendo it brings together all the specters, all the sour hallucinations that haunt the hero throughout the book. The story contains some hint of what could have been, what might be. It is a giant hallucination, perhaps a prolonged drunken stupor. In it the narrator at one time imagines himself to be Blackburn, a wealthy Hecate County socialite and party giver. He imagines his girl friend Jo Gates to be Mrs. Blackburn. The significance of the Blackburns is more than clear, as is the special significance of their being "at home." For some time the narrator had been thinking of the Blackburns as representing home, the solid established virtues of Hecate County. But in this last fierce struggle to set things right, to put things in perspective, he sees the Blackburns as representing not something solid, something real, but something as artificial in its own way as the more obviously damnable Milhollands.

The story is entirely one of moods, of coming in and out of darkness, perhaps in and out of hell. At the opening of the story it seems as if the murky vapors are beginning to lift from the horizon and the narrator is about to perceive the America he really belongs to and wants to live in. The story begins with these reflections:

I kept thinking all through one summer that there was something about the American landscape which made you feel that it had just been discovered. This was true even in Hecate County, which was so full of gardened and arranged estates and of "developed" suburban roads. *America:* it suggests to us even now a landscape unfamiliar and wild. When I looked out over an inlet from the sea, I would feel, for all the white moored launches and the graded lawns on the opposite side, that we had sailed into some uncharted estuary and weighed anchor in some virgin harbor, with its pale opaque gray-blue waters, brackish and almost tepid, tranquilly rippled with evening: its large birds of which I did not know the names flying slowly by the shore that had bred them; and its wooded and grassy banks that still seemed, though the houses had already been built, such a good place to build a house, to find at one's ready disposal all the best that a rich soil could afford and not to be bothered by neighbors. There were adventures and new forms of life over there beyond the thick summer foliage—there were leisure, refreshment, romance. (395)

After a few more drunken hallucinations of himself as a social arbiter and genteel party giver the narrator begins to see his way back to a simpler more uncorrupted America. He sees that one can go back to a kind of life where neighbors do not matter even if they are near by; that the things that really count are one's personal reserves; individualism; the land; nature.

"Mr. and Mrs. Blackburn at Home" is set in the 1930s, and in the story the narrator finds himself fighting with the demonic forces of socialism, fascism, and unbridled American democracy, the frustrations of which force him to the conclusion that in the end he can find no salvation except in himself and in the more elemental parts of his nature. Rushing from the Blackburns' house he returns to the haven of his "old stone house." He dreams now that he is talking to his old childhood friend Si Banks, that they are recalling their common love for the *Ingoldsby Legends.* This recollected love of literature and the bond of affection for Si remind him of the simplicity and honesty of his youth; remind him that he had once been "silently in love with excellence and unable to take quite seriously the respectable pursuits of my elders." Unfortunately, there is no real hope that the narrator can find a haven in this friendship of his youth: Si Banks has become completely drunken and demoralized, the vestiges of his childhood little more than sentimental slobberings.

In the end the hero is forced into isolation, to a belief in eccentric individuality as the only possible salvation in his land. But there are some comforts for the individualist who draws from the deepest wells of his experience. There is a reserve of honesty, of culture; there is a place to retreat to, even if there are neighbors there. There is always something about America that makes you believe "that it had just been discovered," that it is there to be discovered over and over again.

8

Our National Wound

Patriotic Gore is Edmund Wilson's finest work. In every sense it is a perfect manifestation of his literary methods, a showcase for his highest talents, and a triumph of the historical style of literary criticism.

The book was many years in the making. Wilson proposed it to the Oxford University Press in 1947, but apparently he had been thinking of it a number of years before that. In the midst of the composition he stated that "my original idea was to write a book about American literature of the period after the Civil War, but I became so interested in the period of the war that I decided to do a book about it." It was undoubtedly the period of his father's youth, a period whose mysteries he had long hoped to unravel, that intrigued him, for in his original letter to the Oxford University Press he mentions authors such as Edith Wharton, Frank Norris, Clyde Fitch, and George Santayana, all of whom were left out of the final Civil War book (*Letters,* 608-9).

In another early description of the book, Wilson said that the book—the title of which had not yet been chosen—"will differ from those of Van Wyck Brooks in being more critical and less historical" (ibid., 609). In the end it was a magnificent work both of literary history and literary criticism that attempted to deal with the literature generated by the Civil War and to show how it reflected our national mood and style. At the same time it illuminated some problems historians commonly neglect, entangled as they are with the outward public surfaces of things. The book assumes that these neglected areas contain some of the most intimate and essential problems of our national life.

Wilson worked on *Patriotic Gore* between 1947 and 1961, and a great many of the chapters appeared in the *New Yorker* during those years. Writing the book was Wilson's major occupation during this period: it governed much of his reading at that time, influenced the political thinking of the latter part of his life, and was the basis for numerous shorter works such as *The Cold War and the Income Tax* and *Apologies to the Iroquois,* in which Wilson's suspicion of modern states, later forcefully expressed in the preface to *Patriotic Gore,* is reinforced.

During these same years, Wilson continued to work in all of his long-established areas. It may be that he surprised the world by the publication of the *Scrolls from the Dead Sea* (1955), but by the 1950s Wilson's breadth of taste was so taken for granted that none of his literary exploits was startling to the public. While working on *Patriotic Gore,* Wilson updated and reissued some of his old travel books, as in *Red, Black, Blond and Olive,* his old journalism, as in *The American Earthquake,* and some plays and poems, both old and new, as in *Five Plays* and *Night Thoughts.*

Wilson also continued his successful and profitable association with the *New Yorker* during these years. After his stint as literary editor, Wilson sent the *New Yorker* many of his short pieces during the forties, fifties, and sixties, and that magazine became in the long run a more reliable outlet for Wilson than the *New Republic* had been during the twenties and thirties. All but a few of the essays in *The Bit between My Teeth: A Literary Chronicle of 1950-1965,* first appeared in the *New Yorker,* and the diversity of the *New Yorker* material gives some idea of the harmony that existed between Wilson and the *New Yorker* editors, and doubtless the *New Yorker* style as well.

The Bit between My Teeth, containing short pieces that came out during the years *Patriotic Gore* was being researched and written, is a collection of rich and generous miscellany. A number of the essays are clearly spun from the Civil War project, including "The Holmes-Laski Correspondence" (the last chapter of *Patriotic Gore* having dealt with Justice Holmes, who had been a Civil War veteran), "Cavalier and Yankee," and "James Branch Cabell, 1879-1958." Of the forty-seven essays in the book, twenty, or nearly half, deal with purely American topics, and many of the others, such as those concerning language, dictionaries, grammar, and so forth, discuss conditions of American culture and American intellectual life.

Readers of *The Bit between My Teeth* will find many of Wilson's American interests represented once again. There are fresh essays (mostly book reviews) on Mencken, Van Wyck Brooks, Scott Fitzgerald, John Peale Bishop, James Branch Cabell, and numerous others. During this period Wilson was doing somewhat less traveling than he was in the thirties and was far less active as a journalist, but his scholarly interests were being newly refined and expanded. In a piece entitled "George Ade: The City Uncle," Wilson exhibits a renewed virtuosity as an Americanist, combining his historical erudition with his deepening interest in language. "George Ade: The City Uncle" was written about the time that Wilson was starting his research on *Patriotic Gore* and shows qualities that Wilson was to display so well in that later work. In *Patriotic Gore* he carved out a large topic from American literary history that had been imperfectly worked in the past and that could call forth the best from his talents and literary training. It was his first and only large canvas of this kind. Because of the breadth and diversity of the final product, because of the stubborn eccentricity of its point of view, the book met with varied reactions from the reading public; it is, nonetheless, clearly one of the best books ever written on American literature.

After many years of research and writing, and after a great many of its essays had appeared separately, *Patriotic Gore* was published in 1962. The public reception was mixed, with some reviewers declaring it to be a major work of American literary history, others professing to find defects either in its historical thesis or in its literary biases. Most of the critical reservations seem to have been the product of false assumptions about the nature and scope of the book. Since the book was publicly reviewed both by historians and literary scholars, it is no surprise to find that criticisms of the book take several different directions.

At the beginning there was a certain amount of confusion about what *Patriotic Gore* was all about. The book, subtitled *Studies in the Literature of the American Civil War,* deals largely with the period between 1850 and 1880, although in the process of treating writers who were strongly influenced by the war, Wilson follows some careers to 1920. In fact, Justice Oliver Wendell Holmes, who is the subject of the long last chapter of the book, was a young soldier in the Civil War and did not die until 1935. The book is not chiefly, as one might immediately expect, a treatment of the literature *about* the war but rather a study of the relationship between the war and the American psyche. It is a highly personal work, idiosyncratic,

allusive, strangely rhythmical—a cloth of many colors and textures—
and its diversity perhaps accounts for many of its real or imagined
weaknesses.

Like all of Wilson's books this is an intimate personal document
that develops his own biases, interests, and thoughts, sometimes to
the exclusion of subjects that most people might ordinarily expect to
find treated in such a book. The book can be nerve-racking to those
who look for every new book about the Civil War to be a mere filling
in of detail within a framework already set out. Bruce Catton complained in his review of it that "the point of view is clearly set forth,
but the 'objectivity' is that of the Debunker; the most impassioned
and pontifical objectivity you are likely to meet in a long long time."*

The objectivity may well be, as Catton insists, "impassioned" and
"pontifical," but it is very doubtful that the book has a *single* point
of view. The thesis that Catton is speaking of, and which is set forth
in the introduction, is not exactly intended as a controlling point of
view for the entire work. The introduction is simply another individual essay of Wilson's, consisting of some accompanying thoughts that
go with the book; but it is by no means the keystone of it. Doubtless
Wilson did not start out with this thesis; the first chapter is surely an
afterthought, in harmony more with his thinking of 1962 than 1947.

The thesis offered in the introduction is that there is a quantum
of violence in human nature, but that man, unlike some of the lower
animals, seeks to put a moral cloak over his violent activities and
develops justifications of his wars; the vast number of men simply
take these moral justifications at face value. The moral hypocrisy and
cant of territorial aggrandizement is easy to see in other people, says
Wilson. We Americans, for example, can see through the process
whereby Russia swallowed up some of the Eastern European nations
under the guise of establishing "people's democracies"—this is just
a matter of greater power overcoming a lesser power, much like a
sea slug gobbling up some simpler organism. "It is, however, very
difficult for us to recognize that we, too, are devourers and that we,
too, are talking cant" (xiii).

The Civil War (and Wilson gives a number of other examples
from American history) was merely a power struggle of our own,
overladen with our own war cant, our own brand of specious idealism. The impulse toward unification was strong in the nineteenth
century, and Lincoln was merely one of the leaders of this movement
—others were Lenin and Bismarck, who functioned as forces for

*In *American Heritage* 12 (August 1962): 110.

unification and the concentration of power in their own nations. We Northerners, of course, cannot see this of Lincoln, for to do so would be to penetrate our own moral armor. The Southerners, on the other hand, perceived the war as a power struggle and spoke quite freely of Lincoln as "a bloody tyrant," but, naturally, they, too, had their myths and, upon losing the war, their own fraudulent reasons for having lost. The conclusion is merely that though war is war—a human weakness and perversity—its moral righteousness must always be justified if it is to be tolerated, if it is to capture human emotions. Power naked and unabashed has probably never been self-proclaimed in any human society. Even Hitler's annexation of Czechoslovakia was done in the name of freeing certain German citizens who were being "mistreated."

Such as it is, this is Wilson's thesis about war—all war, including our own Civil War—but it is in no way *the* thesis of *Patriotic Gore*. The book itself does not have a single thesis; it has an intention, which is to describe "some thirty men and women who lived through the Civil War, either playing some special role in connection with it or experiencing its impact in some interesting way, and who have left their personal records of some angle or aspect of it." In treating these people, says Wilson, "I have mainly presented them in terms of their immediate human relations and of the values of their time and place, and I have tried to avoid generalizations and to allow the career and the character to suggest its own moral" (x-xi). One of the objections to *Patriotic Gore* was that it is not a very complete survey of the Civil War literature. Charles P. Frank, for example, in his study of Wilson, complains that this book is not very satisfactory as criticism because it hardly concerns itself with the major writers of the period—that there is very little about Melville, Whitman, Twain, and James, and when on occasion Wilson does discuss these giants he may refer to a second-rate work. But Wilson's conceptions of literary criticism and of history were not the standard and conventional ones. For Wilson the only imaginable kind of literary criticism was that which fell into the domain of creative literature; the only imaginable kind of history was, as Benedetto Croce said some years earlier, contemporary history, that is, history that had been assimilated and digested for current use. Wilson had very little patience—for himself at least—with what Croce called chronicle, or with what R.G. Collingwood called "scissors and paste" history—a simple reshuffling of conventional and already accepted views. In Wilson's view, criticism and history must be entirely new makings or they are not worth doing. And they must somehow give us insight into our own contemporary life, or they are

wasted efforts. *Patriotic Gore* is a work that weaves together, carefully and methodically, biographical, historical, and textual criticism
into uniquely imaginative writing. Wilson's first commitment is to
the totality of experience—American experience—and biographical
material, aesthetic criticism, and conventional history are brought
into play when needed to shed some light or this experience, never
as ends in themselves. The result is highly imaginative writing in
which Wilson becomes the designer of the rich canvas he sets out to
create. He selects the detail and the points of emphasis, adjusts the
lights and darks, the tone and pigment, the intensity, the spatial
effects—aiming to pull off a fresh portrait of a cluttered landscape.
No assumption is made that the landscape could not be painted a
different way and might well be so by the very same artist on a
different occasion. There is only the assumption that the landscape
needs doing, that it needs to be looked at with a fresh eye, that the
existing visions are stale, flat, and uninspired—drawn only from
stereotyped glimpses, from commonplace judgments. For Wilson,
the art of criticism always involves setting out anew to capture a
completely original portrait.

In *Patriotic Gore* there are a number of essays dealing with some
of the major public figures of the war years (Lincoln, Grant, Sherman,
Alexander Stephens); there are a number of others dealing with
private figures who either had a great influence on contemporary
thinking at the time of the war (Harriet Beecher Stowe), or who
somehow, through individual creative gifts, cast light on American
life of the day, and who have not been adequately treated in standardized accounts of the period (the southern women, Kate Stone,
Sarah Morgan, and Mary Chesnut, for example); there are portraits
of a number of people who were deeply affected by the war, having
been exposed to shocking combat (Ambrose Bierce), and others of
people who avoided combat entirely but were psychically involved
in it nevertheless (Henry James); there are studies of figures whose
exposure to the war was short (Justice Oliver Wendell Holmes) but
who, on close examination, mirrored the war and its aftermath in an
important way and continued to be influenced by the war over a
period of many decades.

The first essay of the book discusses Harriet Beecher Stowe who
provided, in *Uncle Tom's Cabin,* one of the most compelling literary
documents of the nineteenth century—one that can serve as an excellent point of entry into the literature of the Civil War. But ultimately the study of Mrs. Stowe is a variegated one, contributing a
number of ingredients to Wilson's panorama, and the actual influ-

ence on the public of *Uncle Tom's Cabin* is only one of a number of points Wilson raises about Mrs. Stowe and her work.

Wilson's approach to the main figures in his drama is to look at them from a number of different angles—using biographical detail or psychological analysis, historical background or close textual study, where needed, always with the intent of arriving at a contemporary vision, a fresh portrait of a person who has been treated in stale, shopworn, or stereotyped ways. In the case of Mrs. Stowe, a number of new things need to be said, so it is naturally in the ultimate selection of new angles that Wilson's peculiar gifts as a critic sparkle.

Naturally, the essay begins with *Uncle Tom's Cabin*. Wilson gives us first some curious facts about the popularity of the novel that might superficially seem unimportant. One does not wonder at all that the book sold extremely well in the 1850s—in the first year after it appeared in 1852 it had sold 305,000 copies in America, and something like two and a half million copies around the world. Its influence in the prewar years was tremendous, and it is no wonder that Lincoln greeted Mrs. Stowe at the White House with the remark, "So this is the little lady that made this big war." Needless to say, after the war, the novel declined in popularity and eventually went out of print (not to be reprinted until 1948, when it was taken up by the Modern Library series). It is often assumed that the reason for this decline is that the novel was merely a piece of propaganda and did not deserve to live in its own right. Curiously, however, the book continued to be read in Europe and was a very popular book in Russia until the Revolution of 1918.

Uncle Tom's Cabin is quite unlike our working stereotypes. The stereotypes were formed in the post-Civil War years when adaptations were made for the stage and emphasized either the absurdly comical or the absurdly melodramatic elements of the novel. By the late 1870s, *Uncle Tom's Cabin* had become "half a minstrel show and half a circus." For people born late in the nineteenth century or in the twentieth, the public knowledge of the main characters is distorted: many grew up believing that Simon Legree was a Southerner rather than a New Englander, an overseer rather than a plantation owner (these ideas probably arose from a telescoping of episodes in the more far-fetched versions of the play).

But with the stereotypes and popular mis-readings cast aside, what have we? Coming to *Uncle Tom* as mature adults in the middle of the twentieth century we have a startling experience awaiting us. "The first thing that strikes one about it is a certain eruptive force." The story came suddenly upon Mrs. Stowe, and she expressed the opinion that some power had taken hold of her and made her write the book—almost as if God himself were writing it. And this, said Wilson, is precisely the impression the book makes on the reader.

Out of a background of undistinguished narrative, inelegantly and carelessly written, the characters leap into being with a vitality that is all the more striking for the ineptitude of the prose that presents them. These characters —like those of Dickens, at least in his early phase—express themselves a good deal better than the author expresses herself. The Shelbys and George Harris and Eliza and Aunt Chloe and Uncle Tom project themselves out of the void. They come before us arguing and struggling, like real people who cannot be quiet. We feel that the dams of discretion of which Mrs. Stowe has spoken have been burst by a passionate force that, compressed, has been mounting behind them, and which, liberated, has taken the form of a flock of lamenting and ranting, prattling and preaching characters, in a drama that demands to be played to the end. (5-6)

The book is exceptional in a number of other ways as well. For all the awkwardness in the writing, the poor quality of the narrative, the deeper we get into the novel the more we become aware of a critical mind at work. We feel that the author has a firm grip on the characters and carefully controls and coordinates their interrelations. Also, we have before us a "whole drama of manners and morals and intellectual points of view which corresponds somewhat to the kind of thing that was then being done by Dickens, and was soon to be continued by Zola." More important, though, as far as Mrs. Stowe's intellectual qualities are concerned, there is the taut, intent objectivity of the work. *Uncle Tom* is a piece of moral and intellectual analysis on a high level, and Mrs. Stowe was able to look at the subject of slavery—kept so discreetly hidden and undiscussed before the appearance of her book—with a candor and objectivity that startled all her readers. "She has nothing of the partisan mentality that was to become so inflamed in the fifties. . . . She is national never regional, but her consciousness that the national ideal is in danger gave her book a desperate candor that shook South and North alike" (8).

But Wilson finds a great deal more of interest in Mrs. Stowe than what he has to say about *Uncle Tom's Cabin.* In fact, he devotes only nine of the fifty-five pages of his essay on Mrs. Stowe to that work, though he is quite adamant that none of her later works are of comparable quality. Apparently he believes, and this is characteristic of all his critical writing, that if we are to draw close to the essence of Mrs. Stowe, we must do a lot of spadework around the periphery; we must approach her again and again, from this angle and that. He

follows his discussion of *Uncle Tom* with a long biographical segment
that shows us how deeply interwoven her works are with her theological background. Her father, Lyman Beecher, was a famous Presbyterian preacher of his day, and she was married to a less successful
clergyman, Calvin Ellis Stowe (with whom she enjoyed something
less than an idyllic relationship), so naturally the theological background sheds light on her point of view in writing *Uncle Tom.*

The psychological analysis and biographical detail that are spun
out at considerable length have an even more important aesthetic
significance. With this analysis we get some clues to Mrs. Stowe's
strengths and weaknesses that might otherwise be hard to come by.
For example, Wilson leads us to see that for all her national idealism
in *Uncle Tom,* Mrs. Stowe's life was largely circumscribed by the
conditions and partially oppressive atmosphere of the parsonage.
What accounts for the disappointing quality of Mrs. Stowe's later
novels? Why is there the slackness of the narrative line, the failure
of dramatic imagination, the wordiness "that tends to blur con-
tours"?

The answer is largely that Mrs. Stowe was not really strongly
interested in imaginative literature. She believed, of course, in books,
ideas—in religion as an organ of morality. But "Mrs. Stowe did not
much care to read novels; the sermon was undoubtedly the literary
form by which she had been most deeply influenced. . . . It evidently
bores her to contrive a plot, and she comes to depend more and more
on conventional Victorian devices, which she handles in a more and
more perfunctory way" (33). Doubtless, too, this lack of genuine
interest in literature is responsible for some of the vagaries of her
language, for the clichés and "homely incorrectitude" that charac-
terize all her work from beginning to end.

Yet, despite this great deficiency, Mrs. Stowe continues to be an
interesting writer today. She never writes rubbish; all her works
manifest an ability to think critically. She has an obvious talent for
pinning down character. Even if she has no ability to thrill the reader
of today as a teller of tales, she does manage to shed light on nineteenth-century America. Arthur Schlesinger, Jr., once remarked of
her that she is a "great repository" of American history. The area in
which her observational powers are keenest, the area in which she
is most obviously a repository of some value, is the religious life,
perhaps we should say the religious ambiance of the nineteenth
century. She was a bit of a religious thinker herself: she was familiar
with all the hotly contested issues of New England theology; she
knew with precision the ins and outs of contemporary church politics

and history. Harriet Beecher Stowe knew what the insides of ministers' households were like—how they were furnished, how the housework got done, how ministers related to their families, and she was able to preserve for us a wealth of information on these subjects that might otherwise be lost to posterity. The characters in her novels of clerical life, like those in *Uncle Tom,* are quite vivid and forcefully "present the varieties of religious experience in terms of milieu and character."

The essay on Mrs. Stowe is a fine example of one side of Wilson's considerable achievement as a critic. I refer to his achievement as a man of humane letters, to his concern for his readers, to the broader educational and public-spirited side of his work. For what he has tried to do is explain why we should be interested in Mrs. Stowe, whether the effort of looking into her is worthwhile, what she can and cannot tell us about her time—he weighs the pros and cons of all this painstakingly. He does this more with a view to giving us an educated general portrait of her and her work than he does to developing elaborate aesthetic judgments—although he brings in a great many aesthetic judgments along the way. This kind of generous consideration of his reader's interests is an abiding characteristic of Wilson's literary criticism. Consider for example, the variety of perspectives in the following reflection:

The conversations in Mrs. Stowe's novels are likely to become rather boring because they go on too long—verbosity is one of her most serious faults—but they always show a very strong sense of what human beings are as well as of what they think or what they think they think. The feature of Harriet Beecher Stowe which prevents us from reading her today and doing justice to her exceptional intelligence is not only, however, this verbosity but our reflex shying away from the accents of the old-fashioned parsonage in which she habitually addresses us: the earnestness and fervor of the minister's wife who sympathizes so much with sorrow, who mimics the humble so charmingly, who does hope so very sincerely that the weak and misguided will mend their ways. The best way to read Mrs. Stowe—except, of course, *Uncle Tom's Cabin*—would be probably in a volume of extracts which gave specimens of her social criticism, her intimate historical insights and the scattered reminiscences of her own life which she wrote down in various connections. (47-48)

Here Wilson is sharing with us his own tastes, the drift of his own thinking, but he is also keeping in the forefront of his mind such questions as: Should the educated public of today read Mrs. Stowe? If so, how should she be read? What work of hers should we look at? What way might she be most congenially studied? Such diversity is one of the main ways in which Wilson's criticism differs from so much scholarly criticism: he never starts with the assumption that there is a standardized body of problems to be tackled, that the critic's own interests must necessarily be everyone else's interests simply because the critic has happened to set foot in this or that bailiwick. For Wilson, every topic must be weighed and evaluated in general terms, in the human idiom, to find some common way of discovery, some shared area of interest that all people of our time might have in common.

The essay on Mrs. Stowe is not by any means the most important in the book, but it illustrates most of Wilson's virtues as a critic—his ability to reread the shopworn and find something new in it, his matchless skill in creating a well-balanced medley of a number of themes (psychological, historical, aesthetic), and his ability to direct of all these toward the general reader who might be devoted mainly to literature, but who might also be devoted to history, or to the American character. Wilson's charm is that he can speak to any and all of these interests with perfect clarity and vigorous expression.

The essays in *Patriotic Gore* are sometimes of surprising length and scope. The essay on Lincoln, for example, is quite short, and not one of Wilson's best, but we need not assume that Wilson was completely uninterested in Lincoln, although he has said that he was uninspired by his father's large collection of Lincolniana and made "a point of knowing as little as possible about Lincoln" (*Piece of My Mind*, 226), or that he played Lincoln down because it fitted the thesis of his book to do so; it is more likely that because this ground had been plowed so often and so long Wilson could not whip up much enthusiasm for it, and hence he paints a lukewarm and unambitious portrait.

The essays covering several of the other major public figures of the North turn up some of Wilson's best writing. The studies of Grant and Sherman are masterpieces of their kind and dazzle us with their skill. Grant and Sherman are distinctly different personalities, but one thing they have in common is that neither has come into focus in any of the strictly historical interpretations. By and large, both have been much in need of generous applications of the imagination, although they have largely been denied this treatment in the past.

Consider the portrait of Grant, the better of the two, although there are some respects in which the Sherman essay is more spectacular and treads upon even more difficult ground. Grant's rise to fame, his deep reserve of strength, has always been something of a mystery, and Wilson makes an attempt to fathom these. But there is also the considerable mystery of Grant's literary style, which glimmers in luminous intensity in his *Memoirs* and had already become apparent in his battle commands and memoranda. Quite interestingly, the *Memoirs* have intrigued a number of writers besides Wilson, including Matthew Arnold (who mentioned them favorably in his *Civilization in the United States*), Gertrude Stein, and even Henry James, who, in a review of a volume of Grant's letters, spoke of "a ray of the hard limpidity of the writer's strong and simple *Autobiography.*" Wilson believed Grant's *Memoirs* to be one of the most remarkable documents of its kind, and he fully agreed with Mark Twain, Grant's publisher, that it ranked quite favorably with the *Commentaries* of Julius Caesar. It is also, he said, "like Herndon's *Lincoln,* or like *Walden* or *Leaves of Grass*—a unique expression of the national character."

What is so unusual about Grant? In what sense is he a unique expression of the national character? His rise was much stranger than Lincoln's since Lincoln had always been politically ambitious; at the very least he had always been hardworking and effective: there had been no slumps in his career. Grant's career was one of ups and downs. He never gave the impression of having much ambition. He went half-willingly to West Point; he opposed the Mexican War and had no real desire for a military career; he tried a number of occupations—selling real estate, clerking in a customs house, running for county engineer—and failed at all of them. At one point, when he was living in St. Louis, he was considered a hopeless deadbeat, and people sometimes crossed the street so as not to meet him—fearing that they might be hit up for a loan.

But, says Wilson, "It was characteristic of Grant that a period of moral collapse should have been followed by a period of intense concentration." Wilson saw in Grant a number of American traits: the ability to set in order a turbulent personal life, the ability to achieve singleness of purpose when put under pressure, fearlessness, simplicity, modesty, clarity of mind and thought. It was the bringing together of these virtues out of the ashes of a broken career, an ordering of them into a coherent whole, that accounted for Grant's greatness as a general and as a writer.

Not all of these virtues were clearly evident to Matthew Arnold, who met Grant in England and was not impressed; Arnold found Grant's bearing and manner undistinguished (Arnold, of course, discovered *no* really distinguished or highly refined Americans). The language of the *Memoirs* Arnold at first believed to be without charm and breeding, but when he looked at the *Memoirs* again, some of its virtues started to come into focus.

> But at the same time I found a man of sterling good-sense as well as the firmest resolution; a man, withal, humane, simple, modest; from all restless self-consciousness and desire for display perfectly free; never boastful where he himself was concerned, and where his nation was concerned seldom boastful, boastful only in circumstances where nothing but high genius or high training, I suppose, can save an American from being boastful. I found a language straightforward, nervous, firm, possessing in general the high merit of saying clearly in the fewest possible words what had to be said, and saying it, frequently, with shrewd and unexpected turns of expression.*

Wilson is even more generous in his praise of Grant's *Memoirs*. He finds Grant's style vigorous, terse, epigrammatic, and, above all, like the orders he wrote on the battlefield, models of perfect clarity. The *Memoirs* are not only of high literary quality, they are perfect expressions of the man behind them and reveal the nature of his military genius. "These literary qualities, so unobtrusive, are evidence of a natural fineness of character, mind and taste; and the *Memoirs* convey also Grant's dynamic force and the definiteness of his personality. Perhaps never has a book so objective in form seemed so personal in every line. . . . What distinguished Grant's story from the records of campaigns that are usually produced by generals is that somehow, despite its sobriety, it communicates the spirit of the battles themselves and makes it possible to understand how Grant won them" (143-44). *Memoirs* stands as a revelation of his military skill and vision and also as an expression of his own strength of character and inner reserve.

The extended treatment of Grant's prose style is a matter of recurring importance as the tapestry of his book is enlarged. In the next to the last chapter of the book, there is a long discussion of "The Chastening of American Prose Style," which considers the changes in American prose style that were being made in the years during and immediately following the Civil War.

In the years before 1850 American prose was generally rather bad, although Wilson does find a few social and moral advantages in the older styles of writing that usually took as their model the sermon or political rodomontade. But the fiction of the time was almost completely dominated by verbose and untidy writing. "Fenimore

---

*From Arnold's *Civilization in the United States,* quoted in *Patriotic Gore,* 139.

Cooper imitated Scott and wrote even worse than he." Hawthorne, Melville, and Poe were, of course, more disciplined, but even these "embroidered, or, perhaps better, coagulated, their fancies in a peculiar clogged and viscous prose characteristic of the early nineteenth century" (636). The same was true of oratory. Wilson agrees with Thomas Wentworth Higginson's view that early nineteenth-century oratory—in the days after the republic-founding era of Washington, Jefferson, and the Adamses—was monstrous, pretentious, contrived, falsely intellectual, verbose, and quite without genuine human passion. Higginson's book, *American Orators and Oratory*, which Wilson quotes at some length, reached the conclusion that Lincoln's Gettysburg Address and John Brown's speech at his trial were "the two high-water marks of our public speaking," and that after this time the American language became more efficient and functional, that the pace became firmer, that the plethora of words was reduced.

The war itself was part of the reason for the marked improvement in American prose style. The war had a startling impact on the pace, the lucidity, the precision of writing. Grant and Lincoln both exemplified this trend, although they came from somewhat different backgrounds. It was not, as some might suspect, that both had come from the West and had a local habit of homely speech. Western eloquence had a drawl about it; it was slow and expansive,

but Grant and Lincoln were both quick thinkers: no drawl is to be heard in their writings or in the framing of their reported opinions. . . . What was it, then, that led Grant and Lincoln to express themselves with equal concision? It was undoubtedly the decisiveness with which they had to speak. They had no time in which to waste words. To temporize or deceive was too dangerous. (650)

The war affected not only the writing of the figures of great public importance, it affected writing everywhere. Newspaper writing changed considerably during the war: editors were insisting upon swifter writing, upon greater brevity and simplicity. Too, Northern efficiency, the progress in mechanical techniques, the growth of American business and industry during and immediately after the war, helped deflate the pompous and time-consuming statement. Eventually all of this had an important effect on our literature. After the war, "a sobriety, a rigor of logic was to impose itself on the writing of essays and fiction." This is striking, too, "in the new kind of craftsmanship that gives its structure to the American story from Ambrose Bierce, let us say, to O. Henry" (648). The American story soon became an art form of surefire effectiveness, of cultivated brevity, and this, needless to say, was a cultural development of utmost significance.

Ambrose Bierce was one of the postwar literary figures whose prose was not only chastened by the war but whose literary art was largely shaped by it: a combat soldier who carried his war wounds throughout his life, Bierce brought the tragedy of war into his writing over and over again. Wilson's study of Bierce weaves together with neatness and precision the psychological, the historical, and the aesthetic, bringing them into a harmonious organic whole—the Wilsonian style of criticism at its best.

First, Wilson sees the war as having had a tremendous impact on Bierce psychologically; it was responsible for his lifelong obsession with death, with the dark and evil side of life. The fact is that Bierce saw the war at its worst, firsthand, and was terrified by it. Not only terrified, he nearly lost his life on the march to Atlanta with Sherman. At Kenesaw Mountain his head was, as he later remarked, "broken like a walnut," and he was actually given up for dead. Stories such as "An Occurrence at Owl Creek Bridge," "Chickamauga," and "The Major's Tale," are obvious fabrications built on his own personal experiences of the war.

There is evidence, however, that Bierce was somewhat obsessed with death before the war—that the war merely reinforced an already existing neurosis. Wilson repeats the content of a dream Bierce had at the age of sixteen that indicates a strong preoccupation with death, solitude, and desolation; so we must conclude that Bierce's psychological trauma was of long standing, going back to childhood. Part of Bierce's trauma was the result of his family background, his lack of an education that he always felt keenly. He had been born in a log cabin and spoke of his parents as "unwashed savages," although this was something of an exaggeration. All the evidence shows there were books in the Bierce family home and some signs of a stable culture. But Bierce became obsessed with his lack of a formal education: he dreaded "the man with the diploma," or anyone who had achieved any kind of eminence in life. It may be, says Wilson, that this also accounts for his preference for unattractive women. He himself was remarkably attractive to all women, but he always sought out the ugly ones, perhaps so "he would be in the position of conferring the favors on *them* and would not have to fear competition."

But in his shattering wartime experiences we have the clue to Bierce's strengths and weaknesses as a writer. It was because of his sense of insecurity that he "developed the standards of literary style that he carried to such pedantic lengths." He despised American colloquialisms, Wilson tells us, and wanted nothing to do with dialect literature.

> The best qualities of Bierce's prose are military—concision, severe order and unequivocal clearness. His diction is the result of training and seems sometimes artificial. . . . Bierce was aware of his crudeness, and . . . he resolutely struggled against it. But there was something besides the crudeness that hobbled his exceptional talents—an impasse, a numbness, a void, as if some psychological short circuit had blown out an emotional fuse. The obsession with death is the image of this: it is the blank that blocks every vista. . . . His writing—with its purged vocabulary, the brevity of the units in which it works and its cramped emotional range—is an art that can hardly breathe. (631-32)

In this example of the lavishness and scope of Wilson's style of criticism, the biographical and historical substance is a wellspring of supporting detail for the judgment and the close textual analysis of the critic and provides him the wherewithal to shape a disjointed cluster of ideas about an author into an intelligible whole.

The final essay of *Patriotic Gore*—that dealing with Justice Oliver Wendell Holmes—is a fine example of the intense mental effort and well-honed creative imagination necessary to bring a portrait of this kind to fruition. Wilson finds that Justice Holmes, like Bierce, was strangely influenced by the war. He was injured, not once, but at least three times. On one of these occasions he, too, was given up for dead. Still, the horrors of the war never quite took the toll on his psyche that they did on Bierce's—at least not in an overt way. Although Justice Holmes had a very difficult time in the war, he had an obvious ability to insulate himself against it.

In Wilson's eyes, this inner reserve was largely due to the impregnable security afforded by Holmes's Boston Brahmin background. Holmes, unlike Bierce, was raised with the conviction that society persists, that there is something solid to come back to, that however destructive the war, however carelessly war treats its participants, life, experience, society will go on.

The war was less than the ultimately formative experience for Holmes, although his thought, his manner, his personal style, were crucially altered by his wartime experiences. Wilson believed that the war made a tough, purposive, disciplined man out of Holmes. Furthermore, it helped strengthen a strongly bred Puritanism, making it more rather than less severe at a time when Boston religion was heading for the softness of Unitarianism (in the two Holmeses, father and son, "the theology of Calvinism had faded, but its habits of mind persist").

Holmes's actual views of the war itself are exceptionally interesting and shed light on his later legal career. Wilson tells us that Holmes had little interest in reading about the war, or in defending it. Like Wilson himself, Holmes was skeptical of most of the ideals of the war as expressed on either side. He never became sentimental over Lincoln, nor did he hold any brief for the civility of the southern gentleman. Holmes was never impressed by moral absolutes: "Pleasures are ultimates," he wrote to Laski in 1926, "and in cases of difference between oneself and another there is nothing to do except in unimportant matters to think ill of him and in important ones to kill him." Out of the war Holmes developed a philosophy of *force majeure*. In time of war the established authority has a right to suppress a rebellion against that authority by war (that is, killing), if necessary, and in time of peace has the right to enforce the laws that it has passed. The war brought Holmes to a realistic view of the law. He saw that the law was a sacred code, which meant that it must be defended by resort to arms. The law constantly had to undergo change to meet historical circumstances. Holmes "always saw it as a complex accretion, a varied assortment of rules that had been drawn up through more than a thousand years and which represented the needs and demands of people existing in particular places at particular periods of history" (765).

Intellectually speaking, therefore, we can see a bridge between Holmes's conservative view of the state and his pragmatic view of law. We can also see how he earned a reputation as a liberal in later years. His youthful experiences and his family background bred in him both a rigid, conservative side and a flexible, pragmatic, liberal side. And these two sides of his personality combined to make him a thinker of the first rank.

He also became a great American writer, and his greatness was due to the supreme breadth of his interests and to his desire to relate the law to the larger scheme of things—to culture and society.

It is Holmes's special distinction—which perhaps makes him unique among judges—that he never dissociates himself from the great world of thought and art, and that all his decisions are written with awareness of both their wider implications and the importance of their literary form. He was not merely a cultivated judge who enjoyed dipping into belles lettres or amusing himself with speculation: he was a real concentrator of thought who had specialized in the law but who was trying to determine man's place, to define his satisfactions and duties, to try to understand what humanity is. It is this that makes Holmes's correspondence, as well as his more formal writings, so absorbing and so fortifying and a very important part of his *oeuvre*. In spite of his strong negative predispositions, he will not relinquish a fundamental skepticism as to human convictions and systems, and he is always alert and attentive, always inquiring and searching, to find out some further answers. (781)

Still, for all his erudition, for all the clarity of expression in his writing, Wilson finds in Holmes a grave shortcoming that goes back to his wartime background and also to his Puritan heritage. Despite the fact that Holmes, as a justice of the Supreme Court, had a strong sense of the relation of the law to the affairs of man, he also believed that the life of the law is not logic but historical experience. There remained in Holmes a strong feeling that one's purpose is not to change others but to justify oneself. In Wilson's mind, Holmes was something of a "jobbist," that is, "one who works at his job without trying to improve the world or to make a public impression. He tries to accomplish this professional job as well as it can be accomplished, to give it everything of which he is capable. The jobbist is alone with his job and with the ideal of touching the superlative—which in his grandfather Abiel Holmes's time would have been called being chosen for salvation" (789-90).

It was Holmes's great weakness that he cared much more for "general propositions" than for facts. "I never knew any facts about anything," he wrote to Sir Frederick Jackson Pollock, in 1904, "and always am gravelled when your countrymen ask some informal intelligent question about our institutions or the state of politics or anything else. My intellectual furniture consists of an assortment of general propositions which grow fewer and fewer and more general as I grow older" (792).

How much this tendency toward abstract thought is due to Yankee austerity and want of human generosity, how much of it is due to Holmes's wartime experiences, and how much to other factors (Wilson does not mention the possibility, which is exceedingly strong, that the law itself as a discipline and as a lifelong vocation contains pitfalls that lead to a generalizing of all thought processes), is difficult to determine. Still, we see Holmes not only as a product of his own historical time but as a representative American type. At the end of the essay on Holmes we see not only an effort to understand Holmes's literary skills and the breadth of his education and culture but the probing of an American life-style that has long been with us and that Wilson always found intriguing—partially, of course, because it is the kind of experience he had been trying to fathom since his youth and upon which he became our most definitive authority.

Patriotic Gore contains a great many more essays, some of which are every bit as powerful and original as those already discussed. Some of these concern political figures, others literary figures. On the other hand, some major figures are slighted or not even mentioned. Henry James is slighted, albeit wittily and craftily, although what Wilson has to say in ten pages is worth a book-length study by a lesser critic. Wilson spends a great deal of time with three Confederate women—Kate Stone, Sarah Morgan, and Mary Chesnut—whose diaries are, for the most part, long-forgotten, but who, although not of high importance either to our history or to our literature, succeeded in probing beneath the surface of the slogans and catchwords that grew up about the war both in the North and South. Again, these seemingly minor works are not so minor when rescued by the skilled historical critic; they serve to catch some of the flavor, the nuance, the more subtle vibrations of the Civil War period, the essence of *Patriotic Gore.* This work searches for the elusive, the nonobvious; it seeks to penetrate every crevice where there is a possibility of guiding light. The effort requires both the intuition of the artist and the vision of the historian.

Patriotic Gore is Wilson's best book. It ties him firmly to the American experience to which he always belonged and from which he could never conceive of being separated. *Patriotic Gore* is both a great intellectual synthesis and a magnificent product of our imaginative literature. As an investigator of the subterranean passages, the roots of our literature, Wilson stands out above all his contemporaries. He not only knew how our civilization has flowered, but why—he probed beneath the soil and knew the extent and direction of its source. In *Patriotic Gore* he has told us how we lived and breathed.

9

The Decadence of
the Democratic State

In the last several decades of his life Edmund Wilson became an increasingly dyspeptic critic of democratic politics and of the generally lax moral tone of the government of the United States. His writings of this period reveal a growing disenchantment with big government in all its forms—not only the totalitarianism of the communist states but also the overblown bureaucratic democracy that he saw getting out of hand in his own country.

Wilson's attitude was somewhat perplexing to many of his friends and perhaps to the intellectual community at large. What had become of Wilson the liberal thinker of the 1930s? What had happened to the *New Republic* writer who had visited the coal mines, the dust bowl, the urban tenements, and who had hoped to light the way in America for some healthy brand of European socialism?

Actually Wilson's essentially humanitarian sympathies never wavered. They were always firmly rooted in individualism and in a cussed independence from all large and impersonal institutions. For this reason he found little more that he liked about the political developments of the 1950s and 1960s than he did about those of the 1920s and 1930s.

Often during this period Wilson's friends tried to draw him into one or another political orbit, usually without success. During the brief Kennedy interregnum, Arthur Schlesinger, Jr., who accepted a public office himself, tried to convince Wilson of the Kennedy charm and of the righteousness of the "new frontier." Although Wilson was ready to believe that Kennedy was a step above the platitudinarian

Eisenhower, he remained skeptical and held to the belief that even
the best of politicians in a large state must remain half charlatans.
Wilson pretended to be pleased, if a little incredulous, that both Jack
and Bobby Kennedy had read his works (*Letters,* 632), but he never
had any faith that they were either statesmen or serious thinkers.

Wilson saw the great Kennedy bubble of the early 1960s as an
extravaganza. In 1962 he wrote about Jack Kennedy to Alfred Kazin:
"I think you somewhat overrate his literacy. His historical allusions
are likely to be inaccurate in a way which suggests that he cannot
really have read much history. I suspect that his pretensions to 'culture' are largely worked up by Arthur Schlesinger." But it was not
so much an absence of culture that bothered Wilson about the Ken-
nedys; it was their close identification with the unsavory game of
politics. Wilson could hardly fail to perceive the irony when President Kennedy (probably at the behest of Schlesinger) awarded him
the Freedom Medal, even as the United States government was
prosecuting him for income tax evasion. A decade later he was stung
by another irony when President Nixon gave the same "Freedom
Medal" to DeWitt Wallace, publisher of the *Reader's Digest* (ibid.,
739). What, he thought, could the medals of politicians mean to
writers or individualists of any stripe?

Through all these years Wilson strenuously denied affiliation with
any of the usual political persuasions in America. In the middle sixties
he wrote to his old friend John Dos Passos, that "I have never regarded myself as a liberal, because the word doesn't mean anything
definite" (ibid., 643). According to Wilson, the liberal of recent vintage had completely given up all skepticism and swallowed all the
stale elixirs about the American way of life, the free world, and the
rights of man.

On the other hand, Wilson could tolerate even less the various
new flowerings of conservatism in the 1960s. John Dos Passos, who
would have agreed with some of Wilson's stabs at the stereotypical
liberal mind, wrote during the 1964 election to sell Wilson on the
Goldwater candidacy. Wilson's long affection for Dos Passos could
not keep him from delivering a stinging rebuke: "I was glad to get
the stimulating postcard. But I feel obliged to tell you that your
article about the San Francisco convention sounded like a teenager
squealing over the Beatles. What on earth has happened to you? How
can you take Goldwater seriously? His utterances make no sense and
have never made any. But you seem to have arrived at a state of pure
faith where such questions no longer mean anything." He saw Dos
Passos as having fallen into the trap laid by John Foster Dulles and

others of seeing Russia as threatening America with invasion. "I don't understand how at your age you can continue to believe in these bugaboos and see everything in terms of melodrama. It seems to me you are just as gullible as you were in the twenties" (ibid., 653, 643).

Wilson identified with none of the political faiths that captured Americans in the 1960s and continued with his sweeping skepticism of all forms of government, all political theories as we know them in the twentieth century. He continued his old Jeffersonian faith that some good ought to be able to rise from the will of a people. Like Jefferson, too, he believed that the governmental mechanism should be diminutive and unobtrusive.

᠀

Wilson's most incisive statement of his later political views is the one contained in the introduction to *Patriotic Gore.* This view surfaces again and again in books such as *Apologies to the Iroquois, The Cold War and the Income Tax, O Canada,* and *Upstate,* and in his correspondence and shorter pieces of the 1950s and 1960s.

For the Wilson of these later years, the most dismal tendency of the modern world was the growth of large, impersonal, and irresponsible political states—states that grow, swallow up all around them, and are unanswerable to the people who support them. In *Patriotic Gore,* Wilson illustrates this theory by making a historical comparison of the wars of the past two centuries. He believed that wars—most especially the American wars—show that the proliferation of states is directly related to a kind of biological power drive of which we can find numerous examples from nature: sea slugs, army ants, birds, baboons. From this evidence he concludes that "all animals must prey on some form of life that they can capture, and all will eat as much as they can." Man only differs from the lower form of animals in that his higher form of social organization and powers of linguistic reasoning allow him "to justify what he is doing in terms of the self-assertive sounds which he utters when he is fighting and swallowing others: the songs about glory and God, the speeches about national ideals, the demonstrations of logical ideologies" (xi-xii).

Whether and to what extent we can accept Wilson's view that the biological foundations of human life condemn mankind to be a devouring organism always pushed to eat as much as he can is not clear; yet there is a certain persuasiveness in the view that American history has largely been a history of territorial aggrandizement, settling down in the twentieth century into a kind of ideological aggressiveness in which we try to push our interests with such modified warlike cant as "The American Dream," The American Way of Life," "The Defense of the Free World."

Much of the introduction to *Patriotic Gore* is given over to Wilson's version of the growth of the American power drive since the infancy of the Republic. He shows that the Mexican War in the 1840s was nothing but a bold take-over of land coveted by the American government and partly inhabited by English-speaking settlers. The Civil War was a more successfully disguised development of the power urge. It was nothing but the struggle for dominance of two factions "that had become so distinct from one another that they were virtually two different nations; they were as much two contending power units—each of which was trying to expand at the other's expense—as any two European countries."

Certainly there can be little doubt that America's economic growth in the nineteenth century was largely achieved by aggressive acts of one sort or another and by the power surges of the federal government. There were the long struggles to wipe out the North American Indian and steal his lands. There was the obvious theft of much of the Southwest from a weak and disorganized Mexico. At the end of the century there was the notorious "Spanish American War," which even the more gullible historians have now seen as an undisguised power play.

For the Spanish American War there was the immediate provocation of the sinking of the battleship *Maine,* "though there was never any reason for believing that this had been done by the Spanish, and there is some reason for believing that it was engineered by William Randolph Hearst in order to set off a war." But even if the sinking of the *Maine* was not organized to feed the gaping jaws of yellow journalism, the war was a convenient front for American territorial expansion.

The jingoistic spirit of the 1898 war is undeniable, although Americans have never been ashamed of it nor of the gunboat diplomacy of Theodore Roosevelt that followed shortly thereafter. But in Wilson's eyes, Americans are never really comfortable unless their wars have a deep altruistic or missionary patina to them, unless they can discover, as in the case of the Civil War, a "treasury of virtue" about which songs can be sung and slogans generated.

World Wars I and II were the sorts of wars that Americans have immediately warmed to and readily taken to heart; in neither case were the purposes or the national involvement questioned by the populace. In both cases, the opposing sides were made to appear as calculating villains. In the First World War the "fatuous Kaiser" was blackened in a home front propaganda campaign even as President Woodrow Wilson at first assured everyone that we had no quarrel with the German people themselves. But once the United States got caught up in the power struggle and once we got involved with our European allies, President Wilson "was dragged into subjecting the enemy to an unnecessary unconditional surrender and imposing on them such heavy penalties that a second war with Germany was inevitable." With a real "Beast of Berlin" on the stage and concentration camps hovering in the background, the Second World War became even more "salable" to the general public than the first. Yet it was Wilson's belief that we were "furtively brought into it by President Franklin D. Roosevelt, who had been making secret agreements with the British but pretending, in his public statements, that he had not committed himself." What is perhaps less evident, but equally true, is that it was not Hitler's massacre of the Jews that brought us into the war—this was already far underway when the United States entered the war. "Roosevelt of course disliked Hitler just as Lincoln disliked slavery; but it was not the mass murders of Hitler that drove us into going into war, any more than it had been the wrongs of slavery that made us go to war with the South." Rather it was our fear of an expanding German sphere of influence, perhaps in South America by way of Africa, perhaps directly across the Atlantic if the German forces succeeded in defeating England (xxvi).

Too, the war with Japan was secretly hoped for by the government of the United States because the Japanese were threatening our commercial interests in China and had "become a new power unit expanding across the Pacific and making us uneasy about the Philippines." Of course the Pacific War was sold to the public on the grounds that we were invaded by Japan, but Wilson belonged to the not small minority who found room for skepticism on this little page of history. "The attack on our fleet at Pearl Harbor has become, in our popular history, an act of moral turpitude more heinous than the firing of the Confederates on Fort Sumter; but it has been argued, to me quite convincingly, by Charles A. Beard, Harry Elmer Barnes and others that this act was foreseen by our government and—in order to make our antagonists strike the first blow—deliberately not forestalled at a time when a Japanese delegation was attempting to negotiate peace" (xxvi-xxvii). However much truth there may be in this, there can be no doubt that the Pearl Harbor attack was a rallying point for the American people and made possible the vigorous pursuit of a war that otherwise might have appeared farfetched and gratuitous. There is much to Wilson's idea that the war with the Japanese, as with the Germans, was not a war of ideals but of conflicting interests—a struggle for supremacy.

The same may be said about the smoldering long-term conflict between Russia and the United States in the years after World War II. With Russia expanding her influence both in Europe and Asia during these years the people allowed themselves to be sucked into a government-sponsored paranoia about communism that was said to be a threat to the American way of life, though the threat to our shores was never clearly demonstrated. This hysteria led us into two wars, both very foolish, the Korean War and the Vietnam War, which were damaging to American power and American prestige. Above all, the great flourishing of arms and the name calling between the United States and Russia seemed to have no rational foundation, but simply to be the war whoops and jeers of two powers moving in on lesser peoples, most of whom found these two new powers no more popular than the earlier German and British empires:

The Russians and we produced nuclear weapons to flourish at one another and played the game of calling bad names when there had been nothing at issue between us that need have prevented our living in the same world and when we were actually, for better or worse, becoming more and more a-like—the Russians emulating America in their fanatic industrializing and we imitating them in our persecution of non-conformist political opinion, while both, to achieve these ends, were building up huge government bureaucracies in the hands of which the people have seemed helpless. (xxvii)

This view intensified in Wilson's mind during the 1960s, as is evident in the many letters and several books he wrote during that period that reinforce the same thesis from one angle or another. The thesis has never been popular in the United States, although it may have become ever so slightly popular during the Viet Nam War. It has never been popular because the United States government has become enormously efficient (perhaps more than any government in history) in disguising its intentions and anesthetizing its citizens to the proliferation and scope of its power.

In the years after he wrote *Patriotic Gore*, the United States became involved in the Viet Nam War—probably the most meaningless war in our history. During this period Wilson was to become increasingly involved with the more subtle questions of the style and conduct of our government. He never devoted himself fully, or even significantly, to the Viet Nam issue, but his writings of the period relentlessly searched out the primal causes that made such a foolish exploit possible. For the first time since the 1930s Wilson turned his sights on the larger political and social problems of our national life and tried to show the practical applicability of his theory that modern states act blindly, unfeelingly, in their insensate drive for power and self-expression.

In the last two decades of his life Wilson was neither young enough nor healthy enough to be a working journalist. We have from his pen no work that is the counterpart of *The American Earthquake* with a frontal attack on social problems of contemporary life. On the other hand, in books like *Apologies to the Iroquois* and *The Cold War and the Income Tax* Wilson used his old eccentric vision of things, his astigmatic individualism to make a characteristic attack on the flank. Sidestepping the monstrous complexity of the political giant, he instead took the sidelong historical approach to seek out the monster in its den, to discover how it came to be what it is, how it went off the track. The typical American of the present wants to confront the monster of government only as he has become habituated to it from the daily newspaper. He believes that its abuses are minor peccadillos that may with luck be talked away—or voted out. Never is the question raised of where the monster came from and whether its presence does us ill.

Wilson believed that Americans take too much for granted about their national government and that they are among the most guileless and easily duped of people where politics are concerned. They are repeatedly fooled by the abstractions and the shibboleths of politics and politicians, even when in many other respects they are a skeptical and doubting people. Wilson's counterstrategy was to come at our entrenched beliefs from an odd angle, to get deep down into the physiological processes of our intimate history; in differing ways, this was his approach in books such as *Apologies to the Iroquois, The Cold War and the Income Tax,* and *O Canada.* In these books he hoped to catch us off balance by returning to complex questions of fundamental morality, common humanity, and the universal sense of simplicity and fair play.

Apologies to the Iroquois was conceived and written during the years that Wilson was doing his monumental work on the literature of the Civil War. It appeared, however, three years before *Patriotic Gore* and was published by Farrar, Straus and Cudahy in 1959. It is a book that received relatively little attention for a reason that Wilson himself clearly understood. Americans are not very much interested in their native Indians unless they are framed in a romantic or otherwise contrived and harmless setting. But this fact makes it even more important to observe that *Apologies to the Iroquois* is one of Wilson's best books—inventive, searching, idiosyncratic, eruptive, and disarming. In the end he catches, naked and exposed, one of the great American character weaknesses, the tendency to believe that if you take no notice of the disagreeable it will go away. The Indian problem has not gone away and will not go away; it has lingered on as a thorn in our side, long after Indian civilization has been knocked down and paved over by an encroaching urban society. Wilson began the book as an apology to the Indians who lived in his own beloved upstate New York and about whom he knew shockingly little. In the end he offered his readers further evidence of the mindlessness and injustice of the state and further evidence of America's lack of historical sensitivity, our inability to live except in the present, our inability to get nourishment from our cultural roots, from the land we live in and the air we breathe. *Apologies to the Iroquois* reaches out for a fragmented and much concealed piece of Americana, but in doing so it brings us up with a start. It thrusts before us a picture of ourselves as it might be seen from a mirror at some strange angle—a view of our national image that we prefer to remain shadowed in darkness. Here is a book about Indians, a people still in our midst who can show us—if we give them a moment's thought—that we latter-day Americans have given up our once-cherished independence, our love of the land and open spaces, our love of a real indigenous culture in the face of one that is meretricious and standardized.

Wilson took time out of his long labors on *Patriotic Gore* to write *Apologies to the Iroquois* because he had been drawn to the subject through a curious set of circumstances. In the summer of 1957 he knew virtually nothing about American Indians and smugly assumed, like most Americans, that there was not much to know. But that summer he was visited by a young English writer at Talcottville and, driving back from the county fair, the visitor asked what had become of the Indians that lived in that part of the country. Wilson replied that there were only a few of them left, almost all in reservations. In answer to a question about the Mohicans Wilson told his young friend that these were the same as Mohawks.

Shortly thereafter Wilson learned some unsettling things about New York state Indians. He read a story in the *New York Times* about a band of Mohawk Indians, under a chief called Standing Arrow, who had established a new settlement on Schoharie Creek, near Amsterdam, New York. These Indians claimed that they were occupying land that had been granted to them by the United States in a treaty of 1784. In reading this account Wilson was amazed to find that the large tract of land that was granted to the Indians in 1784 included, or nearly included, the piece of land his own forebears had acquired at the end of the eighteenth century.

His curiosity aroused by this strange discovery, Wilson paid a "journalistic" visit to the claimant, Chief Standing Arrow. He soon began learning some very startling things about New York Indians. He learned right away that the Mohawk Indians were not the same as Mohicans, as he had confidently told his English visitor, but rather one of the six tribes of Iroquois people in upstate New York that had formed themselves into a league, or confederation, around 1570. These six tribes, which have linguistic similarities, are the Mohawks, the Senecas, the Onondagas, the Oneidas, the Cayugas, and the Tuscaroras. By the middle of the twentieth century all of these tribes still existed, just as they had both separately and collectively long before Europeans arrived in North America.

Wilson learned a number of other things about the Iroquois Confederacy. In the early days of European expansion, the confederacy was the only group of Indians recognized as a real nation by the governments in Europe. England, Holland, and France sent ambassadors to the confederacy. The Iroquois Confederacy was the only nation of Indians on the new continent that was never conquered and the only one recognized as a sovereign government. This was well known in colonial times; indeed Benjamin Franklin had been influenced by the example of the Iroquois Confederacy in an early proposal of uniting the American colonies.

Standing Arrow told Wilson a few things about the social life of the Iroquois, explaining that though the six nations are the political unit of the league, the fundamental social unit is the clan. The clans are all named after totems of various sorts: mammals, fish, birds, even plants. Men are free to marry women from other clans but cannot marry women from their own clans. Too, a man's wife's brother, who belongs to the wife's clan is responsible for his children; every man is responsible for the children of his sisters. In the argot of the anthropologist this is called a matrilineal society, which means not only that the clan line descends through the mother but actual authority is vested in her as well. "The senior woman of the clan, known as the 'clan mother' names the chief or chiefs for the clan" and thus maintains a very elemental kind of control. "This dominance of the female," observed Wilson, "has made for a certain conservativism and hence guaranteed a certain stability" (52).

The Iroquois were a people of strong social traits, of national and historical solidarity. It is no wonder that they were dealt with gravely and respectfully by the European settlers and their governments back home.

After the Revolutionary War was over, the Continental Congress agreed to dismiss all grievances against the Iroquois tribes that had fought for England, and the treaty of Fort Stanwix (now Rome, New York) which Standing Arrow showed to Wilson, recognized the equalities of the two nations—Iroquois and the United States—and "recognized the sovereign title of the Confederacy to their title forever, and agreed to protect them in the event of any encroachment whatsoever 'as long as the grass grows and the water runs.' "

But if the Continental Congress intended to be fair to the Iroquois, the state of New York immediately proceeded to cheat the Indians of their land. Over the protest of the United States government, and without any authority from the six-nation government, the state of New York set about systematically taking over Indian lands, so that of the original 18,000,000 acres there are only 78,000 acres left.

One of the problems the Indians had, not only in New York but throughout the United States, was that they frequently made agreements in the white man's language that really gave up things they had no intention of yielding. Most Indians had no notion of land individually held and had no idea that in handing over land to the white man, they were excluding their own interests. The Indians who sold Manhattan Island to the Dutch for sixty guilders (twenty-four dollars), thought that they were selling hunting and fishing rights under conditions where white men and Indians would coexist and share the fruits of the land. The idea of exclusive rights of fee simple ownership was beyond anything in their social experience and their language. Linguistic barriers to communication, and the sheer deceit and dishonesty of the white man, reduced the great Iroquois nation to a negligible force and a vastly diminished population.

But in visiting Standing Arrow and other New York Indians Wilson discovered that despite everything the Iroquois had not been completely eradicated. The few that were left were well prepared to fight for their cause and prevent their remaining lands from being taken away. Wilson wrote his book before the new Indian movement began sweeping across the nation in the 1970s, but his book is devoted in no small part to the active efforts that had been made by Indians to stand up against governmental efforts to rob them of their few remaining lands.

Wilson discovered, for example, that a Mohawk reservation south of Montreal had been destroyed to make room for the Saint Lawrence Seaway. Wilson visited this site and was told that bulldozers had simply broken down the homes of the Indians who refused to leave. One woman even saw her home crushed before her eyes while she was hanging out clothes on the line. "I saw one of those bulldozed houses on the St. Regis reservation," said Wilson, "as a symbol of the fate of the individual at the mercy of modern construction."

Indian power was only beginning to reassert itself during the 1950s, but *Apologies to the Iroquois* contains the stories of some tenacious Indians and their efforts to overcome new bureaucratic assaults on Indian landholding. One chapter deals with the resistance of the Tuscarora Indians to the attempts of the New York State Power Authority and its autocratic chairman, Robert Moses, to build a 700 million dollar hydroelectric plant that was supposed to use the power of Niagara Falls. This project involved condemning part of a Tuscarora reservation, 1,383 acres, in order to flood it as a storage reservoir in seasons when the water runs low. Slyly, Moses picked on the Tuscarora reservation because it was free from property tax and thus no property revenue would be lost by taking it. Furthermore, "it seemed to Mr. Moses much simpler to evict from their humble-looking homes a hundred and seventy-five Indians living in thirty-seven houses than to disrupt the neighboring town of Lewiston, in which, as Moses later explained, it would be necessary to dig up two cemeteries, to demolish a million dollar schoolhouse and to destroy three or four hundred houses" (145-46).

The high-handed Moses, long an important power in the affairs of both New York City and New York state, tried to grab off the lands without so much as giving the Indians a hearing. But in the nick of time, before their houses were bulldozed, the Indians gained a hearing in Washington before the Federal Power Commission. Asserting the claim to undeniable use of the land that was guaranteed to them in the eighteenth-century treaties, the Indians began a long uphill fight in the courts, which they eventually won. (This was only the second time that one of Mr. Moses' improvement schemes had ever been thwarted: the first was when a group of women with baby carriages blocked bulldozers in New York City's Central Park from putting in a parking lot. The women got a playground instead.)

Indians had finally come alive to the fact that they could exert some force publicly, that they had certain quixotic public relations skills, and that they could tip things to their advantage in the mass media. In the next decade or so they would also gain substantial victories for themselves in the courts and some nationwide sympathy and understanding. Wilson's interest in the Indian cause was probably sparked not so much by their newly discovered social and legal weapons but by their persistent individuality, their dogged determination not to give up their older values and way of life.

The author of *The Cold War and the Income Tax* must have taken a certain delight in learning that the Mohawk Indians were resisting attempts by the federal government to withhold income taxes from their wages. They did so on the rather eccentric ground that as Indians they were "wards of the government" and thus not subject to taxation. When this nice ploy was thrown out of the courts, the imagination of the Indians grew even bolder. The hereditary confederacy chiefs appealed to President Eisenhower, pointing out that they were heads of a sovereign nation. They even threatened to take their case to the United Nations. They insisted that they were not citizens of the United States and thus not subject to its laws and obligations. (Indians had all been given citizenship by federal legislation in 1924, but the Indians claimed that they had not consented to this act.) Mainly, though, they did not conceive of themselves as living in the United States, so they could not be made citizens of it (97).

The plain truth is that the Indians had been robbed, tricked, cheated, and deprived not only of their land but of their culture. Only the most hardy and tenacious remained. In the two centuries since the Revolution, the Indians who were not killed off in the ways shown in Western movies succumbed to the white man's diseases. Indians were supremely susceptible to the newly found demon, whiskey, and alcoholism was long a blight of the Indian experience in America—further numbing the powers of resistance to external authority, further reducing the stability needed to maintain a culture and a state.

Still, strong pockets of Indian strength were maintained as America became industrialized and standardized. Wilson comments at length on the Indians' moral reserves, their passivity, their love of nature, their inexplicable whimsey. Wilson began his book by reprinting a 1949 piece from the *New Yorker,* "The Mohawks in High Steel," by Joseph Mitchell. The Mitchell piece told the curious story of how Mohawk Indians became bridge builders in North America. There was a Caughnawaga (Mohawk) reservation near the Saint Lawrence River where the Canadian Pacific Railroad wanted to build a cantilever bridge. The work was to be done by the Dominion Bridge Company, which, in obtaining the right to use some reservation land for the bridge abutment, had promised to employ Indian laborers whenever possible.

Much to the surprise of company officials, the Indians were excellent bridge builders. They were crazy about bridges and great heights. It was impossible to keep them off the structures and they were always walking around on the spans with the agility of mountain goats. A company official later wrote: "They would walk a narrow beam high up in the air with nothing below them but the river . . . and it wouldn't mean any more to them than walking on solid ground. They seemed immune to the noise of the riveting, which goes right through you and is often enough in itself to make newcomers to construction feel sick and dizzy" (14-15).

In time, the company decided to train Indians as riveters, and it was one of their most fortunate decisions. Putting riveting tools in the hands of Indians "was like putting ham with eggs." More than this, the training of these seemingly natural born workers on the high beam had important consequences for the Indians themselves. The Mitchell article describes how the Mohawks from the Caughnawaga reservation later took to the trail and followed major bridge construction projects around the United States. They were involved in the building of the Soo Bridge at Sault Sainte Marie, Michigan. In 1907 they worked on the great Quebec bridge over the Saint Lawrence River. In the years following they began activities in the United States where bridge building was obviously to become a much greater industry. In 1915 or 1916, a Caughnawaga bridgeman named John Diabo came to New York and got a job on the Hell Gate Bridge. He was followed by others and there eventually came to be something of a Caughnawaga settlement in the North Gowanus neighborhood of Brooklyn.

At Wilson's writing eighty-three Caughnawagas were members of the Brooklyn local of the high steel union (officially called the International Association of Bridge, Structural, and Ornamental Iron Workers, AFL), and another forty-two in the Manhattan local—although all lived in Brooklyn. In the years since the settlement of the Indians in Brooklyn they worked on a number of major bridge-building projects in the United States: the George Washington Bridge, the Bayonne Bridge, the Pulaski Skyway, the Triborough

Bridge. In New York City's building boom of the twenties and thirties they were hired in the construction of such buildings as the RCA Building, the Empire State Building, the Waldorf-Astoria Hotel, the Bank of Manhattan Building—and numerous others.

However interesting this piece of American industrial history, it was not as curious to Joseph Mitchell and Edmund Wilson as the persistence of the little Caughnawaga enclave in Brooklyn. Most of the Caughnawagas continue to own property on the reservation in Canada and go freely back and forth using a card issued by the Indian Affairs Office that they called a passport. They never became completely assimilated like other ethnic groups, perhaps because they continued to be birds of passage but also because their native traditions were almost impossible to stamp out. The children attend American schools for a while, read comic books, listen to the radio, play stick ball in vacant lots. But all adult Caughnawagas speak Mohawk; they are usually multilingual, speaking French and English also. The North Gowanus housewives are like American housewives in some respects, but they spend their spare time making Indian souvenirs: dolls, handbags, belts with traditional Iroquois signs. In the fall of the year, when not employed in structural steel, the Indians take vacations to state fairs in New York, Connecticut, or Pennsylvania where they sell some of their products. The men wear buckskins and feathers at these fairs and sleep in canvas tepees pitched in fairgrounds. They even make an awkward try at a wahoo or some half-forgotten Mohawk dance.

The life of the bridge-building Iroquois of Brooklyn may be untypical of the American Indian in the twentieth century. But Wilson must have enjoyed in this bit of curiosa some sense of his own identity with a small group of individualists who refused to melt in a melting pot, even as close as they were to the fire itself in the streets of Brooklyn. Like Wilson himself, the definitive trait of the Iroquois was their insistence on a strong stamp of historical individuality, their determination not to let their values fall apart in the face of unsympathetic social movements, ambiguous moralities, and heartless bureaucracies.

Edmund Wilson started his *Apologies to the Iroquois* because he was ashamed to find that he knew nothing about Indians—even those who lived in his own backyard. In concluding his book, though, he expressed the notion that not only he but many a white American might find in common with the Indian a desire to keep the cherished landscape from being obliterated, familiar sites and monuments from being bulldozed in the name of progress.

Returning last summer to the village in New York State in which I am writing this, I found that—to the horror of many of the inhabitants—a planting of splendid elms that had made a majestic approach to Boonville on the road that leads from Utica, was in the process of being chopped down in order to transform this road into a four-lane highway for trucking. I should have said, when I just started out on my travels in Iroquoia, that I myself was almost as much a member of a half-obsolete minority as these even more old-fashioned Americans of twenty thousand years ago, but I have come to believe that there are many white Americans who now have something in common with these recalcitrant Indians, that the condition of being an American, whether from A.D. or B.C. should imply a certain minimum security in the undisturbed enjoyment of our country. (286)

To the average white American of European descent it may seem strange that the Indian is still there to remind us of who we are and were. Strange relics of the past! But with our present so shoddy and uncertain, this firm and tenacious grip on a coherent and intelligible past brings us suddenly in mind of ourselves once again.

During the 1960s Edmund Wilson seemed to be more concerned than he had been even in the 1930s with the relationship between government and society, between the overweening power of the state and the helplessness of the individual. During this period he wrote his little book on Canadian culture, *O Canada,* which did much the same for his neighbors north of the border that *Apologies to the Iroquois* did for his Indian friends. *O Canada* might have been called *Apologies to the Canadians,* for it is another book about a people that most citizens of the United States have refused to know much about. The Canadians, of course, know a great deal about us. We, however, have little, if any, interest in their political life or their culture.

Thinking back to his youth, Edmund Wilson recalls the general neglect of Canada at that time. "We tended to imagine Canada as a kind of vast hunting preserve convenient to the United States. . . . There the men of my father's generation hunted big game and fished for salmon and trout. . . . In my youth, I always thought of Canada as an inconceivably limitless extension of the wilderness—the 'North Woods'—of upstate New York" (36-37).

But of course Canada is more than a hunting and poaching preserve of Wall Street bankers. It is another country with a different kind of people, a different style, a different flavor. Most obviously, although "Americans" tend to forget this, Canada is the English-speaking country that stayed loyal to the crown in 1776. Canadians remained British, are not "Americans." Another aspect of Canada that we seldom think about is that Canadian society is not melded. "It is a compartmentalized, not melded, community." Paradoxically, the United States, which has had many more peoples to absorb, has done a far better job of actually blending them than Canada. The most striking compartmentalization in Canada is between English- and French-speaking inhabitants. But there are others—the Scots, who have remained pretty much to themselves in Ontario. Even Nova Scotians are likely to refer to the rest of the "Dominion" as "Canada" or "Upper Canada." Inside Nova Scotia there is a kind of Cape Breton nationalism. There are Irish Catholics who do not mix with the French, and there are the Ukrainians, Poles, Russians, Icelanders, and Hungarians, all of whom "have been left to themselves," with no pressure to assimilate into the English-speaking culture (42-43).

O Canada is a collection of miscellaneous essays documenting Canadian distinctiveness and individuality. There is a long study of the Canadian novelist Morley Callaghan, and shorter notes on Canadian poets, novelists, short story writers, painters, and social thinkers. There is a thoughtful history of the French nationalist movement in Quebec, now woefully out of date but useful for the period it covers.

Wilson had been in Canada as a ten-year-old boy in 1905 but did not return until the 1950s, at which time he attended the Stratford Festival and paid a visit to Toronto, which was completely different from the one he had known five decades before. His interest in Canadian matters was piqued at this time and he talked the *New Yorker* into sponsoring an even more extensive Canadian tour in 1962. After returning from this Canadian tour, Wilson wrote his old friend Leon Edel: "I have just spent a month in Canada—Toronto, Montreal and Quebec—and had a delightful time." For the first time in history, he added, Canadian literature was becoming interesting. To another friend he wrote that "My Canadian trip did me good. . . . Montreal is now a delightful city—French restaurants, French theatre, French press—which is far from what it used to be; and it is a relief to visit Canada, because the Canadians are not under the horrible pressure that we are in the United States" (*Letters*, 631).

In *O Canada* Wilson was prompted to recall what Americans, especially those of the genteel classes, had thought about Canada in his boyhood. He was reminded of the myth of Antaeus that seems to have governed a peculiarly indigenous American pattern of experience—the necessity of renewing life by occasional contact with the land or primitive conditions of life, or the exploration of the wilderness. By the early 1900s there were few places left in the United States that held out much promise of openness or primitive wilderness. There was the West, perhaps, for the few who could get there. But for easterners of Wilson's father's generation it was Canada that seemed to keep alive the myth of Antaeus. "It was their pride to come back with trophies in the shape of mounted moose or stag heads or unusually large fish and glazed and exhibited on oval slabs. They liked to think they had been losing themselves, escaping from the trials and anxieties of a precarious commercial society, which was always uncomfortably oscillating between booms in which people made fortunes and crashes which might leave them stripped—a society in which genteel convention now ran contrary to the poker and whiskey which had been necessary to sustain their forebears" (36-37).

For the youthful and bookish Wilson, Canada was partly the evocation of the stories of Ernest Thompson Seton—a land of "huge forests, frozen lakes, large and dangerous animals," or of Frederic Remington's pictures of hunters and Indians shooting rapids in canoes and confronting towering antlers thrusting out of the dark woods. But when he returned to Canada in the 1950s it became immediately apparent to him that none of the Canadian visions that he had inherited from his father's generation, whether those of wildness and isolation or of an openness filtered through the gentility of art, really brought Canada to life.

Wilson's tour of 1962 was, as much as anything, an effort to ask certain questions: Who are the Canadians? How do they differ from us? How are they like us? What can we learn from them? How can we shake Canada loose from all of the working stereotypes? The quest was a moral and historical one, always resisting the customary formulas of the travel book or polite cultural exposition. Wilson attempts to capture the subject from a variety of perspectives, some of which are nothing but the obvious slipped in at an extraordinarily unexpected angle.

Among the most startling and unsettling of Wilson's truisms is the one with which he begins his book; namely, the simple fact that Canada was that part of the English-speaking colonies of North America that did not revolt against the king in 1776. Americans tend to forget that there is a long tradition in Canada according to which the United States and its people were troublesome and disloyal citizens of the king. These people the Canadians began referring to rather contemptuously as "Americans," as if *they* were not Americans also. "The Canadians remained British, so were never in this sense Americans, and we were for long and are sometimes still disapprovingly regarded as a society founded on disloyalty to the sovereign and the destruction of ancient traditions and devoted to exploits of a vulgar success which are impious in both their mutinous origins and their insolence in surpassing the mother country" (35).

It could be that in achieving its dominion status and a relative degree of independence, the traditional Canadian way of looking at the United States has shifted in emphasis. But there can be no doubt that the vast majority of Canadians (like many Europeans) continue to look upon Americans as upstarts who have charged recklessly down this pathway or that, neglecting ties with the parent civilizations, and failing to set down new and lasting traditions of their own. Canada, on the other hand, which kept its ties with the motherland, was not only able to profit by the wisdom of old-world civilization but was also able to develop its own native traditions more sanely and cautiously.

What does Wilson say of the Canadian claim to stronger and firmer traditions, to a more sedate and deeply rooted civilization? On some levels at least he seems in accord with it. He seems to have found that Canada as a whole, despite strong evidences of Americanization in cities like Toronto, had profited by its ties with European, and especially British, tradition. Even in Toronto, perhaps the most American of the large Canadian cities, you get a "British tradition of good order and capable handling." Everything in Canada seems less nervous than in the United States. You usually get better service at the airports and in the hotels, and the people in such public services are less hurried and more polite. In Canada things move at a more leisured pace. "To a man of my generation, it seems closer to the old American world."

Wilson found a number of things that annoyed him in Canada. For example he found the drivers in Toronto more reckless than in any American city; nevertheless, on the whole, he found Canadians less harassed, more willing to listen to rational argument, and more refined in conversation than their American counterparts. Above all, throughout the book runs Wilson's conviction that Canadians respond to the world with slightly more propriety and decorum than Americans.

Whether or not these generalizations are true, there seems to be no doubt that the causative factor is not that Canada has a less diverse or more homogenous civilization than the United States. Such is not true, as Wilson has said in another of his interesting reflections about Canadian culture. Canada has a much smaller population than the

United States, and most of this is clustered in certain areas, but one of the fascinating things about this smaller population is that its various ethnic parts are much more resistant to assimilation than those in the United States. Canada is "a compartmentalized, not a melded community; that is, it is not really a community." Thus in some ways (and surely in ways that must have appealed to Wilson with his pioneer individualism and hatred of worn-out communities), Canada has much more room for individual eccentricities and ethnic indissolubilities.

Everyone knows, of course, how the French, at least in eastern Canada, have refused to assimilate linguistically or culturally, and on this question Wilson devotes a great part of his book. But this was not the only significant compartmentalization in Canada.

The Canadians of Scottish extraction, with their parades led by kilted bag-pipers and their ritual dancing of the Highland reel, have imposed on the whole of Canada their pronunciation of words like *about* as something not far from *aboot,* but they do not seem to mix much with anyone else. There is even a distinct difference between the Highlanders of lower Ontario and the Highlanders of Nova Scotia, where Gaelic is still sometimes spoken. Nova Scotia regards itself, in fact, as more or less a country in its own right, much closer to maritime New England than to the prosperous Scottish business world of Montreal. (42-43)

It is a shame that Wilson, with his interest in language, did not do a bit more in *O Canada* to discuss the question of the difference between Canadian and American English. In general it is safe to conclude, as Mencken did years ago in *The American Language,* that Canadian English is more closely related to American English than it is to English English. And this is becoming more rather than less true. There are a number of holdovers of English words in Canada such as *charwoman* for 'cleaning woman,' and *pram* for 'baby carriage.' But non-American pronunciation is fading. *Clark* for 'clerk,' heard in Canada fifty years ago, is heard no more. There are other oddities mentioned by Wilson, but many deviants that seem to be holdouts are fanciful and contrived. On Montreal and Toronto radio stations one hears the word *schedule* pronounced with the *sch* soft in the English manner, but this must be an affectation since one does not hear it from the man on the street. Perhaps it is preserved as a means of maintaining some kind of un-American nicety and national self-identity on the radio.

Undoubtedly the ethnic minorities and perverse regionalism of Canada appealed to Wilson, who found such forces being stamped out in standardized America. Not only are they accountable for a greater individualism and deeper toleration of cultural diversity, but doubtless they are responsible for much of the charm of the large Canadian cities. New York and Chicago, especially the former, have always been melting pots of the foreign born, but whatever cosmopolitan air these cities have has not been due to this cultural melange but to strictly uniform American qualities; Montreal and Toronto, on the other hand, seem genuinely cosmopolitan cities, where various ethnic groups flourish with some style and gusto, not merely waiting for the inevitable melting and standardizing process to catch up with them.

It might still be that much of the reason for the greater toleration of ethnic diversity in Canada is related to the fact that the country is much more sparsely populated than the United States, much less urbanized, and there is always a greater chance of using the vast land area of the country as a safety valve that guarantees people the kind of respite that the moving frontier gave to Americans in the nineteenth century. At the very least, as Wilson said, "It is true that the people of Canada, widely scattered and with their rugged climate, are more conscious of geography and weather than we usually are in the United States" (76)—a fact that Wilson nicely documents in Canadian novelists like Hugh MacLennan. Above all, a closeness to nature and a feeling for space is much more highly developed in Canadians than in Americans, at least in recent times.

Of course Americans had their great nature lovers in the nineteenth century—one need only think of writers and artists like Emerson, John James Audubon, or William Cullen Bryant—but invariably American literature of the twentieth century treats closed places, people living too close to one another. Even a writer like Robert Frost, who celebrates the desolate upland hills of Vermont and New Hampshire, really has as a primary concern the fact that people breathe too heavily on one another, that "good fences make good neighbors." Of course this is not to suggest that the densely industrial and conformist world of twentieth-century America has no rich possibilities for literature—obviously quite the reverse is true—but Canadian culture continues to hold out promise of the commodiousness and airiness of a more orderly and dignified social life than that enjoyed to the south, and this has clearly contributed to what might be called the Canadian national style.

This is not to suggest that Canada lacks its own social problems and social diseases, some clearly of its own making, others imported from the United States and abroad. There is nothing in Wilson's book to suggest that he thinks that Canadian politics are less silly and destructive than the politics of the United States, although a small population and a greater land area may always give the impression of a political life slightly less frenzied and corrupt. But the truth is that Canada suffers from most of the disorders of populism that plague the United States and adds to them some of the British diseases of mindless and suicidal strikes and trade unionism. Self-destructive social welfare is rampant in many provinces and perhaps even at the national level, and this has often brought governmental agencies to the point of bankruptcy. The financial condition of the province of Quebec is nearly as hopeless as that of the city of New York, with much less excuse.

Some of these problems, admittedly, have arisen or become exaggerated since the time of Wilson's book, but Wilson was never one to hold out hopes for intelligent government in the modern industrial and populist democracies—he was, after all, an apologist for the more elitist forms of responsible citizen democracy advocated by the founding fathers of the United States. In recent years the Canadians have deviated as far from these ideals—if not further—than the Americans. Government is largely by factions and pressure groups with few visible signs on the part of the citizenry of a sense of commonweal.

One salient feature of Canadian life that was certain to have attracted Wilson's attention was the schism between the French and English languages and cultures, a phenomenon that is most striking in Quebec but not limited to that province by any means. Additionally, it is obvious that Wilson would have been instinctively somewhat sympathetic to the French movement, which in the early 1960s had not yet fully become a separatist movement (the separatists were not nonexistent at that time but were a decidedly small minority of French-speaking citizens).

With his love for eccentric social behavior, his love of stubborn independence, his championship of the underdog, and his long-standing interest in the phenomenon of language, it is only natural that Wilson should have become interested in and even sympathetic to the French Canadian cultural plight. Thus it is not surprising to find that nearly a third of Wilson's book deals with the French Canadian problem, even though that problem had not yet caught the attention of American newspaper readers and cultural observers.

Americans had long been aware, of course, that in Quebec there was a cultural and linguistic schism and that this had existed throughout Canadian history (or more precisely from the time of the English conquest of Quebec in 1759). But the details of the friction between the two cultures—to say nothing of the history of it—were shadowy in the land to the south, even a few miles away in New York state or Vermont.

Wilson provided a brief historical sketch of the English/French problem in Quebec that quite clearly made the point that the conquest of French Canada did not in itself give birth to any kind of anglophobia among the French but made conditions ripe for it. At the same time, except for a short period at the beginning, the English gave no thought to stamping out French culture and language or the Catholic religion. But the English moved in to completely dominate trade and commerce while the French were left high and dry by their early masters. The French, said Wilson, "found themselves at a disadvantage in not possessing a bourgeoisie. After the victory of the British ... the French administrators and *commerçants*, who could no longer look forward to careers in French Canada, for the most part packed up and went home. They left a few seignorial estates, a small professional class, an unambitious and illiterate peasantry and a priesthood that came to be the mainstays of the otherwise unenlightened parishes" (179-80).

The result of all this was not immediate conflict, but the development of two cultures of markedly different character. Although the French were independent enough, they lacked the knowledge of the hardheaded business and political techniques, and control of everything important passed to the hands of the sovereign English. The French were not persecuted or disturbed; they were just allowed to go their way as a kind of shabby and poor relation with an inferior language and a backward religion.

Such a situation could eventually be counted on to bring trouble, although with the exception of a few minor skirmishes, the English and French did manage to work out most of their difficulties until well into the twentieth century. French political leadership was either weak or corrupt, or merely exploited for purposes of the personal aggrandizement of its leaders. A good part of Wilson's chapter on the French is a discussion of the long and almost dictatorial rule of French Canada by Maurice Duplessis who for more than eighteen years (1936-1939 and 1944-1959) was the premier of Quebec and ruled over the province much the way Frank Hague ruled over Jersey City or Richard J. Daley ruled over Chicago.

The rule of Duplessis according to Wilson, and according to the various books that have appeared on the man subsequent to his death, rested on two foundations. The first was a belief that French power ought to be able to expand and ought to be felt by the English, even if only as an irritating pinprick. The second was that the whole show had to reflect the power and personal image of Maurice Duplessis. To be sure, now as never before, the power of the French-speaking majority was something to be reckoned with, but its quality was completely circumscribed, hemmed in, by the actions and personality of the premier. As Wilson remarked, Duplessis "created for himself a role as the master of a docile machine that, even with such examples as Tammany before us, seems rather astonishing in North America" (190). Duplessis permitted none but yes-men around him, and he treated most of his subordinates like children, demanding constant adulation and affection.

Duplessis was obviously a man with a certain elemental magnetism, but his knowledge of culture was clearly undistinguished. "He was never to travel any further West than Toronto." His horizons were low and tawdry. He was honestly interested in the improvement of education and did a great deal for the schools of Quebec, but otherwise his contributions to the advancement of French Canadian life were few. He defended only the most backward and traditional form of Catholicism—one that might assure his continued political dominance. Economically he was far to the right, and in the famous asbestos strike of 1949 Duplessis sent in provincial police as strikebreakers, even though it was more than obvious that French-speaking workers in Quebec were grossly underpaid and overworked. Doubtless it was his intransigence and his refusal to do anything that would jeopardize his easy alliance with English-speaking commercial interests that led to Duplessis's slide in the last decade of his life. The years before his death in 1959 must have been disagreeable ones to Duplessis, with the newly invigorated Separatist movement snarling in the background.

Separatism should have been a breath of fresh air after the feudalism of Duplessis, and in some ways of course it was. Wilson writes with a certain amount of sympathy for the need of French Canadians to break loose of the long-standing role as infants in a system of French feudalism (ecclesiastical or political) or English commercialism. His strong libertarian individualism must have moved him to be a coconspirator with the French who were seeking to hold on to their national identity and language. On the other hand, his report of the growth of the Separatist movement in the few years between the death of Duplessis and the publication of his book was not a happy one. He could report little real evidence of the birth of a new national culture and saw only the dreary and sorrowful story of violence and terrorism.

The violence and terrorism subsided, of course, and later on, with the Separatist party under Rene Levesque actually in power, the promise, however distant, of actual separation from the rest of Canada, seemed to make the violence gratuitous and unnecessary.

What would Wilson say about the later achievements of the Separatist party and its control of the Quebec government? We cannot know, of course, because he died in 1972 before the electoral triumph of the Separatists. On the other hand, it is not at all hard to imagine what he would say knowing his political convictions. He would doubtless be skeptical that the cultural life of a people could be made over sheerly by activity in the political domain. Surely he would find that the French Canadian political movement had made some strong cultural gains and there was some kind of intellectual ferment among French Canadians that was not there before. On the other hand, the Quebeçois certainly would not have thrilled him too much, because, with his early American republican spirit, he had little affection for populist, factional politics. More than anywhere in North America, the province of Quebec seems to be a dramatic showcase for the evils of what Richard Hofstadter called "the paranoid style in politics," a style that has often been identified as peculiarly American. In the province of Quebec the paranoid style of politics has been raised to new levels of irritation and self-destruction. Everything seems to proceed by the *via negativa.* The desire is not to figure out what can be done to enhance French cultural institutions but rather to stamp out English traditions and English institutions. All political movement seems to proceed under the notion that if you take something away from English schools or English universities you will somehow make French schools and institutions better. The French eagerly mistake agitation for vigor, thumb-the-nose politics for independence. Any sophisticated outsider might well question whether the French have not just delivered themselves into a new kind of feudalism not really different from that once provided over by the Roman Catholic church or by Maurice Duplessis.

Still, despite his numerous troubled reservations about Canada, Edmund Wilson seems to have concluded that Americans have a lot to learn from their neighbors to the north. Canadian politics is probably just as diseased as American politics. But somehow it usually does not seem so. Most of the social diseases appear milder and more

innocuous in Canada. With a few exceptions, the frenzy of anglophobia in Quebec, suicidal public strikes, and baby-bonus socialism,
Canada still seems to be able to operate all of its main institutions
with more decorum than those below the border. That should be
worth something whatever its cause. One suspects that when everything is weighed in the balance, Canada continues to enjoy two
strong advantages over the United States that pervade all phases of
its life: a small population and vast space. Canada, with its limitless
lands to the north so appealing to Edmund Wilson, Sr., still provides
that extra breath of fresh air once cherished in America when the
more individualistic settlers passed beyond the frontier.

The problem of inept and even corrupt big government in the
United States continued to be a major preoccupation of Wilson's
during the 1960s and was the ulterior subject of his elongated pamphlet, *The Cold War and the Income Tax,* first published as a magazine article.* Wilson's personal discovery of the intricacies of the
Internal Revenue Service and the complexities of the tax law is itself
a detailed revelation of the dark and irrational powers of government. But a good part of the book gets beyond those miseries Wilson
suffered when he failed to file an income tax return for five years; it
seeks an interpretation of the historical background of bloated
American government and irresponsible bureaucracy.

On one level, the book is Wilson's analysis of what has gone
wrong in America since the Second World War and a diagnosis of
government excess and the decline of individual liberty. In one of the
chapters of the book, "The Point of View of a Former Socialist,"
Wilson answers a question that he expected many of his readers to
ask: How can a former socialist who looked to government as a cure
for the abuses of wealth and the excesses of big business now count
himself one of the opponents of big government? Had the liberal
turned reactionary and lost the faith?

Not at all, said Wilson. But as a youth he had the naive belief that
government could do what it had to do in the way of reform without
itself becoming unwieldy and corrupt. "I must confess with com-
punction," he wrote, "that I was naive enough at thirty-one to take

*The text was originally published in *Liberation Magazine* in 1963, and subse-
quently published in hardback by Farrar, Straus. Quotations in this chapter are from
the Signet edition of the New American Library.

seriously Lenin's prediction in his *State and Revolution,* written in 1917 on the eve of his return to Russia, that the clerical work of a socialist government could easily be attended to in the spare time of ordinary citizens who were otherwise occupied with higher things, and that the State, under the new regime, no longer needed by a governing class, would inevitably 'wither away' and cease to harass the individual" (49).

As we now know, nothing of the sort happened in the Soviet Union; the bureaucracy became bigger and more threatening than it had ever been under the czar. In the United States bureaucracy developed somewhat differently, but with similar growth and infringement of individual liberties. Before 1930, the United States government was simple enough: President Harding could play poker three or four evenings a week and Calvin Coolidge could take a long nap every afternoon. But the trouble with the United States government was that it did nothing to curb big business and remedy economic injustice. The New Deal did much to reverse this situation but only at the expense of introducing new complexities and new abridgments of human rights. "There is hardly any longer in the United States any such thing as the old-fashioned farmer who finds himself sold up by the bankers, or the old-fashioned sweated factory worker. Both of these are now dependent on bureaucracies to whom they may appeal or protest: the former on the Department of Agriculture, the second on the labor unions" (50).

In both the United States and the Soviet Union this dependence on bureaucracies has resulted in a kind of complacent and easily deceived citizenry. "The workers with their hands in the Soviet Union as well as those in the United States now have as their principal aim what would once have been called middle class comfort, and in societies which pretend to be governed by opposite 'ideologies' they have both become extremely docile" (50). Although we no longer have the sweatshop or the bankrupt farm, our ease and complacency come at a high price: we lose many of our liberties and whatever check we may have once had on the expansion of bureaucracy and governmental supremacy.

As the title of his book indicates, Wilson sees a strong connection between big government and the cold war. It was his belief that in the years after World War II the United States government sold the public on the notion of communist aggression as a way of building and sustaining big government and an elaborate military. How real the threat of Stalin was in these years will be debated by historians for a long time to come; but there can be small doubt that the cold war resulted in much larger military appropriations and much greater reliance on government operations of all kinds.

Wilson links the tax bureaucracy and the military in an ingenious way. The two systems are interlocked and self-supporting, but even more important, both are murky and clandestine operations carried on behind a cloak of secrecy leaving the general public uninformed of their most complex and important workings. The military can augment its expensive technology without effective public scrutiny on the grounds that giving out too much information would be playing into the hands of the Russians. The compelling need for secrecy allows the military to grow unchecked.

The supporting tax bureaucracy operates in a less secret way perhaps, but the end result is no less confusing and mysterious to the public. The tax laws in the United States are so complicated and inscrutable that the average citizen has no possible way of understanding them in depth. When Wilson began his long struggle with the IRS he assumed that at least the agency was guided by "definite statutes"; that dealings with them might be complex but certainly also precise. "I was gradually brought to the conclusion that these laws were more or less of a muddle. . . . Not even the best-trained lawyer can apparently find his way through the forests of those gigantic tax books, through the dense print and obscurely worded sentences of those innumerable exasperating forms which involve supplying endless data about every detail of one's profits and losses, or of one's personal or corporate expenditures. . . . The question of what ought to be taxed and how much and which deductions ought to be allowed has reached a point of fine-spun complexity that— working in terms of a different set of values—recalls the far-fetched distinctions of medieval theology" (39-40).

Wilson might have mentioned, though he did not, the elaborate system of spying and snooping encouraged and used by the IRS; nor did he mention the insidious moral distinction and class wars that it spawns by pitting social and economic classes against one another; nor did he mention the devious ways in which the IRS circumvents tax laws and the decisions of tax courts by not following court precedents and forcing each and every victim of its rulings in certain areas to take their cases to court, knowing full well that this is usually not financially possible. But Wilson's own case from the 1950s documents nicely the capriciousness, the mindlessness, the wild incoherence of IRS practices. The IRS rises out of the quagmire of American life as the queen of bureaucracies, as the keystone of a vast system of Kafka-esque treacheries and inscrutabilities. How can we trust a government that would tolerate at its heart an organization that is so dishonest, confused, and inaccessible?

In the end, it was not so much the IRS or the military in and of themselves that were the sources of Wilson's rage. It was their contribution to a systematic poisoning of our culture, an insidious contamination of our social life and the fabric of individual liberty and personal worth. This poisoning, says Wilson, is like that of some slow progressive disease. We have the vague feeling of malaise or discomfort but we do not know how to identify the source of our problems. "We amuse ourselves with labor-saving devices that compute or wash dishes for us; we drug ourselves with the slop of TV programs or driving on monotonous highways in cars of abominable design." But always there is this suspicion riding us that something is not right. We must drug ourselves or otherwise sedate our minds. And even as taxes are enslaving us (and one wonders what Wilson would have thought of the more recent governmental monstrosity called inflation—that so much more sneaky form of taxation) we are having to put up with shoddy merchandise, a generally lower standard of living and a polluted culture.

The United States, for all its so much advertised comforts, is today an uncomfortable place. It is idle for our "leaders" and "liberals" to talk about the necessity for Americans to recover their old idealism, to consecrate themselves again to their mission of liberation. Our national mission, if our budget proves anything, has taken on colossal dimensions, but in its interference in foreign countries and its support of oppressive regimes, it has hardly been a liberating mission, and the kind of idealism involved is becoming insane and intolerant in the manner of the John Birch Society.... The accomplished, the intelligent, the well-informed go on in their useful professions that require high integrity and intellect, but they suffer more and more from the crowding of an often unavowed constraint which may prevent them from allowing themselves to become too intelligent and well-informed or may drive them to indulge their skills in gratuitous and futile exercises. (102-3)

The Cold War and the Income Tax clearly shows a resurgence of Wilson's old skepticism about the quality of American life. Like the Wilson of the twenties and thirties, the Wilson of the cold war and the Vietnam era rejected all the elixirs of social reform fashionable in the United States. Since the New Deal the typical American liberal looked to the government and to the politicians for the redress of all social ills and inequalities. But by the creation of gargantuan bureaucracies and an indissoluble and uneradicable military monster requiring larger and larger feedings, government produces ten new inequalities, injustices, and social diseases for every one it cures. Yes, Americans are content because they are prosperous, but deep down they know that the individual is too often stifled and must live in a moral climate that is filled with uncommonly stale and unhealthy airs.

10

The Democratic Man
of Letters

In his later years Edmund Wilson was a much less active journalist and involved social critic than he had been in his youth. But as a prophet of our intellectual life, as a demanding and often irritable critic of American scholarship, his powers increased with the passing of time. In his seventies he found himself recognized as a somewhat respectable national seer, but he never mellowed into his respectability. He remained as suspicious as ever of institutions and habitual patterns of thought. He kept up his attacks on government and politicans but never shied away from doing battle with his fellow literary critics and intellectuals over what he regarded as the standardization of learning and scholarship. Thus it was that Wilson's reputation was never allowed to go untarnished for long, and by the 1960s there were many ready and anxious to view him as an old curmudgeon.

In 1968 Wilson published a pamphlet not much larger than *The Cold War and the Income Tax,* entitled *The Fruits of the MLA.* It is, in part, an attack on the Modern Language Association, one of the leading academic organizations in the United States. This book grew out of some squabbling Wilson had gotten into over the reprinting of American classics—squabbling that had been carried out publicly the previous year in the *New York Review of Books.* For this Wilson got himself a bad name in certain academic circles—if he had not already had one—as a man skeptical of the fruits of academia and of professional scholarship. Since scholarship has become so highly departmentalized and institutionalized in the twentieth century, there have been few outsiders willing and able to storm the bastions of the establishment that supports it. But like Mencken in the twenties, Wilson went after the academic world in a big way—much to the annoyance of many.

Wilson believed that it was essential for the writer and the free thinker to stand clear of institutionalized modes of thought. For this reason he never sought a permanent academic appointment, although on numerous occasions he might well have been driven into a professorial chair if only for reasons of financial exigency. In the late thirties he taught in the summer school of the University of Chicago to ease his depleted financial reserves. Later, during the 1960s, he did a fair amount of lecturing at universities, but only under short-term arrangements. Princeton was the recipient of most of his lectures and he continued to return there long after the death of his old mentor Christian Gauss. While working on *Apologies to the Iroquois* he lectured on Indians at Utica College and, starting in the fall of 1964, allowed himself to be maintained and "put on display" by the Center for Advanced Studies at Wesleyan University in Connecticut. "It is delightful," he wrote to an old friend from Bogota, New Jersey, a tavern owner who used to send him Scotch whiskey: "They supply you with everything from a house to postage stamps and pay you for being here" (*Letters,* 653). Nonetheless Wilson preferred not to build permanent ties to the academic community.

Of course Wilson could have selected an academic career at any time in his life. Certainly this is the vocation Christian Gauss would have selected for him. All of Wilson's writings are suggestive of the best in teaching and scholarship, and he had about him something of the air of a professor in the best old sense—the sense of one who has a frank love of his own learning and who enjoys expounding it to others.

To get to the reasons behind Wilson's distrust of the academic environment, behind the suspicion of stale and institutionalized forms of learning, we must go back to visions of the world of learning Wilson had formed in his youth. Wilson had been devoting himself throughout his life to large moral questions about the aims and purposes of scholarship, questions such as: What should be the fruits and ideals of learning in a country like ours? What is the relationship between learning and life, between thought and action? Such urgent questionings were apparent even in *Axel's Castle,* Wilson's most purely aesthetic work. Above all, he asked, why is it that learning so often forsakes forceful modes of expression for others that are anemic, repetitive, and stereotyped?

Much of what Wilson had to say about scholarship is contained in autobiographical fragments, some of which had their roots in his early school experiences. One of the most enlightening of these is the essay "Mr. Rolfe" that later appeared in the 1948 edition of *The Triple Thinkers*. Mr. Rolfe was the Greek master at the Hill School and the first strong intellectual influence in Wilson's life. An aloof but authoritative New Englander, Rolfe was a scholar of such distinguished parts that he might, as Wilson observed, have adorned the faculty of any university. Certainly it was in part his manner, his moral authority, that distinguished Rolfe from the other masters at the Hill School. But more than this there was something in the quality of Rolfe's thinking that formed an indelible impression in Wilson's young mind.

Rolfe was, of course, an outstanding scholar, in what might be called the disciplinary sense of the word. He was a man who pursued his subject with rigor and exactitude. He was a man, said Wilson, "who made you get everything exactly right, and this meant a good deal of drudgery." He was a stern taskmaster who could wither you with a glance if you did an injustice to his subject matter. He kept his classes in a state of tension and allowed nothing less than the fullest respect to the beauty and nobility of the Greek language.

Yet this alone, Wilson came to see, was not sufficient to explain why Rolfe was a great scholar and teacher. He was also a man of supple mind, a man of vigorous imagination: there was nothing of the schoolmaster or the provincial about him. He was a New Englander in the best tradition and had behind him all of the saltiness and brusqueness of innumerable sea captains; his homely and breezy qualities formed "a rocklike base on which the flowers of Hellenism flourished." There was something organic and open-minded in his "comic sense, his exquisite literary taste and the benignant incandescence of his mind."

Rolfe was never limited by the mechanics, the apparatus, of his specific subject matter. He was a man of diverse interests and worldly outlook; his reading tastes far overran the bounds of the classics. Wilson recalls his first visit to Mr. Rolfe's rooms, where he discovered in the bookshelf the plays of Bernard Shaw, an author whom he, at the tender age of fourteen, assumed to be a perverse cynic. In time he came to appreciate the diversity and eccentricity of Rolfe's interests, to see in him something more than a stern taskmaster. He came to see him as a man sensitive to beauty in numerous departments of life, whose specialty was not merely a technical discipline but a window on the world; he came to see that if one really mastered the complexities and subtleties of a single subject one would have some open vistas to all subjects. Rolfe was not without his eccentricities, but these were a part of a well-developed character, so that whether he was sarcastic at times, whether his mind revealed certain perversities—such as his intense dislike of progressive education, about which he wrote amusing short poems in later years—there was always a solidity about him that held his complex nature together and in harmony.

Another important influence on Wilson's youth, perhaps the most important of all—was Christian Gauss, about whom he also wrote publicly on numerous occasions, and who is a central personage in the charming memoir "Mr. More and the Mithraic Bull." (Significantly this essay begins, as "Mr. Rolfe" concludes, Wilson's book *The Triple Thinkers*.) The essay is not only germane to Wilson's thinking about the nature and uses of knowledge; it is surely one of the finest American essays of this century.

The essay has occasionally been interpreted as a criticism of the "new humanism," of which Paul Elmer More was an outstanding representative, from the stance of the liberalism of which Wilson had become a spokesman in his *New Republic* days. However, the contrast between Christian Gauss and Paul Elmer More was more than ideological; instead it was largely one of life-style—a contrast between two worlds of scholarship, one rigid and doctrinaire, bound apparently to an inflexible pattern of thought; another imaginative, open-ended, and humane, capable of growth and development.

Christian Gauss, a professor of French and Italian at Princeton who became dean of the college in 1925, was one of those rare teachers we encounter—if we ever do—only once in a lifetime and who possesses the gift of starting in his or her pupils a train of thought that does not move to a hardened conclusion but that is capable of being picked up, extended, transposed, perhaps even recast in a different form than the original. In short, he was a teacher who inspired one to think, who instilled a love of thinking as a way of life.

This ability is not usually a technique of teaching, or a skill, but a habit of mind that is somehow infectious, in which one becomes immersed. Gauss himself was a man of widespread and exhilarating interests: his mind was constantly developing, growing, moving on to new fascinations. "His own ideas on any subject were always taking new turns: the light in which he saw it would be shifted, it would range itself in some new contest." He was, as one might suspect, a man of tremendous erudition, who gave the impression of having intimate knowledge of every subject that interested him: "If one asked him a question about the Middle Ages, one absolutely got the impression that he had lived in Europe then and knew it at first hand."

But, as with Rolfe, erudition alone was not at the heart of Gauss's inspirational qualities as a teacher—it was his imagination and the flexibility of his mind. Whereas Paul Elmer More was also a man of redoubtable learning, it was learning of a firmly set and inflexible nature, a sort to which one seldom looks for development, spontaneity, and forceful expression. More's mind is revealed in Wilson's essay as lacking spaciousness, liberality—perhaps humor—and one suspects that all of his ideas were permanently formed and incapable of development.

Outwardly, the nostalgic memoir "Mr. More and the Mithraic Bull" is an account of a conversation Wilson had with More in December 1929, a conversation that took place during a visit he and Dean Gauss paid to More's Princeton home. Sitting in More's living room, discussing Mithraism, about which More, as a student of the history of religions, was supposed to be an expert, Wilson looked at these two great men of Princeton. Here were two men of undoubted scholarship, of the widest imaginable erudition—yet how different they were. There was about Gauss a soft and pliable romanticism. The strength of More was that he "always knew precisely what he thought and was always ready to face anybody down." Wilson sat listening to them discuss Mithraism and its relationship to Christianity:

I looked at Gauss: his golden locks were gone and had left a prodigiously high domed forehead. With his fine profile of a blond South German Dante, in his Princetonian soft shirt and tweed golf suit, he sat today, lying back in his chair, the great expounder of French romanticism, hobnobbing with the great anti-romantic. So much subtler a mind than More, with so much wider a range of imaginative sympathy, and correspondingly so much less fixed in his opinions, he looked out cooly through his eyeglasses without rims on those prejudices and principles of More's which years ago had aroused his indignation. The amenities and responsibilities of Princeton had dimmed the flamboyance of his romanticism. But Paul Elmer More, still just as positive, still nearly as narrow as then, sat attentively forward in his chair, still ready to face anybody down. (14)

Once again, it was not the doctrinal difference with More that lay behind Wilson's irritation with that literary luminary as much as an impatience with his rigidity of thought, his inability to bring the scope of his own learning into question, his lack of desire to expand his horizons beyond what he already knew. Later, when the discussion turned to some modern authors, More's intellectual arrogance "started up from behind his deliberate urbanity." He apparently could not discuss Joyce (whom he had evidently not read) without considerable agitation, and when the suggestion was made that there might be a parallel between Joyce's *Ulysses* and Homer, More bristled and cut sharply down on the discussion. "The same confounded old academic inertia! I thought; the same old proprietary interest in the classics"—that a living upstart like Joyce could presume to hobnob with one of the major classical writers.

Once more we have the insight that was raised in the essay "Mr. Rolfe": there is nothing about learning, about the largeness of erudition, that by itself guarantees the worth of scholarship. Not that deep learning, rigorousness, exactness, count for nothing, as Rolfe had so well taught his young charges. They do count—but they are not enough. Without imagination, without openness of mind, a capability to change, to develop, to learn something new, scholarship is not a window on the world but an accumulation of old materials that will eventually suffocate the mind.

Wilson's distrust of academia is the distrust that the literary man, the imaginative writer, has for forms of learning that are pedantic, stultified, compartmentalized, incapable of moving beyond professional training and habitual patterns of thought. "Mr. More and the Mithraic Bull" offers some of Wilson's main criticisms of the academic type in capsule form, for here we see in dramatic relief the professional traits—impatience with new ideas that invade one's specialty, that get under one's skin and require motion out of the scholarly armchair; laziness and inertia; and the preference to direct one's interest toward already well-worked problems that require little expenditure of imaginative effort.

Another expression of the same viewpoint can be found in a later essay of Wilson's, " 'Miss Buttle' and 'Mr. Eliot,' " that appeared in *The Bit between My Teeth*. This essay starts out as a discussion of the popularity of T.S. Eliot among literary scholars. One might suppose that Eliot's contribution to poetry is of no greater importance than, let us say, that of Robert Frost, although assuredly there are many, many more articles in academic journals dealing with Eliot than with Frost. But why is this true? The answer given by Wilson in his essay " 'Miss Buttle' and 'Mr. Eliot' " is revealing. Eliot's work, he tells us, is of a sort that is especially suited to the kind of criticism in which English teachers like to indulge; it is the kind of poetry that is especially suitable for the classroom. "In the first place, there is very little of it: you can get through it all in the evenings of a week. These English professors are lazy. They rarely know anything but English Lit., and they rarely read anything in English that they do not have to read for their degrees and their courses or to get themselves a little credit by writing in some critical organ about one of their accepted subjects." The trick is to find yourself a few books that can easily be commented on in a highly specialized way. Such scholarship is like Talmudic *pilpul,* the "method of rabbinical exegesis by which the criterion of excellence came to consist in the degree of farfetched-ness that could be compassed by subtle argument." For this kind of exegesis, which permits the professor's laziness, Eliot has provided the ideal text.

Not only is it small in bulk; it presents in the shortest space a maximum of out-of-the-way references that the researcher may hope to run down, of apparently symbolic images that the interpreter may hope to illuminate and of often unavowed quotations that, working in some other connection, one may joyously stumble upon. The commentators have been preying on Eliot's work, like sandpipers pecking for sand fleas, so persistently for many decades that they seem to have been getting on Eliot's nerves and to have goaded him into telling them that they have unearthed more revelations than the poet had buried secrets. (382)

Wilson's scorn for the various forms of explicatory and micro-scopic literary criticism is amusingly presented in a little spoof that came out while he was artist-in-residence at Wesleyan University in the mid-1960s. The spoof took the form of a play "The Lamentable Tragedy of the Duke of Palermo, by Henry Chettle and William Shakespeare, Now First Discovered and Transcribed by Homer R. Winslow, M.A. Hillsdale, Ph.D Harvard." Homer Winslow is a tradi-tional but mellow Shakespearean professor at Hillsdale College who is put upon by one of the new fire-breathing professional types, Ned ("Spooky") Simms, who has taken over as head of the department. Simms hopes to put Winslow into the back seat; and Winslow, who uses the old methods of getting students to love literature, is nearly reduced to teaching "freshman English"—the dreaded bugaboo of English professors.

A literary-hoax play eventually brings the unsuitable and ungen-tlemanly Simms to a bad end—and Winslow is allowed to continue teaching Shakespeare in the old-fashioned manner. But not before Wilson has had his fun with all kinds of literary pedantry and banal-ity. Spooky Simms is Wilson's parody of the Talmudic, explicatory scholar—always tracking down some intellectual trifle or obscure reference. In a particularly mirthful encounter with poor old Winslow, Simms professes to have unearthed the secret of Yeats's poem *The Wild Swans at Coole.*

Spooky: I've cracked *The Wild Swans of Coole.*
Winslow (smiling): Not irreparably I hope.

And of course what Spooky has done is read all kinds of preposterous nonsense into the poem.

Spooky: The poem is crammed with homosexual allusions. The Wild swans —Wilde—remember that Yeats knew Oscar—we don't know how well. And swans—that refers to Proust. *Swann's Way* had come out in 1919 — just six years before the poem.*

The Duke of Palermo is a farcical rendering of a number of Wilson's pet peeves about academia—the old-maidishness of the politics, the narrowness and mirthlessness of the disciplines, the rigid compartmentalization of thought. Mainly, though, Wilson's distrust of scholarship is based on practical, utilitarian grounds. The trouble with too much academic scholarship in the vast and cumbersome system of higher education is the uselessness and triviality of it. Throughout his career Wilson was a strong advocate of the public uses of learning. He believed the only kind of scholarship that ought to be tolerated is that which justifies itself, which has some public use —some use for what Wilson frequently liked to call the ordinary reader. The totally private and special use of scholarship for purposes of academic achievement was always annoying to Wilson, as can be seen in *The Duke of Palermo* and many of his essays of the 1950s and 1960s.

A good example of the sort of useless scholarly project that ruffled Wilson is described in *The Fruits of the MLA,* a book in which he is sharply critical of the plans of the Modern Language Association to publish some of the American classics long since out of print.

For a number of years Wilson had had a project of publishing major American classics in an easily accessible form, such as that of the thin-paper *Editions de la Pléiade* of France or the *Scrittori d'Italia* of Italy. What he wanted were inexpensive, convenient, compact, well-edited volumes for the general reader. His original plans to produce such a series were thwarted by the Modern Language

* The Duke of Palermo and Other Plays, 9-10. The title play cited here originally appeared in the *New York Review of Books,* January 12, 1967, 13-23.

THE FRUITS
OF
THE MLA

EDMUND WILSON

A New York Review Book

George H. Douglas photo

Association, which had a project of its own that whisked away the funds set aside for Wilson's scheme by the National Endowment for the Humanities.

The brouhaha over the idea of having an edition of the American classics for the general reading public began with an article in the *New York Review of Books* in 1967 by Lewis Mumford, who objected to a new edition of Emerson's *Journals* put out by the Harvard University Press because "it included too much material which Emerson had left directions to destroy and that it presented this material in a totally unreadable text, the editor of which, by resorting to no less than twenty diacritical marks, had made it look like something between an undecoded Morse message and a cuneiform inscription."

The projects of the MLA, which seemed to be adopting Wilson's idea in name but not in spirit, revealed to Wilson some of the same kind of scholarly abomination. One of the projects he described was a text of William Dean Howells's *Their Wedding Journey*, about which Wilson raised some troubling questions. Why did the MLA spend an exceedingly large sum of money publishing this first—very poor—novel of Howells's at all? "What, especially, is the point of reprinting it with thirty-five pages of textual commentary which record the variations of nine of the existing texts?" Why must we be given spelling variations of all the texts? Why does the editor trouble himself to paste into the volume excerpts from Howells's travel writings from his diaries that were not made use of in the composition?

"What on earth," asked Wilson, "is the interest of all this? Every writer knows how diaries and articles are utilized as materials for books, and no ordinary reader knows or cares. What is important is the finished work by which the author wishes to stand" (13). Which brings us back again to the matter of public usefulness. Wilson freely admitted that scholarly exercises of this sort may have some usefulness to Ph.D. candidates who may find the work valuable in the writing of a thesis, but in every other way they are quite useless. For the general reader—and Wilson, as a man of humane learning, puts the general reader in the forefront of his thinking—they have no interest whatsoever.

Furthermore, projects of this sort may be harmful in other ways —at least they are harmful in that they keep literature out of the hands of the reader. Some of the projects of the MLA are to be drawn out over many years, with the result that the reading public will not have access to them for a long time to come. Most of the volumes are too expensive for the ordinary reader. Many of them are monstrosities of the bookmaker's art. (The fourth volume of the Centenary edition of the works of Nathaniel Hawthorne is, says Wilson, a good example of MLA bad bookmaking—the book weighs nine pounds and is two and three-eighths inches thick, printed on heavy grayish paper.) But above all, most of these projects manage to take the joy out of reading, and instead of serving to bring American literature to the reading public, they shunt it off to a corner to be used only by literary scholars according to their own cheerless ways.

Not that Wilson is condemning categorically scholarly activities such as the scrutinizing of variants. There are times when these activities may be of considerable interest—where a mystery is involved, as in *Edwin Drood,* or *The Turn of the Screw,* for example. Or in the case of Russian writers such as Pushkin or Tolstoy, who were the object of the czar's censors. But one must exercise some judgment, some discretion, and not be caught up in the false belief that there is some magic in the machinery of scholarship as an end in itself.

Wilson's main grievance against so much modern scholarship is that it is neither gentlemanly nor discriminating nor humane—judgments that can surely be extended to academic fields beyond that of literature. All of the major academic disciplines in fact have their counterparts of the MLA as well as their arcane professional languages and scholarly mumbo jumbo. But what all kinds of scholarship of this type have in common is the inability to weigh, to judge, to question the value of their own work as part of the larger human framework. In other words, academic, as opposed to humane scholarship (perhaps we may adopt these two terms as an essential dichotomy of Wilson's thought), refuses to bring the fruits of its own labor into question; refuses to let in light from the outside; allows no air of humor or playfulness to fall upon its privately held subject matter; refuses to believe that learning belongs to humanity rather than solely to that part of it set apart in accord with certain self-appointed rules of professional competence.

Wilson's views on scholarship, expressed in many books and articles over the years, are both peculiarly American and peculiarly democratic in character. Again we have to go back to Wilson's rugged and individualistic New York state forebears for an understanding of his refusal to accept the stuffiness and rigidity of conventional and institutional scholarship. For Wilson, academic scholarship has a strong elitist tendency, a hankering after exclusiveness, a desire to hoard the private subject matter, and these tendencies are no less reprehensible when found in the intellectual realm than when found in the political or economic realms. Scholarship, to be worth anything, must be a free and open offering to society. Even if it is obvious that not all members of society can grasp the fruits of scholarship, one must write as if they could. One must write as if there were a single general language to which all of the educated public can respond—not a series of fractured cultures, each with its arcane subject matter, a series of microcultures where English professors speak only to other English professors, philosophers to other philosophers.

But Wilson did not intend to popularize scholarship. Wilson's own literary scholarship is as thorough and painstaking as that of professionals who pore over their variant spellings or their Hinman collating machines. In the end the difference between humane and academic scholarship is one of expression, communication, language. The true scholar must always be one who can talk with his fellow man, who can interact with him in a fundamental way. Which is another way of saying that at the heart of scholarship is art—poetry in the broadest sense. He who has the gift of tongues, who can speak to his fellow man and has taken the full breadth of humanity as his subject matter, he alone will have an honest outlet for scholarship.

In Wilson's eyes, the nonimaginative, nonliterary manifestations of scholarship can only give rise to conveniently packaged products of a commercial nature—products that can be sold and traded to other scholars in the market for precisely that kind of product and no other. Such, in fact, was his final conclusion about the usefulness of the MLA. Not that there is anything about the commercial usefulness of the MLA as a job market for college teachers that must be objected to. "This is all of course perfectly legitimate; the Modern Language Association has no doubt performed a useful role." But it is in the claim that the MLA offers more than a commercial service that Wilson felt the need to question.

Something of this claim does in fact accompany literary scholarship, especially. The literary scholar has as his or her subject matter one of the most universally human of all subject matters; thus there is the tacit assumption that writings about this subject are not only *about* it but somehow also *of* it. But there is no such guaranteed connection. In modern academic life literary scholarship is often merely another subject area, like mechanical engineering or business administration, useful only to others following the field.

But naturally and rightfully this is not as it should be. Literary scholarship was traditionally believed to be at the center of all humane studies because it dealt with language—that most vital and distinguishing trait of the human condition—with poetry, and with literature in the broadest sense. But experience in recent years has shown that literary studies have given up their leadership in academic life, resulting in a lack of direction to the entire range of learning in our time. If the literary studies are not humane it is hardly likely that any of the other academic fields of learning will be so.

To Wilson true scholarship is literate scholarship, which is the same thing as saying humane scholarship—that which is able to speak out to men of good taste and sensitivity wherever they may be found. Of course, specialization may and should be built on top of literate scholarship, but when such specialties lose their moorings in humane or literate learning they have lost most of their reason for being. This is what is wrong with much of the academic life in the twentieth century. It must do a better job than it has of reinvigorating and refreshing itself in the common and shared experience of humanity.

11

Upstate

It was Edmund Wilson's great power and distinction that he was immersed in the America of his lifetime and curiously detached from it at the same time. In his later years, unkind critics found him to be an old curmudgeon who had lost the ideals of his youth and found no new ones to take their place—a faded and cantankerous aristocrat who scorned all of the alleged material and spiritual advances of America. But it was Wilson's tenacious grip on the American past, his never-ending attempts to dredge up the values of his forebears and the ambiance of the old America that make his views on the new so refreshing and invigorating. If Wilson was irritable and contemptuous of the world around him, it was not because he had given up on his homeland, but because he was struggling desperately to find in it permanent values that could make life worth living. We Americans are committed to change, but we also surrender to mindless changes, intellectual fads, and social nostrums. Wilson fought to preserve not so much an ideal past but his own little patch of moral ground, his own individuality. In his fierce individuality and self-direction we find Wilson's irritability with America credible and, at the same time, inspiring.

Upstate, the last book Wilson published before his death in 1972, is in many ways the most inspiring of his works. Curiously, although a good deal of it was written during a period when his health was bad and when the infirmities of age might have encouraged a bleak and pessimistic outlook, the book seems full of subdued optimism. *Upstate* is a far more genial, more forward-looking book than *Memoirs of Hecate County.* Although it is occasionally morose, sometimes cynical, it conveys the joy of discovering that one's roots can provide solace and strength after all, and that the wild phantasmagoria of the present moment is but a passing wave in the vast ocean of history.

Like many of Wilson's books, *Upstate* is a strange, eccentric collection of essays and impressions. The book consists primarily of selections from Wilson's diaries for the years between 1950 and 1970—at least the parts that refer to his annual summer visits to the old stone house at Talcottville. At the beginning there are several longer essays—one on New York state religions, two on upstate and local history, and one on Dorothy Mendenhall, Wilson's cousin who loved the house at Talcottville and spent summers there when Wilson was a boy. A prologue and an epilogue draw the book together, although so powerful is the unifying force behind the book that the essays and the diary entries might almost stand on their own. Wilson has said that the landscape of the northeastern part of New York "overwhelms the people," and one might add that the isolation of the land and the people stamps a uniqueness and individuality onto any human drama that takes place there.

"The Old Stone House," Wilson's early essay on upstate New York and his New York state ancestors was written in the early 1930s. The house at Talcottville and its environs continued to be a lingering presence in his work throughout his career, although for a period of seventeen years Wilson did not take his vacations there. He returned in the summer of 1950, and every year thereafter, becoming the owner of the house after the death of his mother in 1951.

The house at Talcottville had never been completely abandoned during this time, although neither Wilson nor his mother had stayed there for many years. It was maintained by Wilson's cousins, Otis and Fern Munn, who lived there year-round and acted as caretakers. Mrs. Wilson had hoped to make inspection trips in her later years and even spoke of being able to spend one summer there, but her health always prevented this. She did not love the house as her husband and son did, but it was never totally out of her thoughts.

Wilson became suddenly concerned about the house the year before his mother died and went there from his home at Wellfleet on Cape Cod in a taxicab (none of his family members were able to drive a car at that time). This trip, made with his grown daughter Rosalind and his twelve-year-old son Reuel, took place in June 1950 and was, said Wilson, "as it had always been in my youth—and now in a special way, after so long—a rather emotional experience."

Upstate New York is a wild and in many ways inhospitable land. And by "upstate" here we refer not to that popular subdivision of

New York state known to followers of the political scene—that part of New York state that is outside of New York City. For New York state consists of many upstates—the kindly old Hudson River valley, the busy city belt between Albany and Buffalo, the Finger Lake country, the misty Catskill Mountain area, celebrated in painting by George Inness and Thomas Cole. The upstate referred to here is really upstate—far from the centers of civilization, far from the gentle valleys of Rip Van Winkle. "Far away" New York state is the vast and lonely land that juts north to the shores of Lake Ontario and the Canadian border, a land that repels all but the hardiest of people and seemingly all forms of commercial enterprise.

Talcottville lies in a trough between the lower ranges of the Adirondacks and a large wild plateau once known as the Lesser Wilderness, now simply called Tug Hill. The almost nonexistent town of Talcottville is officially in Lewis County, which has an area of 1,270 square miles, but a population of only slightly over 20,000—a population that has remained constant for over sixty years. There has been nothing to draw people here, and Wilson quotes an article from the *Conservationist,* a publication of the New York State Conservation Department, that proclaims that this uninviting and unrewarding area "should never have been cleared at all." At one time spruce from the area was in demand, but in the long run logging turned out to be unprofitable, as did the few cheese factories and creameries that had once been established. No railroad ever prospered here, and Tug Hill is inhabited by deer, wildcats, bear, otter, beavers, even, it is said, by wolves and panthers. "It is dangerous on this account to stray without a gun very far from the roads, and it is easy to get lost in the miles of forest." Winters are unbearable in Lewis County, and on Tug Hill snow sometimes continues to fall for ten months of the year, often reaching a depth of between eighteen and twenty feet.

Upstate New York was originally settled by New Englanders, and although New Yorkers later made much of their contempt for Yankee values, there was always a good deal of affinity between the people who had moved to New York and those who stayed behind. A constant struggle with poor farming land and scarce natural resources made the settlers of northern New York state strangely eccentric and individualistic. To begin with, only the hardy—perhaps only the foolhardy—would be drawn to the stony slopes that defy all forms of farming. Those who remained were somehow different. A recent New York state historian has said that residents of these lonely

mountains and hills "have developed an independent spirit border-
ing on eccentricity."* Like the flinty lobsterman of the New England
coast and the laconic Vermonter, the upstate New Yorker has never
been anything like the standardized American type.

When Wilson began again to live in the old stone house—and he
had much refurnishing to do: painting, papering, repairing, updating
the water system, digging a new well—he wrote that he felt, "after
many years of absence, that I was visiting a foreign country, but a
country to which I belonged." He never completely sold Elena, his
fourth wife, or his children, on the virtues of the place. They all
preferred their more civilized year-round home at Wellfleet. Elena
Wilson believed that she saw ghosts there, "although ordinarily she
was not at all interested in ghosts." Most of the family did not feel
comfortable in this godforsaken corner of the universe. "I, on the
contrary," wrote Wilson, "am quite at home here—the only place,
perhaps, that I feel that I belong. Everybody knows me—and, quite
unlike the general attitude in New England, where anyone from two
miles away is 'a foreigner'—everybody seems good natured and comfortable; even the dogs are not yappy and snappy, as they are likely
to be in Wellfleet." Above all, the stone house and the community
was an outlook on the world, a powerful center of gravity.

This little town is at once a point of permanence for me—since we always
came back in the summers—and a phase in the flux of American life. You feel
both the struggle of the settlers to make themselves a place in the wilderness,
the will to found a society, and the spirit of adventure, the thirst for freedom,
the need to make new lives for themselves, that carried them farther and
farther West. (*Upstate*, 87-88)

Above all, it seemed to Wilson that the vast woodlands of upstate
New York, despite their isolation, gave rise to a feeling of human
intimacy. He had the notion from his earliest childhood that "everybody was related to everybody else or, at no matter what distance
from one another, were neighbors or very old friends." Was not this
the original flavor of the older America before the urban bacillus
infected everywhere—a place where one could breathe free, be left
alone, but at the same time have in the vicinity neighbors one could
trust, believe in, and understand. One could enjoy here the dual but
self-supporting virtues of isolation and community. Twentieth-cen-

*David Maldwyn Ellis, *New York: City and State* (Ithaca: Cornell Univ. Press,
1979), 20.

tury America is the place of the lonely crowd. In the older America there were no crowds, but the distant neighbors were real and purposeful.

For the last two decades of his life, Wilson returned every summer to Talcottville, even in the years when he was busy with important projects, or even when his family insisted on remaining on Cape Cod. *Upstate* is an intimate record of those summers, a portrait of the land and people of the northern counties in stark contrast to the world outside. Too, the keeping of the diary dredged up the summers of long ago, the spirit of family members long gone, of eccentric neighbors, of old New York state culture and religions, of loggers and fishermen, of men who tried to work the soil and lost and then moved on leaving the land victorious and pretty much untouched.

Upstate is a charming and inspiring recollection but it defies the usual classifications accepted for the diaries of writers and intellectuals. The book is not usually about Wilson's ideas, or the books that he has read in the summer months; it is concerned with the simpler and truer verities of life and death, of the seasons, of friendship and conversation, and sex—sex ever so lightly intruded here and there, for Wilson is now an old man—of woods gray and dark, of going to town, of orange sunsets and menacing thunderstorms, of transactions with the world outside, and always that smug contentment that the world outside can go to hell—at least for the summer.

When the published diary entries come to an end, Wilson is seventy-five years old and clearly troubled with physical infirmities. He writes in his diaries of his old problem with drinking, of complicated dentistry, of an attack of malaria (contracted he thinks in Jamaica), of flare-ups of angina. But when he is at Talcottville none of these things seem to matter. There are sources of strength and funny satisfactions sufficient to keep the rude world at bay.

Talcottville was a place where Wilson could benignly laugh and thumb his nose at the world, even at himself and his profession. He stocked the library with books that even he, one of the world's most omnivorous readers, would never read. After his mother's death he brought up from Red Bank a number of her girlhood favorites—the stories of Juliana Horatio Ewing, "which I never quite liked or understood." He put on the shelves his father's old travel books that bored him. Later on he laid in some books for "wintertime" reading—*Clarissa,* Hazlitt, Gioacchino Belli, Milton's complete prose—quite a nice expenditure considering the fact that he had not the slightest expectation of returning for the dismal and unpredictable New York winters.

In any case, Wilson did not do a great deal of writing or reading in Talcottville. He preferred to dabble away at family history, hunt up Indian remains, visit a boyhood stream or the swimming hole called Flat Rock, talk to the local inhabitants of any walk of life, turn up long-forgotten artifacts or family heirlooms—"some object, quite blackened from disuse, that had been lying in an old drawer or closet: copper candlesticks, a brass oil lamp on a long spiral stem, a silver napkin ring, silver salt and pepper shakers, a silver-topped inkwell with my great Aunt Rosalind's monogram"—or simply drive around the countryside to watch the passing show.

Although he did not drive a car himself, Wilson liked to be driven to all of the prominent settlements nearby. He would visit Lowville, the county seat of Lewis County, with its handsome old houses and dingy commercial section. Closer by, to the south, and just over the county line in Oneida County, was Boonville where the family did its shopping. None of these places ever depressed Wilson, even Utica, the major metropolitan center of the area, an hour's drive to the south in the Mohawk Valley. Transported to the south or midwest, Utica would scarcely have had interest for Wilson, for it had become a flat, tired industrial center. But "I still, when I go for the day there, look with eagerness into the shop windows and make a point of visiting the museums, which, through the bounty of old textile families, are well equipped and well kept up."

Wilson had to be driven around, and this meant finding a willing native chauffeur. For a number of years the chauffeur was Albert Grubel, a retired German farmer who always had stories to tell about accidental drownings and other gruesome local happenings. The very peculiar Grubel pops in suddenly here and there, now and then, in the diary entries between 1956 and 1966, usually with eccentric views on local mishaps and highway tragedies—especially automobile casualties and the predictions for the death rate for the Fourth of July or Labor Day holidays. Grubel had never been further away than Boonville and refused to drive Wilson to Utica. Like a number of the local inhabitants he saw the world outside in skeptical and suspicious terms that somewhat amused Wilson, but with which he could privately empathize.

Later on Wilson was driven around by another neighbor, Mary Pcolar, a woman of Hungarian background, a predominant figure in the last half of *Upstate*. Wilson met Mary in 1960 when she was working at a pharmacy in Boonville, was smitten by her, and tried to coax her into teaching him Hungarian—he in turn offering to teach her French. He made several appointments with her, but she nearly always got out of them. Several years later, after they became close friends, he found out that she had been a little fearful that she did not know the language well enough to teach it. Also, she had heard that Wilson was a bad character who had a wine cellar and who had been married four times. But after a while, when she had left the pharmacy and did not have a job for the moment, she relented and showed up suddenly at the stone house, saying, "All right I'll teach you Hungarian."

The bond between the two became strong and soon involved more than Hungarian and Mary's services as guide and driver. Her farm and ethnic background brought out all of the instincts of a Pygmalion in Wilson, with sexual overtones muted and subdued, and he gladly took on the role of advisor and teacher to this attractive and appreciative woman about half his age.

Mary Pcolar grew up on a farm in West Leyden (a few miles west of Talcottville). Her high-school teachers urged that she be sent to college, but her parents, being European peasants, had no notion of higher education for women, so she had to carry on her personal education in a haphazard and sporadic way. To get away from the farm she moved after high school to Perth Amboy, New Jersey, a bad-smelling factory town that had a lot of working-class Hungarians in it—a town that Wilson remembered distastefully as part of the murky scenery on the Pennsylvania Railroad between New York and Red Bank. She worked for a time at the Vogue School of Fashion Modeling in New York and at night as a telephone operator. While in Perth Amboy she married a young Slovak, George Pcolar, a World War II hero, by whom she had three children. All of them returned eventually to upstate New York, where George got a job as a steel-worker in the Revere Copper and Brass factory in Rome.

Mary Pcolar was a warm and self-effacing woman ("she is a very handsome girl in whom the Mongolian stock is evident: high cheekbones, slightly slanting gray eyes, set rather wide apart, a figure erect and well built"), a woman of a certain natural intelligence and refinement. Wilson wrote of her: "She not only worked with me at Hungarian, she drove me around, typed my manuscripts and letters, and provided me with a pleasant companion who never got on my nerves. She has a remarkable many-sided competence. . . . I became very fond of Mary and followed her further career, as if she were an interesting niece, and I always felt regret that there was so little I could do to help her" (216-17).

Clearly, though, Wilson did a great deal for Mary Pcolar and she for him. She was his ever-patient and willing Galatea. She was always open to instruction—far more so than his own two daughters, Rosalind and Helen, neither of whom, he remarked, "has ever shown any signs of caring to be instructed by me." More important, though, Mary gave even more to Wilson in return. She was, in a way, a great natural teacher, a civilizer in the best sense. Wilson marveled at her own children, "much better trained than the children of my literary and academic friends," always patient and well-behaved in a European way. If Mary had gaps in her formal education, there were no impurities in her culture; she was solid and firmly rooted.

Wilson developed ties of affection for all the Pcolars—both Mary and her husband, the two teenaged daughters and a son. "They seem very old world, this family. They are closely bound up with one another and have a good time together. George and Mary and the children kid one another amiably. They know intimately all that goes on on their hundred and seventy five acres: birds, animals, plants and trees." Although definitely old world and European, the Pcolars were also American to the core, and reminded Wilson of early American types in their hardihood and geniality. They had spun out of the soil and meager surroundings a kind of natural aristocratic spirit that harmonized with the mood of the manor house life cherished by the Talcotts.

For the last twelve years of his life, Wilson kept up his annual association with Mary, who, when she was not working at several different jobs of increasing responsibility (including, in time, the school teaching she had always wanted to do), was his regular companion and driver to Boonville, Utica, and countless places of local interest. The aging Wilson, always expansive when he reached this northern clime, chronicles in *Upstate* the delights he took in traveling to museums in Utica and the Boonville Library, and in such ordinary and prosaic happenings as the fireman's fair and parade that had delegations from a number of nearby towns and contained both of Mary's daughters, one playing the clarinet. It is doubtful that a fireman's parade elsewhere in the country, in the usual clamorous American setting, would have engaged Wilson's attention in the slightest.

As always, the summers at Talcottville gave Wilson the opportunity to recharge himself, to get a persepctive on the world. Above all, this little patch of ground, so far away from the tumultuous urban America, gave Wilson the lucidity and vision to see that larger world.

Much of *Upstate* is concerned with life in America beyond the bounds of Lewis and Oneida counties, and whenever Wilson left the environs of his homestead his mood could quickly congeal and his critical powers turn up to their full intensity.

In 1970 Wilson recorded a three-day trip to western New York to the place near Dunkirk where the chautauqua was born. This trip—not in the company of Mary Pcolar, but some other friends— gave Wilson the opportunity to glance around at standardized and rubber-stamped America, which he described freely and with unvarnished prose. He did not like the landscape west of Syracuse, which he found monotonous and dreary, perfectly flat. But the evidences of human culture and habitation were even less inspiring.

I had thought that the chain of restaurants on the Thruway farther east was even considerably worse than the chain along the Massachusetts Turnpike, but in the west there is a chain even worse: cafeterias with no trays to carry the food and not even paper plates to eat it on. We decided that the people who went there had no idea how bad it was. These inhabitants seemed very low grade. Not even pretty girls, but pale gray-eyed lean ill-built Polish women and the usual thick loutish men. One wonders how these men and women can feel enough mutual attraction even to breed more of their unattractive kind. The shadow of the Alleghenies looms on the sky near Fredonia—this is the furthest western corner of New York State. Lake Erie is so polluted that swimming in it has been forbidden, and the fish from it are dangerous to eat. The huge bulk of a Niagara-Mohawk Power Company building, squatting in the water at the edge of the lake, looks menacing in the half-darkness. (360)

Wilson's trips outside of Lewis and Oneida counties, except perhaps to Canada, where he is to some extent able to relax because it is off on the margin of the continent—"the Canadians are not under the same pressure as we are"—left him limp and unfulfilled. He was unmoved by American stainless steel and tinsel, computers, color television sets, and all forms of popular culture.

In the summer of 1969, Wilson spent quite a bit of time going to the movie houses in Rome and Utica to see whatever films came to town. "We decided to go to *Mayerling* in Utica—which turned out to be a rich, heavy repulsive load of Hollywood grandeur and elegance, with no possible human appeal." He saw *Funny Girl* with Barbra Streisand, "a dreadful woman with a horrible blaring voice ... but who makes no attempt to produce the comic personality of Fanny Brice." Despite the fact that American intellectuals had discovered the movies as an art form (or at least an important folk art), Wilson remained stubbornly unconvinced. He and the Pcolars saw two films with Sidney Poitier and found them to be flatly didactic and simpleminded. "The Negro hero has to struggle against race prejudice and injustice, but of course is made to come out on top as a brave man and good fellow acceptable to suburban whites. In *Guess Who's Coming to Dinner,* the young dedicated Negro doctor marries a devoted white girl; but what we are not allowed to ask—as O'Neill does in *All God's Chillun*—is how this marriage is going to work out" (338-39).

Worse still than the popular culture is American habitation— cities blighted beyond hope of salvation, as Wilson's old friend Lewis Mumford believed. New York in 1969 he found sinister, dirty, tawdry—girls in absurd miniskirts, young people so unkempt that you could not tell which ones were pimps and prostitutes, which simply hipsters or swingers. This same year he paid a visit to Chicago where his son Reuel was living with his wife Marcia and their baby.

This city, which used to have a kind of grandeur and which, before I spent the summer at the University there, and realized that it was rather oppressive, once seemed to me quite romantic, is extremely unattractive now. The high buildings here and there, the products of a desire to compete with New York, upset the proportions of Michigan Avenue; and the Art Institute, seen from a distance, is now almost unidentifiable. Some very ugly structures are going up—a monstrous black towerlike thing—insurance, I think—that is truncated at the top. The people seem less tough and dynamic, pale and measly city dwellers, quite joyless. On the south side, the Negro slum is squeezing against the University, and the University people live in fear of further riots. Reuel tells me there are rumors that, at some point this summer, they are going to begin taking potshots at whites. The Negro streets are full of damage: broken panes and boarded up shops, with sometimes "SOUL BROTHER" painted on them in order to ward off attack. The whole effect is claustrophobic. You find yourself in the middle of the Middle West, and, sitting at the hotel and reading the papers, you feel that all the horrors of a hateful, convulsive and chaotic civilization are closing in on you from every side. (320-21)

A constant thread running throughout the book is Wilson's lament for the decline of American individualism and the parallel rise in collectives, most especially the Federal bureaucracy. During the Viet Nam war, Wilson was visited by some left-leaning college students opposed to the war and capitalism. Wilson found these youngsters naive in that they talked vaguely of some kind of Marxism as being able to work a magic cure in America. But Wilson had long ago discovered that the United States is a kind of tyranny of bureaucrats, differing from the one in Russia only in some surface aspects. All clamor for social and political change presumes that change will be the work of bureaucrats committed to the idea of "an all-controlling government." Indeed the youngsters looking for change in the late sixties could not even conceive of anything changing or improving except through some action of government. From the perspective of Wilson's early American individualism such lunacy was at the core of all our difficulties. He believed that the average twentieth-century American is so addicted to the idea of reform that he cannot see the inevitability of reform itself being sucked into the orbit of bureaucracy and dominated by the spirit of the mindless collective. He concurred with Veblen's belief that the United States would in time be completely governed by technocrats.

Deeper down, closer to the real heart of our problem, the reason why we are stymied by bureaucrats, why our minds are befuddled with ideas like "democracy" that really do not mean much, is that we have lost the superior values and ways of living that once held out hope of a decent civilization. Education is no longer valued and prized, unless of course it is identified with competence in some form of technology or professionalism. Education has become a business where people are produced to fit into pigeon holes. The old ideals of education as producing the commodious life and higher, more refined virtues fall by the wayside. Education and culture become just as institutionalized as politics; indeed the educational system is nothing but a seedbed for the production of a technocracy and mobocracy, an enforcer of standardization, uniformity, and mediocrity.

Still, despite his occasional moments of gloom and pessimism about the future of society in America, *Upstate* is not at all a gloomy book. Wilson's passionate interest in all that goes on around him beats on every page, as does a conviction that somewhere in the interstices of our social system lie living strains of hope and virtue. Throughout the book Wilson is hoping for something new and interesting to turn up and always hoping that America can reinvigorate itself with some of its past and long-standing resources. In 1968, four years before his death, he writes: "Old age has its compensations. I feel that I can loaf in the mornings, be less anxious about what I am going to write and not suffer afterwards so much about the gaffes and errors I have made." Too, "knowledge that death is not far away, that my mind and emotions and vitality will soon disappear like a puff of smoke,"

Edmund Wilson regrets that it is impossible for him to:

read manuscripts,

write articles or books to order,

write forewords or introductions,

make statements for publicity
  purposes,

do any kind of editorial work,

judge literary contests,

conduct educational courses,

deliver lectures,

give talks or make speeches,

broadcast or appear on television,

take part in writers' congresses,

answer questionnaires,

contribute to or take part in
  symposiums or "panels" of any
  kind,

contribute manuscripts for sales,

donate copies of his books to libraries,

autograph books for strangers,

allow his name to be used on letter-
  heads,

supply personal information about
  himself,

supply photographs of himself,

supply opinions on literary or other
  subjects.

Wilson's printed "card of response." *University of Illinois Library*

makes it perhaps a little easier to suffer the fools and knaves of the world and once again make an ordering of priorities in the world, a civilized reassessment of the things that are worthwhile, simple, and enduring.

There is not a great deal that is solid to hold onto in the maelstrom that is twentieth-century America. Upstate New York is something of a refuge, however slight, a patch of permanence and independence. It is still worthwhile going to Talcottville every summer because, as Wilson says in the concluding words of the book, it reminds him that this planet and this country have had a few moments worth dreaming about.

My young vision of New York State now hardly exists, though I do not think, as I did last year, that I shall sell my old place here. In spite of the encroachments of the highways and the element of impoverished ambitionless inhabitants, I have still, I think, just enough money to keep the old place going, and I am still as comfortable here as I can hope to be anywhere. That the old life is passing away, that all around me are anarchy and what seems to me stupidity, does not move me much any more. I have learned to read the papers calmly and not to hate the fools I read about. As long as my health holds out, I shall have to go on living, and I am glad to have had some share in some of the better aspects of the life of the planet and of northern New York. (386)

Even if age proves the general futility of life on this rapidly extinguishing planet, even if one cannot abide the foolishness of the vast majority of mankind, one still does have one's vocations and pastimes, and if there is a decent patch of land here and there, and a few breaths of freedom—and America has offered that—life can still have some rewards.

Epilogue

Edmund Wilson died at his old stone house in Talcottville on June 12, 1972. He was cremated and his ashes later removed to Wellfleet for burial. He was fortunate, as many writers are not, that some of his best writing had not yet been released to the public, with the result that interest in his work has continued unabated since his death. With the publication of his diaries from the twenties and thirties, withheld during his lifetime, a much fuller and richer picture of his life and outlook became available to the general public. But by 1972 it was already clear to the obituary writers and editorialists that Edmund Wilson had carved for himself one of the most enviable literary reputations in twentieth-century America.

Of course Wilson continues to be difficult to place intellectually. Some pointed out that he had forsaken his great promise as a literary critic, had traveled too far afield to contribute to any narrowly specialized field of scholarship. Some found Wilson lacking in aesthetic depth and sensitivity. Then again, Richard Gilman, writing in the *New Republic* a few years before Wilson's death, complained that "the primness of Wilson's imagination" had kept him estranged from some of the most powerful modern writers, kept him from writing about or dealing with "the really disturbing and aberrant writers of our time." Still others have been turned off by the later Wilson who seemingly became remote from American life, responding to it with peevish and atrabilious disdain.

Such criticisms, however, missed the most important truth about Wilson, namely, that he never abandoned his own fiercely individualistic reading of literature, his idiosyncratic vision of things, which had always been the source of his powers. Throughout his life Wilson refused to respond to a publicly circumscribed body of problems, to an intellectual framework dictated by an impersonal community of scholars. He did not want to attack the problems that were expected of him, only those he agonized over himself. His lifelong desire was to learn all he could about what interested him, to dig deeply into those things, always putting every scrap of new information through the alchemy of his own sensibility, giving all the stamp of his own authority. If Wilson is one of America's great men of letters, it is because from his earliest years he insisted on seeing the world from a kind of introspective and self-willed patrician detachment. He was an intellectual who had to feel the world for himself, and an often frenzied introversion, a loneliness, a personal honesty, is what he offered to the world outside.

If there was a certain amount of debate during his lifetime about what Edmund Wilson was—critic, reporter, social critic, writer, or whatever—it remains most sensible to see him as a historian, especially since history, by its very nature, is one of the most variegated departments of letters. Almost certainly one can see strong similarities between Wilson and the great genteel historians of the nineteenth century—men like Parkman, Prescott, and Ticknor in the United States, and Macaulay in England. William Makepeace Thackeray once expressed his admiration for Lord Macaulay by noting that immense learning and erudition alone did not account for the genius of Macaulay. Rather it was rooted in his ability to distill what he knew and present it to the reader without ostentation, as a free and open offering to society—a politeness. Thackeray's description of Macaulay's literary skills might be applied to Wilson without having to change so much as a comma:

Take at hazard any three pages of his Essays or History, and glimmering below the stream of the narrative, you, as an average reader, see one, two, three, a half score of allusions to other historical facts, characters, literature, poetry, with which you are acquainted. Your neighbor, who has *his* reading and *his* little stock of literature stored away in his mind, will detect more points, allusions, happy touches, indicating, not only the prodigious memory and learning of this master, but the wonderful industry, the honest, humble, previous toil of this great scholar. He reads twenty books to write a sentence, he travels a hundred miles to write a line of description.

This determined politeness of manner, this compulsion to treat history artistically, impressed Wilson's friend and fellow critic Alfred Kazin. Wilson harks back, said Kazin, to the time "when the great novelists were still on the parlor table and there were Americans still detached enough from our 'commercial ideals' to see the country in focus." Above all, everything Wilson tells us must be shown clearly, simply, and with eloquence. Wilson's writing starts from "a tensely balanced effort to seize control, to portray, to consummate." His first obligation is always to engage the passions and intellect of the reader. He always has to grasp the whole figure of some writer or historical personage. "He has to show his subject," says Kazin, "as a character in a story and each book as an action; he has to find what is most permanent in a writer yet be not so much in the writer as behind him, in the force of the age that is backing him up; he has to make a point each step of the way and to show a case all around; he has to do it solidly, in his own style, gathering up all of the details into one finally compact argument, like a man whose life hangs on the rightness of a sentence."

If we Americans have something to be grateful for in the achievement of Edmund Wilson it is undoubtedly his steadfast devotion to the literature, history, and culture of the United States. There are, of course, those who said that Wilson went sour on the United States, that with the passage of time he became more remote from things American. Wilson often seemed to do little to dissipate this wrongful notion, as when he remarked, in *The Cold War and the Income Tax,* that "this country, whether or not I continue to live in it, is no longer a place for me." But such assertions, found in many letters and utterances of Wilson's later years, are the products of mood and moral outrage, rather than substance and conviction. Wilson had always been out of phase with the America of the twentieth century. He took his strength from being solidly rooted in the early republican America of his forebears. But he was at one and the same time the most assiduous and contemporaneous of Americanists. He never had a desire to live abroad. When he learned foreign languages and read foreign literatures it was always as grist for the mill of American experience. He traveled through America first; he read American books first and devoted most of his energies to these books. His very individualism and elaborate irritability hints at why he was first and foremost an Americanist. He wrote of and for his own needs and ours; he addressed mainly his fellow countrymen experiencing similar pains and joys of living in America in the middle of the twentieth century.

If Wilson is remembered several generations from now, it will certainly be as one of the most enlightening and original critics of American life. Already there is good reason to suspect that his work stands favorably in comparison with other critical historians of the American experience—men like Tocqueville and Henry Adams.

Sometimes opinionated, sometimes even wrongheaded and perverse, often cantankerous in expressing his dislikes; nonetheless his views of the American scene remain clear, powerful, and penetrating. Wilson's writings are historical syntheses on the highest plane, and over the years they will continue to reveal to Americans more and more truths about themselves.

Chronology

1895 Edmund Wilson, Jr., born May 8 at Red Bank, New Jersey, the son of Edmund and Helen Mather Kimball Wilson.

1912 Graduated from the Hill School in Pottstown, Pennsylvania. Edited the *Hill School Record.*

1916 A.B. degree from Princeton University. Edited *The Nassau Literary Magazine.*

1916 Worked as a reporter on the *New York Evening Sun,* at a salary of fifteen dollars a week.

1917 Enlisted as a private in the United States Army and served with Base Hospital Unit 36; later was sergeant in the Intelligence Corps, until July 1919.

1920 On staff of *Vanity Fair,* New York.

1921 Joined the staff of the *New Republic,* with which he would be associated for nineteen years.

1922 Publication of first book, *Undertaker's Garland,* in collaboration with John Peale Bishop.

1923 Married actress Mary Blair. (Daughter, Rosalind Baker Wilson.) Wilson's father died.

1926 Associate editor of *The New Republic.*

1928 Divorced from Mary Blair.

1929 Publication of *I Thought of Daisy,* his first novel.

1930 Married Margaret Canby, no children.

1931 Publication of *Axel's Castle,* which established his reputation as a literary critic.

1932 Traveled around United States, studying the effects of the depression. Publication of *The American Jitters.*

1932 Accidental death of Margaret Canby Wilson.

1935 Trip to Russia on a Guggenheim Fellowship, May to October.

1936 Publication of *Travels in Two Democracies.*

1938 *The Triple Thinkers.*

1938 Married Mary McCarthy. (Son, Reuel Wilson.)

1939 Taught in the summer session at the University of Chicago.

1940 *To the Finland Station.*

1940 Relationship with the *New Republic* came to an end.

1941 *The Wound and the Bow.*

1943 Publication of *The Shock of Recognition,* a collection of American responses to American literature and culture.

1943 Literary editor of the *New Yorker* (until 1948).

1946 *Memoirs of Hecate County.*

1946 Divorced Mary McCarthy and married his fourth, and last wife, Elena Mumm Thornton. (Daughter, Helen Miranda Wilson.)

1947 *Europe without Baedeker.*

1950 *Classics and Commercials.*

1952 *The Shores of Light.*

1955 *The Scrolls from the Dead Sea.*

1958 *The American Earthquake.*

1959 Taught Harvard seminar on Civil War literature (material later published in *Patriotic Gore*).

1959 *Apologies to the Iroquois.*

1962 *Patriotic Gore.*

1963 Received from President John F. Kennedy the Presidential Medal of Freedom, the highest civilian honor given by the United States government.

1963 *The Cold War and the Income Tax.*

1964 Received the Edward MacDowell Medal for "outstanding contribution to literature."

1965 Publication of *O Canada* and *The Bit between My Teeth.*

1966 Awarded the National Medal for Literature, and the Emerson-Thoreau Medal "for distinguished achievement in the field of literature."

1969 *The Fruits of the MLA.*

1971 *Upstate,* Wilson's last book before his death.

1972 Wilson died at Talcottville, New York on June 12; buried in Wellfleet, Massachusetts, on June 15.

The Books of
Edmund Wilson:
A Checklist

Except for significantly revised editions, only the first editions of the
works are listed.

The Undertaker's Garland [with John Peale Bishop]. New York: Al-
fred A. Knopf, 1922. Stories and poems.
Discordant Encounters: Plays and Dialogues. New York: Albert and
Charles Boni, 1926.
I Thought of Daisy. New York: Charles Scribner's Sons, 1929. Novel.
Poets, Farewell! New York: Charles Scribner's Sons, 1929. Poems and
essays.
Axel's Castle: A Study in the Imaginative Literature of 1870-1930.
New York and London: Charles Scribner's Sons, 1931. Criticism.
The American Jitters: A Year of the Slump. New York and London:
Charles Scribner's Sons, 1932. English title, *Devil Take the Hind-
most.* Journalism.
Travels in Two Democracies. New York: Harcourt, Brace, 1936.
This Room and This Gin and These Sandwiches: Three Plays. New
York: New Republic, 1937.
The Triple Thinkers: Ten Essays on Literature. New York: Harcourt,
Brace, 1938. Criticism.
*To the Finland Station: A Study in the Writing and Acting of His-
tory.* New York: Harcourt, Brace, 1940. Biography and history.

The Boys in the Back Room: Notes on California Novelists. San Francisco: Colt Press, 1941. Later included in *Classics and Commercials.* Criticism.

The Wound and the Bow: Seven Studies in Literature. Cambridge, Mass.: Houghton Mifflin, 1941. Criticism.

Note-Books of Night. San Francisco: Colt Press, 1942. Poems and essays.

The Shock of Recognition: The Development of Literature in the United States Recorded by the Men Who Made It. Garden City, N.Y.: Doubleday, Doran, 1943. An anthology of "literary documents," mostly essays, by contemporaries of American writers.

Memoirs of Hecate County. Garden City, N.Y.: Doubleday, Doran, 1946. Novel.

Europe without Baedeker: Sketches among the Ruins of Italy, Greece and England. Garden City, N.Y.: Doubleday, Doran, 1947. Journalism.

The Triple Thinkers: Twelve Essays on Literary Subjects. New York: Oxford University Press, 1948.

The Little Blue Light: A Play in Three Acts. New York: Farrar, Straus, 1950.

Classics and Commercials: A Literary Chronicle of the Forties. New York: Farrar, Straus, 1950. Criticism.

The Shores of Light: A Literary Chronicle of the Twenties and Thirties. New York: Farrar, Straus and Young, 1952. Criticism.

To the Finland Station: A Study in the Writing and Acting of History. New York: Doubleday, 1953.

Eight Essays. Garden City, N.Y.: Doubleday, 1954. Criticism and biography.

Five Plays. New York: Farrar, Straus and Young, 1954.

The Scrolls from the Dead Sea. New York: Oxford University Press, 1955. Journalism.

A Piece of My Mind: Reflections at Sixty. New York: Farrar, Straus and Cudahy, 1956. Essays.

Red, Black, Blond and Olive: Studies in Four Civilizations: Zuni, Haiti, Soviet Russia, Israel. New York: Oxford University Press, 1956. Journalism.

A Literary Chronicle: 1920-1950. Garden City, N.Y.: Doubleday, 1956. An Anchor Book containing selections from *Classics and Commercials* and *Shores of Light.*

The American Earthquake: A Documentary of the Twenties and Thirties. Garden City, N.Y.: Doubleday, 1958. Journalism. Most of this was previously published in *American Jitters* and *Travels in Two Democracies.*

Apologies to the Iroquois (with "The Mohawks in High Steel" by Joseph Mitchell). New York: Farrar, Straus and Cudahy, 1959. Journalism.

Patriotic Gore: Studies in the Literature of the American Civil War. New York: Oxford University Press, 1962. Criticism, history, and biography.

The Cold War and the Income Tax: A Protest. New York: Farrar, Straus, 1963. Polemical essay.

O Canada: An American's Notes on Canadian Culture. New York: Farrar, Straus and Giroux, 1965. Journalism, criticism.

The Bit between My Teeth: A Literary Chronicle of 1950-1965. New York: Farrar, Straus and Giroux, 1965. Criticism.

Europe without Baedeker: Sketches among the Ruins of Italy, Greece and England together with Notes from a European Diary: 1963-1964. New York: Farrar, Straus and Giroux, 1966. Journalism.

Galahad and *I Thought of Daisy.* New York: Farrar, Straus and Giroux, 1967. Fiction.

A Prelude: Landscapes, Characters and Conversations from the Earlier Years of My Life. New York: Farrar, Straus and Giroux, 1967. Autobiographical essays.

The Fruits of the MLA. New York: New York Review, 1969. Essay.

The Duke of Palermo and Other Plays, with an Open Letter to Mike Nichols. New York: Farrar, Straus and Giroux, 1969.

The Dead Sea Scrolls, 1947-1969. New York: Oxford University Press, 1969.

Upstate: Records and Recollections of Northern New York. New York: Farrar, Straus and Giroux, 1971.

A Window on Russia. New York: Farrar, Straus and Giroux, 1972. Essays.

The Devils and Canon Barham: Essays on Poets, Novelists and Monsters. New York: Farrar, Straus and Giroux, 1973.

Letters on Literature and Politics, 1912-1972. Edited by Elena Wilson. New York: Farrar, Straus and Giroux, 1977.

The Twenties. Edited with an introduction by Leon Edel. New York: Farrar, Straus and Giroux, 1975. Notebooks and diaries.

The Thirties. Edited with an introduction by Leon Edel. New York: Farrar, Straus and Giroux, 1980. Notebooks and diaries.

The Forties. Edited with an introduction by Leon Edel. New York: Farrar, Straus and Giroux, 1983. Notebooks and diaries.

Bibliographical Essay

BIBLIOGRAPHIES

The only recent and exhaustive bibliography of Wilson is *Edmund Wilson: A Bibliography,* by Richard David Ramsey (New York: David Lewis, 1971). This bibliography is quite good for the period before 1971 and offers a fairly complete listing of Wilson's published writings up to that time. It is weaker on unpublished writings and letters. It has a fair-sized list of critical items about Wilson, but not all of these have annotations.

Also helpful are: "Edmund Wilson: A Bibliography," by William J. Lewis, in *Bulletin of Bibliography* (May 1958), 145-51, and the earlier "Edmund Wilson: A Checklist," by Arthur Mizener, *Princeton University Library Chronicle* (February 1944), 62-78, which is very complete up to that time. Easily accessible is the bibliography on Wilson in the *Bibliographical Supplement* of the *Literary History of the United States,* edited by Robert B. Spiller, et al. (New York: Macmillan, 1959), 238-39. The supplement itself was edited by Richard M. Ludwig.

There is a short but useful selected bibliography in *Edmund Wilson,* by Charles P. Frank (New York: Twayne Publishers, 1970), 197-204.

BIOGRAPHY

There is as yet no biography of Wilson. Of the several books already devoted to Wilson, *Edmund Wilson: A Study of Literary Vocation in Our Time* by Sherman Paul (Urbana: University of Illinois Press, 1965), takes a somewhat biographical approach but is essentially a literary study.

Of course Wilson has provided us with rich material for biography in his own writings, not only in books like *A Prelude* and *A Piece of My Mind,* but in those parts of his diaries that have thus far been made available (*The Twenties* and *Upstate*). Nevertheless, Wilson's autobiographical writings, however extensive, are extremely selective and do not provide sufficient material for a biographer. At times they reveal certain dimensions of his daily life with great passion and in full detail, but they leave other dimensions almost completely untouched or neglected. He wrote very little about some phases of his marriages, for example, or about his relationship with his children. We have from Wilson's hand no comprehensive idea of what it was like to be the literary editor of the *New Yorker* and no firm picture of the workaday conditions during his nearly two decades on the *New Republic.* Much information can be pieced together from published and unpublished sources, but one suspects that a fully rounded biographical portrait of Wilson will be possible only if one of his intimate acquaintances accepts the mission of providing some continuity and coherence to Wilson's own rich but highly selective autobiographical offerings.

WILSON'S WRITINGS

A convenient checklist of Wilson's books can be found preceding this essay.

As a writer whose works never fell into the best-seller category, Wilson was relatively fortunate in his publishers. His first published book, *The Undertaker's Garland* (with John Peale Bishop) was published by Alfred A. Knopf in 1922, but it was not until the appearance of *I Thought of Daisy* in 1929 that Wilson found a publisher who was committed to his work. Wilson had made the acquaintance of Max Perkins, now long-famous as the editor of Fitzgerald, Hemingway, and Thomas Wolfe at Scribner's. Thanks to Perkins, Charles Scribner's Sons became Wilson's first regular publisher. With Perkins's advice and consent, the Scribner firm published *I Thought of Daisy, Poet's Farewell, Axel's Castle,* and *The American Jitters.* But the relationship with Perkins and Scribner's cooled in time. Wilson was not happy with what Scribner's had done with *The American Jitters* and, accordingly, gave *Travels in Two Democracies* to Harcourt Brace. Perkins hoped, nevertheless, to keep Wilson on his list, and wrote numerous times with an expression of interest, but Wilson flung back the charge that Scribner's was not really interested in him as an author. On October 18, 1938, he wrote to Perkins: "I remember that on one occasion some years ago I came to you with a request for what was certainly the very moderate sum of $75. . . . You wouldn't do anything for me . . . at a time when you were handing out money to Scott Fitzgerald like a drunken sailor. Naturally you expected him to write you a novel which would make you a great deal more money than my books seemed likely to do. But even so, the discrepancy seemed to me to be somewhat excessive." Perkins tried to get Wilson back into the fold at Scribner's—but without success.

From 1936 to 1950, at which time Wilson began his long-time association with Farrar, Straus, Wilson had a few publishers who took his work on generous terms, although he never concluded an arrangement with any of them to be his exclusive publisher. The two most prominent of these were Harcourt Brace (who did *Travels in Two Democracies, The Triple Thinkers,* and *To the Finland Station*), and Doubleday (who published *The Shock of Recognition, Memoirs of Hecate County,* and *Europe without Baedeker*). Scribner's nearly got back in the act during these years and gave Wilson a contract to publish *The Wound and the Bow,* but when Perkins read the chapter about Hemingway he insisted on its removal. When Wilson stood firm, Scribner's broke the contract and the book went to Houghton Mifflin. At the time Wilson admitted that Perkins had been very enthusiastic about the Hemingway essay, but Hemingway "has been getting worse (crazier) of late years, and they are scared to death that he may leave them." There may have been some justification in this fear, though the Hemingway essay was, on the whole, sympathetic. Hemingway got hold of it (it had already been published in *Atlantic Monthly*) and threatened to get an injunction to prevent Houghton Mifflin from publishing it. Nevertheless, the book came out as scheduled.

In 1950, the firm of Farrar, Straus (later Farrar, Straus and Young; Farrar, Straus and Cudahy; and, finally, Farrar, Straus and Giroux) took over as Wilson's publisher, and it has continued to publish his work until the present time. It has now published several posthumous volumes. Before he began his association with Farrar, Straus, Wilson had already sounded out the editors at Oxford University Press about the book that was to become *Patriotic Gore;* Oxford published that book when it finally appeared in 1963 as well as *The Scrolls from the Dead Sea,* which Oxford published in 1955. Except for works in one or two special categories, all of Wilson's other books from 1950 to the time of his death in 1972 were published by Farrar, Straus.

The firm of Farrar, Straus was a rather new one when Wilson went with it in 1950. Farrar and Straus had joined forces in 1945, although before that John Farrar, the senior partner, had been a prominent New York editor for many years. Farrar, nearly Wilson's age, had been an editor for George H. Doran since 1925 and had also served as editor of *The Bookman.* Roger Straus, Jr., the partner with whom Wilson had most of his dealings, was only thirty-three in 1950, but he, too, had had extensive experience as an editor in New York. Both Farrar and Straus were interested in quality publishing and have always eschewed highly commercial ventures.

Farrar, Straus did a great deal for Wilson. They agreeably reissued a number of his earlier books, made new volumes out of collections of his essays from the twenties and thirties, and sold all of these assiduously (they even made a boxed set of the three volumes, *The Shores of Light, Classics and Commercials,* and *The Bit between My Teeth,* which they originally sold for $18.50). They successfully marketed Wilson material to the Book-of-the-Month Club and went along with nearly all of Wilson's schemes for reissuing his out-of-print material.

Relations with Roger Straus were nearly always amicable. Wilson urged on the firm his prejudices for compact books and they usually acceded to his insistence on the uncommon 4¼" X 7¼" format. This format is not really desirable for books over, say, 250 pages, as Wilson may not have fully appreciated. Still, Farrar, Straus continued to use that format even after Wilson's death, although they mercifully abandoned it for the 768-page *Letters on Literature and Politics, 1912-1972,* where it would certainly have been an abomination.

A good deal could be written about Wilson's success in the field of paperback books. When the so-called quality paperbacks became a vogue in the early fifties, Edmund Wilson found a champion and devoted servant in Jason Epstein of Doubleday's Anchor Books. (Anchor Books was the first quality paperback line.) Wilson wrote to Roger Straus in 1953: "Young Epstein of Doubleday came up here to see me. . . . He is the only publisher I have ever met whom I have felt I have had to caution not to over-interest in my books." Still, it was with gratitude that Wilson allowed Epstein to put out a paperback edition of *To the Finland Station*—a book that was a natural for a fresh and vigorous resale. Wilson, in turn, suggested possible selections for Epstein's list, and in later years tried to interest Epstein in his project to do a compact edition of the American classics.

During the 1960s and after, Wilson was less needful of the services of Epstein for paperback publishing since Farrar, Straus got into their own paperback line. Needless to say, they reissued Wilson titles as aggressively as possible.

Wilson's publications in magazines over the years can be described fairly briefly. Most of his articles during the twenties and thirties appeared in the *New Republic*. After 1943, the *New Yorker* was far and away the biggest outlet for Wilson material.

While these two magazines carried the vast majority of Wilson's pieces during the time periods involved, Wilson had a number of other magazines to which he would send things occasionally. During the twenties and thirties Wilson published in *New Statesman and Nation, Vanity Fair, Theatre Arts Monthly, Modern Monthly, New York Herald Tribune Books, Dial, Atlantic Monthly, Partisan Review,* and *Scribner's Magazine,* among others.

During the forties, fifties, and sixties, Wilson published in *Encounter, Nation, New Statesman, Atlantic Monthly, Partisan Review,* and, quite expectedly when it came along, the *New York Review of Books.* The whole of *The Cold War and the Income Tax* was originally published in *Liberation Magazine.*

Students of Wilson will not want to neglect Wilson's earliest journalistic endeavors, which appeared in the *Hill School Record* and the *Nassau Literary Magazine.*

LETTERS

The most important collection of Wilson's letters to date is *Letters on Literature and Politics, 1912-1972,* selected and edited by Elena Wilson with an introduction by Daniel Aaron (New York: Farrar, Straus and Giroux), 1977. In a brief foreword to this work, Leon Edel, Wilson's literary executor, makes it clear that "a more comprehensive collection is planned for a later date." It may be regretted that more of Wilson's personal and intimate correspondence could not be made available at this time. Nevertheless, this collection was made in accordance with Wilson's wishes and is in every way excellent.

Of more recent and specialized interest is, *The Nabokov-Wilson Letters: Correspondence between Vladimir Nabokov and Edmund Wilson, 1940-1971* (New York: Harper and Row, 1979).

The most important repository of Wilson's correspondence is the Beinecke Rare Book and Manuscript Library of Yale University.

BOOKS EDITED BY WILSON

The most important work edited by Wilson was his splendid anthology of American literature, *The Shock of Recognition* (New York: Doubleday, Doran, 1943). Wilson was never one to freely accept editorial assignments and only took them on as a labor of love. This explains most of the books that he did edit: *The Last Tycoon*, by F. Scott Fitzgerald (New York: Charles Scribner's Sons, 1941); *The Crack-Up; with Other Uncollected Pieces, Notebooks and Unpublished Letters*, by F. Scott Fitzgerald (New York: New Directions, James Laughlin, 1945); *The Collected Essays of John Peale Bishop* (New York: Charles Scribner's Sons, 1948).

COMMENTARY AND CRITICISM

BOOKS ABOUT WILSON

The most important books about Wilson to date are *Edmund Wilson: A Study of Literary Vocation in Our Time*, by Sherman Paul (Urbana: University of Illinois Press, 1965) and *Edmund Wilson*, by Charles P. Frank (New York: Twayne Publishers, 1970). These two books complement one another nicely. The Paul volume is a searching intellectual analysis that attempts to make a coherent framework of Wilson's entire literary output. Frank's study is more of an overview, devoted to simple accounts and expositions. It is somewhat more readable than Paul's earlier work but probably less penetrating. Since Frank's book devotes a great deal more space than Paul's to Wilson's poetry, plays, stories, and novels, it may be safe to say that he is avoiding the center of Wilson's contribution as a writer. Still, his book is a good overview and general introduction to Wilson and comprehensively covers many works that are seldom if ever mentioned in usual accounts of Wilson.

Of much less interest than either of the above is Leonard Kriegel's *Edmund Wilson* (Carbondale: Southern Illinois University Press, 1971). Most of this book is devoted to an analysis of *Patriotic Gore* and accepts the criticism of that book from a stance of rather hidebound literary history.

MEMOIRS AND REMINISCENCES

The recent collection, *Edmund Wilson: The Man and His Work*, edited by John Wain (New York: New York University Press, 1978), contains some interesting reminiscences of Wilson by Edith Oliver,

Alfred Kazin, Angus Wilson, and Bette Crouse Mele. Rather detailed and interpretive personal material is also to be found in Alfred Kazin's recent book *New York Jew* (New York: Alfred A. Knopf, 1978). See also, Richard Hauer Costa's *Edmund Wilson: Our Neighbor from Talcottville* (Syracuse: Syracuse University Press, 1980).

Much discussion with some penetrating biographical analysis of Wilson can be found in Daniel Aaron's Introduction to Wilson's *Letters on Literature and Politics, 1912-1972* (New York: Farrar, Straus and Giroux, 1977).

Recollections of Wilson in earlier times and in more specialized environments are "Edmund Wilson, the Campus and the *Nassau Lit.*," by Christian Gauss, *Princeton University Library Chronicle* (February 1944), 41-50; "Edmund Wilson on the *New Republic*," by Malcolm Cowley, *New Republic* (July 1, 1972), 25-28. Also, compare Arthur Mizener, "Edmund Wilson's *New Republic*," *New Republic* (May 9, 1970), 28-30. A view of Edmund Wilson at the *New Yorker* can be found in Brendan Gill's *Here at the* New Yorker (New York: Random House, 1975).

GENERAL ASSESSMENTS OF WILSON

After his death in 1972, a flurry of tributes and evaluations appeared in newspapers and magazines here and abroad. Among these were: L. E. Sissman, "Edmund Wilson," *Atlantic Monthly* (September 1972), 30ff.; T. S. Matthews, "Edmund Wilson, An American Original," *Saturday Review* (May 17, 1975), 19-23; George H. Douglas, "Edmund Wilson: Great Democrat of Letters," *Nation* (August 7, 1972), 86-89.

Among earlier general assessments of Wilson are: Warner Berthoff, "Edmund Wilson," no. 67 in the *University of Minnesota Pamphlets on American Writers* (Minneapolis: University of Minnesota Press, 1968); Alfred Kazin, "The Imagination of a Man of Letters," *American Scholar* (Winter 1964-1965), 19-27; and earlier also by Kazin, "The Critic and the Age," *New Yorker* (November 15, 1952), 181ff., later reprinted in Kazin's *The Inmost Leaf* (New York: Harcourt, Brace, 1955); Donald Robinson, "Edmund Wilson," in Robinson's *The 100 Most Important People in the World Today* (New York: G.P. Putnam and Sons, 1970), 323-25; Irving Howe, "Edmund Wilson: A Reexamination," *Nation* (October 16, 1948), 430-33.

Of a still earlier period, see "Edmund Wilson," in *Bookman* (November 1929), 302, which contains a picture of Wilson in his *New Republic* office; "Edmund Wilson," in *Saturday Review of Literature* (February 3, 1934), 446, an evaluation with picture.

For more strictly factual accounts and reference material, see "Edmund Wilson," in *Twentieth-Century Authors: A Biographical Dictionary of Modern Literature*, edited by Stanley J. Kunitz and Howard Haycraft (New York: H.W. Wilson, 1942), 1529-30, and later revisions; *Current Biography Yearbook*, 1964, 25th ed., edited by Charles Moritz (New York: H.W. Wilson, 1965), 464-66. There are useful articles on Wilson in a number of well-known encyclopedias: *The Encyclopedia Americana; The Columbia Encyclopedia; The Standard International Encyclopedia; The New Funk and Wagnall's Encyclopedia.*

WILSON AS AN AMERICANIST

Articles and essays that identify Wilson as first and foremost an Americanist and historical critic are not plentiful, and more often than not they have been restricted by a greater perceived need to explain and evaluate Wilson on more specialized and restricted ground.

The most perceptive writing on Wilson thus far has been that by Alfred Kazin, who has been writing about Wilson since his youth—in recent years also from the vantage point of personal friendship and affection. Kazin's first treatment of Wilson appeared in his *On Native Ground* (New York: Harcourt Brace, 1942), in which he recognizes Wilson's central importance to the American scene but is, in the intellectual light of the day, obliged to deal more exclusively with problems of sociological and Marxist criticism. When *The Shores of Light* appeared in 1952, Kazin wrote an appraisal of it in the *New Yorker* (November 15, 1952), later reprinted in Kazin's anthology *The Inmost Leaf* (New York: Harcourt Brace, 1955), 93-97. Here Kazin captures the essence of Wilson as a historical critic who melts down all of his materials and submits them to the totality of his personality. He writes:

There are deeper critics, critics less hidebound by indifference to abstract thought; there is no other critic who so evenly and so hauntingly writes criticism as a work of art. Should anyone try to create criticism as an art? The answer is that Wilson cannot help it. The key words of fashionable criticism today are "form," "sensibility," "difficult," "proper," "tact"; his are "grasp," "solid," "vivid," "focus," "lens"; he is a writer among writers, the writer who has taken on the job of explaining them to the world. Writing always from that other shore of memory and good English usage, where the great novelists were still on the parlor table and there were Americans still detached enough from our "commercial ideals" to see the country in focus, he has always to grasp out of time lost, out of the books misread by other critics, the whole figure of the writer in his age, and to present this subject as a new creation. He has to show his subject as a character in a story and each book as an action; he has to find what is most permanent about a writer yet may be not so much in the writer as behind him, in the force of the age that is backing him up; he has to make a point each step of the way and to show a case all around; he has to do it solidly, in his own style, gathering up all the details into one finally compact and lucid argument, like a man whose life hangs on the rightness of each sentence.

In a still more detailed essay, "Edmund Wilson on the Thirties," in Kazin's *Contemporaries* (Boston: Little, Brown, 1962), Kazin expresses to perfection the intimate connection between Wilson's devotion to historical experience and his powers of literary expression.

Wilson is not a reporter but a literary artist driven by historical imagination—like Henry Adams and Carlyle. Such writers are lightning-quick to see the many metamorphoses of modern man. In Europe, where the succession and contrast of different epochs can be seen on every hand, writers who appeal to the historical imagination can be read for their merit as artists. But in this country, where we are likely to overvalue single traditions as such but to overlook the beauty of history itself, the creative side of such writers is unappreciated. Wilson's sense of historical contrast is documented entirely from his own life and that of his family in relation to America. The points of the compass for him are "the old stone house" of his ancestors in upstate New York that he describes so movingly.

If the historical imagination lives on metamorphosis, it expresses itself as personal impressions. Wilson writes cultural reminiscences as novelists and dramatists write scenes and dialogue. His strong suit is never ideas as such (any more than ideas as such were the strength of Carlyle or, despite his pretensions to philosophy, of Henry Adams). . . . What makes Wilson's reporting good is the impression of actual experience brought to white heat on the page; it is the re-creation of a scene that relates Wilson to history, not the significance of history in itself.

These themes are developed more fully and in more personal terms in Kazin's third autobiographical volume, *New York Jew* (New York: Alfred A. Knopf, 1978). Also by Kazin are: "Edmund Wilson: His Life and Books," *Atlantic Monthly* (July 1967), 80-83; and "The Imagination of a Man of Letters," *American Scholar* (Winter 1964-1965), 19-27.

For other essays and articles suggesting the importance of Wilson as an Americanist and as a historical critic, see P. Shaw, "American Heritage and Its Guardians," *American Scholar* (Winter 1975), 733-51; Warner Berthoff, "Edmund Wilson as a Provincial Plutarch," *Saturday Review* (August 28, 1971), 18-21; George Snell, "Edmund

Wilson: The Historical Critic," *Rocky Mountain Review* (Winter 1944), 36-44, an earlier study of Wilson that treats the relation of Wilson to other American historical critics, particularly Van Wyck Brooks; Larzer Ziff, "The Man of Fire: Edmund Wilson and American Literature," in *Edmund Wilson: The Man and His Work*, edited by John Wain (New York: New York University Press, 1978); Norman Podhoretz, "Edmund Wilson, the Last Patrician," *Reporter* (December 25, 1958), 25-28; George H. Douglas, "Edmund Wilson: Our Great Democrat of Letters," *Nation* (August 7, 1972), 86-89, also "Edmund Wilson: The Critic as Artist," *Texas Quarterly* (Winter 1974), 58-72.

It is to be regretted that we do not have from other major historical critics who were Wilson's friends or contemporaries, any extended or substantive evaluation of Wilson's work. There can be no doubt that Van Wyck Brooks admired Wilson and valued him highly as an historical critic. But he did not extensively commit himself in print. Malcolm Cowley wrote at length about Wilson's critical views in earlier days, and in his book *A Second Flowering: Works and Days of the Lost Generation*, Cowley said not once but several times that "I am sorry for not having devoted a chapter to Edmund Wilson"; nevertheless, he did not do so. Brief, but of significant interest are a few other contributions by historical critics: Irving Howe, "Edmund Wilson: A Reexamination," *Nation* (October 16, 1948), 430-33; Perry Miller, "Essays and Asides: A Passion for Literature," *Nation* (January 27, 1951), 87-88; and F.O. Matthiessen, "A Critic of Importance," *Yale Review* (June 1931), 854-56.

WILSON AS A LITERARY CRITIC

Wilson has more often been treated as a literary critic than as a writer in any other mode. Except for the period before 1940, when Wilson's political views attracted a great deal of attention and heated dialogue, his contemporaries more often agreed or disagreed with (and accordingly wrote about) his literary ideas than about any other aspects of his work.

Edmund Wilson: The Man and His Work, edited by John Wain (New York: New York University Press, 1978), contains a recent and very good collection of articles about Wilson as a literary critic. Especially relevant are articles by Angus Wilson, Larzer Ziff, Andrew Harvey, and John Wain. There is a good earlier collection dealing with Wilson as a critic in *A Library of Literary Criticism: Modern American Literature*, compiled by Dorothy Nyren (New York: Frederick Ungar Publishing, 1962). Reprinted here are a number of good articles about Wilson as a critic, including contributions by Perry Miller, Malcolm Cowley, William Phillips, Gilbert Highet, Robert Spiller, and Alfred Kazin.

It hardly needs to be mentioned that Wilson is treated in a good number of histories of criticism, textbooks, and other works of a didactic sort. The main problem to the authors of these was always one of finding a suitable placement for Wilson in some neatly constructed intellectual framework. For example, see Walter Jackson Bate, *Criticism: The Major Texts* (New York: Harcourt, Brace and World, 1952). Also, John Paul Pritchard, "Edmund Wilson," in *Criticism in America* (Norman: University of Oklahoma Press, 1956), 269-76; Charles I. Glicksberg, "Edmund Wilson," in *American Literary Criticism, 1900-1950* (New York: Hendricks House, 1951), 482-85; Walter Sutton, *Modern American Criticism* (Englewood Cliffs, N.J.: Prentice Hall, 1963). Sutton, for example, rightly and fairly treats Wilson as a critic who has contributed to several different critical approaches and includes references to Wilson in chapters on "Psychological Criticism," "Liberal and Marxist Criticism," and "History and Theory of Criticism." (Characteristically there is no chapter devoted to historical criticism, for in the didactic framework provided by the philosophical system builders like Rene Wellek, historical criticism can only be a kind of subcategory of sociological criticism.) Naturally there are also numerous references to Wilson in histories of literary criticism.

Of individual articles about Wilson as a literary critic, the following are devoted mainly to general comment and overview: Gilbert Highet, "The Criticism of Edmund Wilson," in *People, Places and Books* (New York: Oxford University Press, 1953), 29-36; "The Method of Edmund Wilson," *University of Toronto Quarterly* (October 1941), 105-111; Harvey Breit, "Talk With Edmund Wilson," *New York Times Book Review* (November 2, 1952), 18; Richard Gilman, "Edmund Wilson, Then and Now," *New Republic* (July 2, 1966), 23-28; Richard Kostelmetz, "The Other Mr. Wilson," *Twentieth Century* (Winter 1966), 71-72; Delmore Schwartz, "The Writing of Edmund Wilson," *Accent* (Spring 1942), 177-86; Perry Miller, "Essays and Asides: A Passion for Literature," *Nation* (January 27, 1951), 87-88.

There have been a number of Wilson detractors over the years, and most have aimed their sights at Wilson's critical practices and ideologies. Consistently hostile was Stanley Edgar Hyman, who tore into Wilson from a number of different angles in *The Armed Vision:*

A Study in the Methods of Modern Literary Criticism (New York: Alfred A. Knopf, 1948). Hyman objects that Wilson is a popularizer and not a serious critic. He believes that Wilson does not rise much above "plot synopsis and summary." Hyman was a colleague of Wilson's at the *New Yorker,* and apparently the two were antagonistic to one another. Brendan Gill, who knew both men, claims that Wilson once told him, "That fellow Hyman is bad news." The roots of this mutual dislike are not entirely clear.

But Hyman was by no means the only one to follow this line of attack. Wilson's so-called superficiality was the object of a number of discussions over the years. Compare Howard Mumford Jones, "The Limits of Contemporary Criticism," *Saturday Review of Literature* (September 6, 1941), 3-4, 17. Another frequent charge has been that Wilson has no coherent point of view, or that his stance as a critic is not clearly definable. Heading in this direction are: J. Donald Adams, "Masks and Delays: Edmund Wilson as Critic," *Sewanee Review* (Spring 1948), 272-86; J.A. Clark, "The Sad Case of Edmund Wilson," *Commonweal* (July 8, 1938), 292-95.

Most of the attacks on Wilson have not been this sweeping or all-encompassing. Mostly Wilson has had to endure specific objections to his literary prejudices or to strongly held convictions in one area or another. For example, Wilson turned up a number of foes with his psychological approach to literature after the appearance of *The Wound and the Bow.* See Louis Fraiberg, "Edmund Wilson and Psychoanalysis in Historical Criticism," in *Psychoanalysis and American Literary Criticism* (Detroit: Wayne State University Press, 1960), 161-82; Lionel Trilling, "A Note on Art and Neurosis," *Partisan Review* (Winter 1945), 41-48; Elmer Edgar Stoll, "Psychoanalysis in Criticism," in *Shakespeare to Joyce: Authors and Critics; Literature and Life* (Garden City: Frederick Ungar Publishing, 1965), 339-88; Edward Wagenknecht, "Edmund Wilson on Dickens," in *Dickens and the Scandalmongers: Essays in Criticism* (Norman: University of Oklahoma Press, 1965), 114-20. All of the above articles are hostile to Wilson's psychological interpretations and theories.

The vast majority of attacks on Wilson as a critic have appeared in individual reviews of his books rather than in articles of a systematic nature. For citations of these, and for more complete reference to Wilson's literary wars over the years (as, for example, those over detective fiction or academic editing and bookmaking), see Richard David Ramsey's *Edmund Wilson: A Bibliography.*

SOCIAL AND POLITICAL IDEAS

Some of the literature critical of Wilson concerns his political and social ideas. A good deal of this material is now dated since it pertains to Wilson's writings as an active journalist before World War II. During the period since the war, Wilson raised a great many more tempests over literary and cultural matters than over political ones, but, from both a biographical and historical standpoint, the literature about Wilson as a political and social thinker remains important.

Articles in this area are numerous and not all are germane to the present study. But of the period before World War II, the following seem especially relevant: Kenneth Burke, "Boring from Within," *New Republic* (February 4, 1931), 326-29, which is a response to Wilson's "An Appeal to Progressives," in the same magazine; "Stuart Chase Replies," *New Republic* (February 10, 1932), 348-49, being Chase's rejoinder to Wilson's article, "What Do Liberals Hope For?"; Malcolm Cowley, "Flight from the Masses," *New Republic* (June 3, 1936), 106-8 (see Cowley's addition to this, "Postscript to a Paragraph," printed in the same magazine two weeks later; also, Cowley's "From the Finland Station," *New Republic* (October 7, 1940), 478-80, written in opposition to Wilson's swing away from the left; and still earlier by Cowley, "Stalin or Satan," *New Republic* (January 20, 1937), a reply to Wilson's piece "The Literary Left."

Bernard DeVoto, "My Dear Edmund Wilson," *Saturday Review of Literature* (February 13, 1937), 8, 20, is hostile to Wilson's Marxism of the early thirties. In a reprinted version of this in his *Minority Report* (Boston: Little, Brown, 1940), DeVoto softens this view; Edward Fiess, "Edmund Wilson: Art and Ideas," *Antioch Review* (September 1941), 356-67, offers a general treatment of Wilson's liberalism and its relationship to his critical ideas; Joseph Freeman, "Edmund Wilson's Globe of Glass," *New Masses* (April 12, 1938), 73-79; Charles I. Glicksberg, "Edmund Wilson: Radicalism at the Crossroads," *South Atlantic Quarterly* (October 1937), 466-77, which expresses discontent that Wilson refused to ride on the communist bandwagon; Granville Hicks, "The Failure of Left Criticism," *New Republic* (September 9, 1940), 345-47.

Most of the articles listed above focus on Wilson's brush with European socialism during the 1930s, and with his liberal or sociological criticism. Needless to say, with Wilson's retreat not only from socialism but from a narrowly sociological approach to literature, there are fewer articles of this kind in the years between 1940 and 1972. Some of these are retrospective: Daniel Aaron's "Go Left Young Writers," which appears in Aaron's book *Writers on the Left*

(New York: Harcourt Brace and World, 1961), is a very detailed account of the literary left in the thirties, including Wilson; Robert Cantwell, "Wilson as a Journalist," *Nation* (February 22, 1958), 166-70; Malcolm Cowley, "Edmund Wilson's Specimen Days," *New Republic* (November 10, 1952), 17-18; Granville Hicks, "The Intransigence of Edmund Wilson," *Antioch Review* (Winter 1946-1947), 550-62; Irving Howe, "Edmund Wilson and the Sea Slugs," *Dissent: A Quarterly of Socialist Opinion* (Winter 1963), 774, which is not mainly a discussion of *Patriotic Gore* but of the "sea slug image of the Introduction and its political ramifications"; Murray Kempton, "The Social Muse," in his book *Part of Our Time: Some Ruins and Monuments of the Thirties* (New York: Simon and Schuster, 1955), 110-49, being a discussion of the literary left of the thirties, including Wilson; Norman Podhoretz, "Edmund Wilson, The Last Patrician," *Reporter* (December 25, 1958), 25-28, traces Wilson's intellectual development, with special reference to his political views; also by Podhoretz, "Edmund Wilson: Then and Now," in his *Doings and Undoings: The Fifties and After in America* (New York: Farrar, Straus, 1964), 30-58; Robert E. Spiller, "The Influence of Edmund Wilson: The Dual Tradition," *Nation* (February 27, 1958), 159-61, reprinted as "Edmund Wilson: The Dual Role of Criticism," in Spiller's book *Oblique Light* (New York: Macmillan, 1968), 215-20, provides a discussion of the schism in Wilson between aesthetic and sociohistorical criticism. Obviously the inability to find just the right academic pigeonhole for Wilson has been the origin of a good deal of the critical discussion of his work.

Index